The Anatomy of the New Poland

To Alan and Adam

STUDIES OF COMMUNISM IN TRANSITION

Series Editor: **Ronald J. Hill**
*Professor of Comparative Government
and Fellow of Trinity College,
Dublin, Ireland*

Studies of Communism in Transition is an important series which applies academic analysis and clarity of thought to the recent traumatic events in Eastern and Central Europe. As many of the preconceptions of the past half century are cast aside, newly independent and autonomous sovereign states are being forced to address long-term, organic problems which had been suppressed by, or appeased within, the communist system of rule.

The series is edited under the sponsorship of Lorton House, an independent charitable association which exists to promote the academic study of communism and related concepts.

The Anatomy of the New Poland

Post-Communist Politics in its First Phase

Frances Millard

Principal Lecturer in Politics
University of Portsmouth
Portsmouth, England

Edward Elgar

Published by
Edward Elgar Publishing Limited
Gower House
Croft Road
Aldershot
Hants GU11 3HR
England

Edward Elgar Publishing Company
Old Post Road
Brookfield
Vermont 05036
USA

British Library Cataloguing in Publication Data

Millard, Frances
   Anatomy of the New Poland: Post-communist
   Politics in Its First Phase. - (Studies
   of Communism in Transition)
   I. Title II. Series
   320.9438

Library of Congress Cataloguing in Publication Data

Millard, F. (Frances)
   The anatomy of the new Poland: post-Communist politics in its
  first phase / Frances Millard.
      p.   cm. — (Studies of Communism in Transition)
    Includes bibliographical references and index.
    1. Poland—Politics and government—1989–   I. Title II. Series.
  DK4449.M55 1994
  320.9438—dc20   93–34443
                                    CIP

ISBN 1 85278 924 7

Electronic typesetting by Lorton Hall

Printed in Great Britain at the University Press, Cambridge

Contents

Figures

Tables

Preface

Students of Polish politics have long been familiar with its dramas and its absurdities, its flights of vision and its sullen slumps. After 1989, with the collapse of communism throughout Eastern Europe, the stage changed, swivelling westwards away from the USSR on which it had for so long been dependent, and numerous actors reversed their roles. The Polish case is an exceptionally interesting one because of its history of working-class protest, the flourishing of its Catholic Church under the communist regime, and the originality of its creative intelligentsia. Poland was the awkward ally of the USSR. Its population refused to accept the legitimacy of its style of imposed socialism, its peasantry refused to collectivize, its workers took action to put into practice their allotted place as the leading force in society, and its dissidents stood up for humanism and universal values.

In 1988 the Polish communist elite took its first hesitant steps in the direction of a negotiated settlement with the opposition. The conservatives within the Communist Party were bankrupt and bereft of ideas. A new outburst of workers' protest in 1988 augured the breakdown of the fragile peace which had prevailed since the introduction of martial law in December 1981 and set in motion a final acceptance of the option of dialogue, which had been resisted for so long. The communists did not intend to relinquish power, nor did they expect to do so. Yet it was the Polish Round Table agreement of April 1989 that set in motion the processes which led to the installation of the first non-communist prime minister in Eastern Europe since the communists had taken power. Solidarity's performance in the June 1989 election surpassed the wildest expectations of its supporters and the blackest nightmares of its opponents. For all that, Solidarity did not win a majority. The assumption of power was itself a risk.

Poland's opposition was as prepared for power as an opposition could be after nearly a decade of illegality and lack of direct government experience. Its intellectuals and scholars were aware of the wide range of possible institutional solutions for ordering political and economic affairs. They had good tactical sense and negotiating skills. In Lech Wałęsa they had a figure of nationally-recognized appeal and wide political experience and the prospect of a revived Solidarity movement to channel the national consensus for change. On the other hand, the problems they faced were formidable. The economic crisis was severe, and the country was mired in debt to Western creditors and to the USSR. The economy was inefficient and geared to outmoded industries with little experience of technological adaptation. Popular expectations were very high that evicting the communists would quickly bring freedom and prosperity. How the USSR would react was uncertain. Communist officialdom was entrenched in the state administration. Solidarity had prepared itself to be a leading, legitimate opposition force within the communist system, not itself to take the commanding heights and thence construct a new one. They took the risk and erected the scaffolding almost overnight. The new structure was to be a longer-term project.

This book sets out to examine the processes of democratic and capitalist restructuring of Polish society in the first period of the post-communist transition. I have tried to describe and assess as clearly and simply as possible the factors that are operative in contemporary Polish political processes, their origins and their implications. The same ingredients are now in a different pot, but they have not yet changed. One might expect strikes and protests if things began to go disappointingly wrong; the disillusionment of capitalism can be as grindingly miserable as that of 'real socialism'. One might also expect a strong Church to place its own moral concerns on the agenda and to oppose the licence that freedom brings. What was and remains uncertain was what sort of political institutions would emerge from the interplay of interests that coincided in the face of a common enemy but that now would inevitably diverge. The basic question is whether democracy can survive and evolve in a stable fashion without a thriving bourgeoisie to support it and with social dislocations and disappointed expectations to undermine it.

So far the answer must be a qualified affirmative. Although the spectacle of institution-building has not always been edifying, the essence of the old system has been destroyed and the shell of a new one is in place. The formal institutions are democratic. The social structures needed to maintain and nurture them, notably the political parties, however, are feeble and mostly self-serving. The private sector of the economy has also shown a welcome dynamism, in gloomy contrast with the stolid position of the large state enterprises. Unemployment is severe and it will get much worse, but the whole economy has not collapsed overnight.

It will be apparent from the chapters that follow that the pendulum could still swing in the other direction. There are grievances building up among all sections of the community. There is great insecurity, as high levels of inflation continue and job security has become a thing of the past. There are corruption and exploitation and poverty, especially among the elderly. There is even nostalgia. For the present these tensions cannot be expressed through a clear social-democratic alternative strategy, for the communists' successors are still paying for the sins of the past. Those who fear populist demagoguery have some cause for their anxieties. That the warnings of authoritarianism, populism or a new form of dictatorship have not proved sound is a tribute and credit to the new political elites and the patience and endurance of the population.

I have benefited from the help of my many Polish friends and colleagues, directly and indirectly, in my attempts to understand their politics over almost three decades. I hope my affection and appreciation have always been apparent. I am also indebted, as a modern woman must be, to my team of computer advisers, particularly Robin Prior and above all to Adam Millard-Ball. My colleagues Fergus Carr, Stephen Cope and Peter Starie have helped and supported me, as always. My thanks go also to the Series' General Editor for his assistance, support and encouragement. Finally, I want to express my deep gratitude to Alan Ball, who has done everything I have asked of him and more; his criticism and comments have helped shape every chapter. I cannot guarantee I have done them justice.

F.M.
July 1993

1. The Communist Regime and Its Legacy

The election of June 1989 provided a symbolic end to the communist regime in Poland. For many it offered real opportunities for a new beginning. The communist abscess would be excised and the energies of the fundamentally healthy, talented society would be released. Forty-five years of alien rule would be expunged and the historical seams invisibly rejoined to the 'real' Poland of the pre-communist period.

Of course, such views did not materialize overnight. The atmosphere in Poland in the summer of 1989 was one of enormous anxiety and uncertainty. There were also those who warned that the experience of communist rule had left its enduring mark on the character of the Polish people, as well as on social, economic, political and cultural attitudes and behaviour. The Communist Party itself had come to power with the aim of revolutionary transformation in all spheres of life, which would reject the past and lead ultimately to the creation of a new communist society. In the event it achieved neither. For the new post-communist leaders, too, shedding the past is no easy matter. The experience of communist rule in Poland remains embedded in institutions and structures, as well as in memories, attitudes and patterns of behaviour. It is this embedded experience which forms the subject of this chapter. The legacy of the communist period lies in its shaping of a distinctive socio-economic formation, in the structure of interests created by the economic system, and in the particular character of the political culture.

THE EARLY YEARS OF COMMUNIST POWER

We may identify several phases in the development of the 'communist' system in Poland. In the first period, from 1944 to approximately 1954, the Soviet Union played a dominant role, in the first instance by supporting the tiny Communist Party (the PPR or Polish Workers' Party and then, following merger with elements of the Socialist Party, the PZPR or Polish United Workers' Party) with the Red Army, security forces, Soviet advisers and other personnel. The USSR was the key international actor, establishing (roughly) the old Curzon line as Poland's eastern boundary with the Allied Powers at Teheran in 1943, serving as the guarantor of a 'united democratic regime' at Yalta in February 1945 and fixing the western boundary on the Oder–Neisse line at Potsdam in August that year. Poland's geopolitical location made it of vital strategic importance to the USSR.

Indeed, the whole experiment in Polish socialism has often been seen as the result of an external revolution, imposed upon Poland and moulded by the strategic, economic and ideological interests of the Soviet Union. 'The Polish Communists did not seize power ... They were installed, protected and directed by the Soviet Union'.[1] It is indeed impossible to ignore either the key role played by the Red Army in the coming to power of the Polish Communist Party or the continuing direct influence of Moscow. There was strong Soviet influence in the establishment on 22 July 1944 of the Lublin Committee (the Polish Committee of National Liberation, or PKWN), which administered the lands liberated from German occupation; in the emergence of its successor, the Provisional Government of the Polish Republic (January–June 1945) and in the post-Yalta broadening of the latter in the (putative) Provisional Government of National Unity. Soviet security forces and 'advisers' played a direct role.

The Polish Communist Party itself was small and isolated, not least because of historic hostilities and the strong religiosity of the population. Traditional anti-Soviet sentiments had been exacerbated by the Soviet secret police (NKVD) massacre of some 20,000 Polish officers, symbolized by the burial site discovered during the war at Katyń. (It was not until 1990 that the Soviet government acknowledged its culpability; only in 1992 did the Russian President Boris Yeltsin provide the Polish government with documents showing Stalin's personal responsibility for the murders.) The inactivity of the nearby Soviet

1   Patrick Brogan, *Eastern Europe 1939–1989*, London, 1990, p.52.

army during the Warsaw Uprising, when the cream of the non-communist resistance perished at the hands of the Germans, also fuelled Polish anger.[2]

It is also the case that the Polish communists were divided, not only between the Moscow-based Poles and those operating at home, but also within these two groups. Yet they cannot be seen merely as Soviet stooges (though some like Bolesław Bierut came close), but also as individuals sharing a broad set of political aims and values with the Soviet elite. They were dependent upon the USSR, but the Soviet presence also caused them problems. Their policies were often undermined by the behaviour of the Red Army, and both the Lublin Committee and the PPR itself protested against it. For example, mass arrests and deportations of members of the mass resistance movement, the Home Army (AK), rendered inoperable the Committee's efforts to woo the AK,[3] and indeed subsequently provoked the latter to armed resistance. Red Army looting weakened hopes that Soviet liberation from the Germans would undermine traditional anti-Soviet attitudes: 'The debauchery of Red Army units returning from Germany, gang violence, and in addition the shortage of bread are turning people against the Soviet Union.'[4]

The relationship between Stalin and the Polish communists was, then, both dependent and reciprocal. They had common aims and served each other's purposes. However, the communists did not simply perch uneasily on the top of a hostile society. Large numbers joined the party, and communist membership increased from some 20,000 at the time of the establishment of the Lublin Committee to over a million by 1948.[5] The acquisition of German territory in the west provided scope for land distribution and patronage, exploited by Władysław Gomułka in his position as Minister for the Recovered Territories. Increasingly, economic reconstruction and planned indus-

2   In Ciechanowski's view the Polish resistance wrongly assumed that Warsaw was a priority for the Red Army; he also concludes that the Red Army's failure to take Warsaw in early August was due chiefly to military reasons: Jan Mieczyslaw Ciechanowski, *The Warsaw Rising of 1944*, Cambridge, 1974, pp.243–80.

3   Antony Polonsky and Boleslaw Drukier, *The Beginnings of Communist Rule in Poland*, London, 1980, p.272.

4   Polonsky and Drukier, op. cit., p.429; see also p.292.

5   M.K. Dziewanowski, *The Communist Party of Poland*, Cambridge, MA, 1959, p.253.

trial development created conditions of considerable social mobility, whose beneficiaries also had cause to support the communists.

With the onset of the Cold War and, at Stalin's insistence, the rejection of the Marshall Plan, came a general tightening of Soviet control of Eastern Europe and a great push towards uniformity. The split with Tito's Yugoslavia in 1948 heralded a purge of communist leaders, including Gomułka, the Polish Party's Secretary General, perhaps the most genuinely 'Titoist' of them all. Gomułka was known for espousing a distinctive 'Polish road to socialism' to take account of specific national conditions and characteristics.

By the end of 1948 the vestiges of armed resistance had been virtually eradicated and the communists were firmly entrenched. Soviet institutions and processes became the model for the Eastern European countries. Stalinism was omni-faceted: economic, political, social, cultural. It meant a massive industrialization campaign based on heavy industry, with a concomitant proliferation of bureaucratic structures to direct the central planning mechanism. It aimed at wholesale collectivization of the peasantry, at that time comprising nearly 70 per cent of the population. Politically, it sought to entrench communist party control of state institutions, including strict censorship of the media to impose ideological conformity. The party assumed control of the trade unions, the Peasant Self-Help Association, the Women's League and numerous other organizations. The apparatus of repression was highly developed, and the purges affected not only allegedly dangerous social elements (such as the clergy) but the PZPR itself. The Stalinist personality cult was ubiquitous, symbolized by the Palace of Culture, built as a monument to Stalin and dominating the Warsaw skyline. Literary and cultural expression became aridly sycophantic and excruciatingly dull.

Stalinism never achieved the complete control of Polish society, however. It was less violent in Poland than elsewhere and in marked ways less successful. Anti-Soviet and anti-Russian sentiments remained pervasive. Collectivization of the peasantry proceeded slowly, while the Catholic Church resisted attempts to mould it into a compliant instrument of party policy.[6] Gomułka himself, although

---

6   Throughout 1949 the PZPR leadership expressed anxiety about the small numbers of secret agents and their poor quality: see documents in *Polityka* 52, 29 December 1990.

arrested and expected to face charges, remained physically unscathed and became something of a national symbol of resistance through his defiant stance.

DE-STALINIZATION AND THE CRISIS OF 1956

After Stalin's death in March 1953 the Soviet Union intervened less directly in Poland's domestic politics, although it determined the broad military, economic and political framework within which the PZPR operated. The Stalinist legacy of central planning and mechanisms of party control remained dominant, but they were also moulded by bouts of social assertiveness which punctuated developments of the next thirty years. De-Stalinization began haltingly in 1954; it focused initially on the activities of the security services, stimulated by the revelations of the secret police defector Józef Światło, broadcast to Poland by Radio Free Europe;[7] but it was given its greatest impetus by Khrushchev's secret speech of 1956. In Poland the process continued in stop–go fashion, with periods of liberalization and reform succeeded by periods of conservative retrenchment. Factional disputes over the party's relationship to society became a permanent feature of the Polish political landscape.

The first major crisis for the ruling PZPR came in June 1956, when workers' protests in Poznań, leaving dozens dead and hundreds injured, signalled the end of proletarian passivity. Workers' councils began to be established at factory level, and their economic demands acquired a political cast, with emphasis on a greater say in the running of enterprise affairs and a call for the reinstatement of Gomułka. The death of Stalin and the inauguration of the Soviet New Course by Malenkov in 1954 had already generated divisions within the PZPR over how to respond. In February 1956 Khrushchev's attack on Stalin at the CPSU's Twentieth Congress presented new problems for the East European elites. Khrushchev could blame the dead Stalin for the terror of the 1930s, but in Eastern Europe the local architects of Stal-

---

7   Światło's revelations were published as *Za kulisami bezpieki i partii*, Warsaw, 1990; see also Andrzej Paczkowski, 'Aparat bezpieczeństwa w Polsce: lata 1954–1956', *Puls*, 54, no.1, 1992, pp.62–9.

inism were still in power. In this respect the PZPR was fortunate in having a scapegoat to hand, namely its leader Bierut, who died suddenly shortly after the Soviet party congress. Hardliners such as Jakub Berman were dismissed and the PZPR seemed to accommodate smoothly the new demands for collective leadership. However, factional struggles intensified between the hardline (Natolin) faction and the reformist (Puławski) wing, associated with Gomułka, who had been quietly released from house arrest in 1954.

The initial response of the party to Poznań reflected the instinctive reaction of Stalinist politics: it portrayed the workers' protests as a result of *agents provocateurs* serving foreign interests. The new party leader Edward Ochab, however, swung to the view of the de-Stalinizers, and the PZPR formally acknowledged the existence of genuine workers' grievances.[8] Warned by party workers from the Zeran factory, the reformers forestalled an impending purge. Ochab retired gracefully and on 21 October the Central Committee elected Gomułka as the new party leader. Despite rumours of Soviet military mobilization and the unscheduled visit of a high-powered Soviet delegation, the Polish communists convinced Khrushchev that they maintained control of the situation. The hated Polish-born but Russified Marshal Rokossovski, the Minister of Defence, was shipped home to the Soviet Union along with others of his kind. The Soviet leaders embraced the notion of a Polish road to socialism and the PZPR gained a brief but genuine legitimacy in the reflected light of the popular Gomułka who had again, as in 1948, stood up to the Russian bear. His achievements appeared still greater in the light of developments in Hungary, where Soviet tanks savagely quelled a mass popular revolt against the communist system. In Poland prospects of a new national reconciliation appeared further strengthened by the release of the Polish Primate Cardinal Wyszyński and his subsequent call to support the regime in the 1957 election.

The year 1956 was momentous for a number of reasons. The dominant themes of communist politics in Poland were all manifest in 1956 and would again emerge with embellishments and variations in all

8   See the documents in Paul Zinner (ed.), *National Communism and Popular Revolt in Eastern Europe: A Selection of Documents on Events in Poland and Hungary, February–November 1956*, New York, 1956, especially pp.126–43.

subsequent political crises. The party itself was unable to maintain unity and cohesion; on the contrary it was divided over means and ends, strategy and tactics. It did not stand firm against society, which itself ceased to be passive. Important elements, notably from the creative intelligentsia and the industrial working class, proved willing to take risks. The intelligentsia began to push unremittingly at the limits of free expression.[9]

The change in intellectual climate was dramatic, but it was the workers' protests in Poznań which affected the PZPR most profoundly; it was, after all, the working class in whose name the party ruled and on which it based its claims to legitimacy. Poznań also saw the surfacing of the anti-Soviet attitudes which the party had hoped to undermine by stressing Soviet protection against a resurgent Germany. The response to the crisis, initiated by Ochab and continued by Gomułka, was to build a positive base of support by reaching accommodation with all major social forces. The intelligentsia benefited from a relaxation of censorship. The working class was promised better living standards through economic reform and the acceptance of workers' councils. The massive spontaneous de-collectivization of the peasantry was permitted to stand, and thenceforth most land remained effectively in private hands. Gomułka's *modus vivendi* with the Church included scope for parliamentary representation of Catholic deputies. The election of January 1957 was the first in post-war Eastern Europe to provide a measure of choice, with 722 candidates contesting 459 seats in the *Sejm* (parliament). A process of legal reform was set in motion in accordance with promises of socialist legality.

The optimism was to prove short-lived. Gradually real gains were clawed back and promises were not met. Gomułka threw his weight back towards the conservative elements of the party and left much of the party *apparat* untouched. Censorship was tightened, controversial journals were closed and the workers' councils dissolved. Economic reform never materialized. Even Gomułka's admirers acknowledge his

---

9　It was inaugurated with the publication of Ważyk's 'Poem for Adults': see Stanisław Barańczak, 'Before the Thaw: The Beginnings of Dissent in Postwar Polish Literature (The Case of Adam Wazyk's "A Poem for Adults")', *Eastern European Politics and Societies*, vol.3, no.1, 1989, pp.3–21; see also Peter Raina, *Political Opposition in Poland, 1954–1977*, London, 1978, pp.26–44.

failure to provide clear and decisive leadership.[10] Internal tensions again surfaced within the party. Gomułka faced a hardline group acquiring a new, nationalist form in the person of General Mieczysław Moczar,[11] Minister of the Interior, and a more pragmatic grouping of so-called technocrats associated with Edward Gierek, provincial party leader in Silesia. Thus by the early 1960s the year 1956 had become a powerful collective memory of shared optimism yielding to smashed illusions. The party itself was worried by signs of increasing 'revisionism' within the ranks of its own intelligentsia, encouraged by the rhetoric of change proclaimed in 1956. The symbol of this tendency was the philosopher Leszek Kołakowski, who, among others, kept alive the humanist current of Marxist thinking. In 1965 two young Marxists, Jacek Kuroń and Karol Modzelewski, wrote an Open Letter to the party espousing the need for a social revolution to remove the new class of the bureaucratic apparatus.[12] Intellectual criticism also came from outside the party's ranks, as in 1964 in the 'letter of the 34', attacking the sterility of the party's cultural policy. Conflict with the Church arose again over issues such as religious instruction in schools. During the celebrations of the Polish millennium in 1966 Cardinal Wyszyński's statements displayed a blunt anti-communism. A number of these strands came together in 1968, when a section of the young Warsaw intelligentsia welded links with the generation of 1956.

THE MARCH EVENTS

Student protests in March 1968 found little echo among the wider society but they had a significant longer-term impact. They focused initially on demands for the freeing of protesters imprisoned after demonstrating against the closure of *Dziady* (Forefathers' Eve), a classic work by Adam Mickiewicz, Poland's foremost Romantic

10   See for example Bronisław Syzdek and Eleonora Syzdek, *Polityczne Dylematy Władysława Gomułki*, Warsaw, 1985, pp.223–7.
11   On Moczar see Michael Checinski, *Poland: Communism, Nationalism, Anti-Semitism*, New York, 1982, pp.156–73; Raina, op. cit., pp.104–6.
12   Lengthy excerpts are available in English in S. Persky and H. Flam, *The Solidarity Sourcebook*, Vancouver, 1982, pp.35–56.

writer of the nineteenth century, and the expulsion of Adam Michnik and Henryk Szlajfer from Warsaw University. They rapidly escalated into generalized anti-regime protests which spread to other major cities. The brutal response to the protests was out of all proportion to the challenge posed by the students, who were left shell-shocked both by savage beatings and numerous arrests and by the sudden, incongruous press revelations that Zionist agents and traitors were responsible for the disturbances. Some have viewed the March events and the anti-Zionist campaign as '... a classic example of political provocation' and a bid for power by Mieczysław Moczar.[13] The hunt for Zionists fed avidly on traditional anti-Semitism in a campaign redolent with echoes of Stalinism. The exodus of Jews from Poland had begun immediately at the end of the war, achieving mass dimensions after the notorious (and not fully explained) Kielce pogrom of 1946.[14] In 1968 another exodus took place, depriving the country of many talented people, exiled or driven abroad by pressure and harassment[15] before Gomułka could restore a degree of tenuous authority over the party. As a result of the experiences of the 'March generation' and its links with the generation of 1956, the nucleus of the future dissident opposition emerged. The party, however, reverted to its conservative mould, with the excoriation, expulsion or exile of leading revisionist thinkers, including Kołakowski. A vigorous reformist strand within the PZPR would re-emerge only in 1980.

THE CRISIS OF 1970 AND ITS AFTERMATH

The absence of workers' support for the student protesters of 1968 was notable. Poland also remained quiescent during the Warsaw Pact invasion of Czechoslovakia in August. It was not to last, however. In December 1970 the PZPR faced another major crisis, provoked in great measure by its own ineptitude. Worried by the increasing burden

13 Norman Davies, *God's Playground: A History of Poland*, Oxford, 1981, vol. II, pp.588–9; Raina, op. cit., pp.146–8 takes the opposing view.
14 Checinski, op. cit., p.36.
15 Ibid., pp.241–53.

of subsidies and by a succession of agricultural failures, the government introduced major price increases just before Christmas, a move so extraordinary that it immediately aroused suspicions of provocation.[16] Repression of the ensuing wave of strikes and protests served only to intensify resistance. Feelings of seething resentment burst out into the open, especially in the Baltic shipyards of Szczecin, Gdańsk and Gdynia. Workers assaulted party headquarters in Gdańsk, looted shops and burnt down the Militia Training Centre in Słupsk. The clampdown claimed over three hundred victims of tanks and bullets.[17] Gomułka's health collapsed and on 20 December Edward Gierek took his place.

Although the workers played a major role in the downfall of Gomułka, their role cannot be seen as the only factor. As in 1956, factions within the Politburo were of major significance.[18] Gierek's reputation in Silesia was high, and it was clearly hoped that he could restore credibility with the workers. He did appear to gain through his direct approach to striking workers in the early months of 1971, when he promised a freeze on prices and a major reform programme, the so-called Second Modernization of Poland.

Gierek's two-pronged strategy was in essence simple. In the economic sphere links with foreign firms and major new investment in modern technology would be financed by borrowing from Western countries. The New Poland would generate sufficient exports to repay the debts incurred. This massive borrowing would also permit concessions in the sphere of consumption to satisfy the material aspirations of the population; great stress was placed, for example, on increased availability of private cars. In the political sphere Gierek promised further democratization and greater investment in social consumption, especially housing.

During the first few years of Gierek's tenure there was a new sense of prosperity. New investment projects got under way, including infrastructural developments, and the shops were full. By the mid-

16 But see the protocols from November and December Politburo meetings in Paweł Domański (ed.), *Tajne dokumenty Biura Politycznego. Grudzień 1970*, London, 1991, pp.7–17.
17 See General Korczyński's diary of 17 December 1970, 'Dziennik bojowy gen. broni Grzegorza Korczyńskiego' in ibid., pp.21–7.
18 Stanisław Kania, *Zatrzymać konfrontację*, Warsaw, 1991, pp.48–52.

1970s, however, it became clear that the Gierek strategy was doomed to fail. Dramatic increases in oil prices heralded a period of economic downturn in Western countries and there was little demand for Polish goods. More important, credits from the West were poorly utilized; they became a status symbol for local party leaders and enterprise directors, who demanded loans without regard to longer-term considerations of economic rationality. Conspicuous consumption by the *nomenklatura* was widespread. The underlying reason for failure was not only the greed and incompetence of the elite, but their failure to reform the economic planning system. The system was geared to producing quantity, not quality, and this was reinforced by the use of performance indicators which linked bonuses to output. Grafting foreign technology on to existing structures could not overcome the fundamental conservatism of the planning arrangements nor the entrenched power of the heavy industry lobby.

The economy entered a downward spiral, achieving negative growth in 1979. In 1976 the regime reneged on its promises to maintain price stability. Subsidies were consuming more and more of the state budget. Yet again there was no consultation over price increases and again major workers' protests broke out.[19] To prevent the spread of unrest the authorities immediately rescinded the price rises, but they wielded a heavy hand against those held responsible for organizing the disturbances. The mid-1970s also saw the re-emergence of political tensions, notably over proposals to amend the Constitution. As a result of protests by intellectuals and Church leaders, the most controversial proposal, stressing Poland's 'eternal and inviolable ties with the USSR', was muted: the new provision stressed 'friendship and cooperation' with the USSR and other socialist states.

The most significant result of the suppression of the workers' protests in 1976 was the forming of links between dissenting workers and intellectuals. This took the form of the Committee for Workers' Defence (KOR), established to provide legal and material support for imprisoned workers.[20] Its subsequent strategy was the mobilization of

19 Michael Bernhard, 'The Strikes of June 1976 in Poland', *East European Politics and Societies*, vol.1, no.3, 1987, pp.363–92.
20 For a history of KOR and its origins see Jan Józef Lipski, *KOR: A History of the Workers' Defense Committee in Poland 1976–1981*, Berkeley, CA, 1985.

'social self-defence' to bring about continuous pressure for concessions from the authorities.[21] Many KOR activists were to become advisers to Solidarity and, still later, prominent members of the post-communist political leadership.

The Church was also proving itself more willing to speak out on human rights issues; Cardinal Wyszyński supported demands for an inquiry into allegations of police brutality against the striking workers.[22] A group of Catholics, including Tadeusz Mazowiecki, went on hunger strike in Warsaw in May 1977 to protest against the arrest of KOR supporters and the continuing detention of workers. The greatest immediate achievement of this still inchoate opposition was the securing of amnesty for those imprisoned in 1976. Within three years Mazowiecki and numerous others would take their place as advisers to the workers of the Baltic coast, the birthplace of Solidarity. The gravity of the situation in Poland at the end of the 1970s was obvious to all save, apparently, the upper echelons of the party. The economy was in dire straits, as debt servicing requirements led to reductions in imports of key industrial components and giant construction projects stood uncompleted. There were drastic shortages of foodstuffs and basic consumer goods and a deterioration in health care, education and housing. The party-inspired expert group of DiP (*Doświadczenie i Przyszłość*, Experience and the Future) produced reports analysing the bankruptcy of the polity, the moral exhaustion of society and the wide gulf between the two.[23]

SOLIDARITY

Two factors worked against the prolongation of social paralysis and malaise. Throughout the late 1970s dissent was spreading and providing the basis of an active alternative culture, notably but not exclu-

---

21 Ibid.; see also Adam Michnik, *Letters from Prison and Other Essays*, London, 1985, pp.135–98; A. Ostoja-Ostaszewski *et al.*, *Dissent in Poland 1976–77*, London, 1977; David Ost, *Solidarity and the Politics of Anti-Politics*, Philadelphia, PA, 1990, pp.55–74.
22 Bogdan Szajkowski, *Next to God ... Poland*, London, 1983, p.46.
23 The English translation is Michael Vale (ed.), *Poland: The State of the Republic*, London, 1981.

sively among the intelligentsia. Discussion groups and illegal publications proliferated. The Flying University, whose name echoed resistance to tsarism and the Polish 'underground state' of the Second World War, challenged the party's monopoly of scholarship and education.[24] The Confederation of Independent Poland, the first modern underground political party, preached a bitter anti-communist and anti-Soviet message. The regime seesawed between repression and uneasy toleration. It was especially sensitive to attempts by workers to organize themselves, as in 1978 in the Free Trade Unions of the Coast, whose founders included Andrzej Gwiazda and among whose members was the future leader of Solidarity, Lech Wałęsa. The second factor was the resurgence of a renewed sense of spiritual community, initiated by the growing activism of the Church in pressing the interests and concerns of believers, stimulated by the election of the Polish Cardinal Karol Wojtyła to the Papacy in October 1978, and culminating in the first papal visit in June 1979. It was 'a psychological earthquake ... A whole generation experienced for the first time a feeling of collective power and exaltation. ...'[25]

Solidarity arose in the course of the third major crisis faced by the post-war communist regime. A wave of industrial unrest was yet again triggered by rising prices, which served as an issue in their own right but also as a vehicle for channelling multifarious grievances. Protests began in July 1980 and spread rapidly. The authorities made substantial concessions; on 12 August foreign journalists were officially informed that the worst was over and that settlements were being reached amicably.[26] Two days later the strike spread to the Lenin shipyard in Gdańsk, and thence along the coast and south to Łódź and Wrocław and into Silesia. Politburo figures showed 700,000 workers on strike by the end of August.[27]

The settlement reached at Gdańsk was the *de facto* birth of Solidarity. For the population, Gdańsk became the spearhead and symbol of

---

24 See *Survey*, vol.24, no.4, 1979, and vol.25, no.1, 1980, for documents emanating from different elements of the opposition.
25 Szajkowski, op. cit., p.72.
26 Kevin Ruane, *The Polish Challenge*, London, 1982, p.10.
27 *Protokół 29* of the Politburo meeting of 30 August 1980 in Z. Włodek (ed.), *Tajne dokumenty Biura Politycznego. PZPR a 'Solidaność' 1980–1981*, London, 1992, pp.90–92.

what rapidly developed into a mass movement. There were several major factors in the success of the Gdańsk negotiations. The first was the mass character of workers' protest. The second stemmed from the strikers' refusal to permit the government its traditional divide-and-rule tactics of bilateral enterprise-by-enterprise negotiations; the workers formed the Inter-Enterprise Strike Committee to negotiate on behalf of a group which rapidly expanded to embrace several hundred enterprises; linked to this was the tactic of occupying the factories instead of mounting street protests. The third was the nature of the demands made, most notably for the recognition of independent trade unions buttressed by the right to strike; here the workers benefited from the legal and tactical advice of their intellectual advisers. This insistence on new trade union structures was the culmination of a collective learning experience dating from 1956:[28] most important, the workers refused to countenance any restructuring or 'democratization' of the existing trade union movement.[29]

The effective government accession to all of the 21 demands in the Gdańsk Agreement[30] represented a dramatic departure from the canons of communist politics, not least because it accepted the principle that autonomous organizations might exist, free of direct communist party control. Holmes calls the Agreement 'one of the most important events in the history of the communist world...'.[31] The PZPR, according to its future leader Stanisław Kania, was unconcerned about the right to strike, but independent trade unions were altogether a different matter; they would provide structures which could be exploited by the political opposition.[32] Indeed, Solidarity

---

28 Alex Pravda, 'Poland 1980: From "Premature Consumerism" to Labour Solidarity', *Soviet Studies*, vol.XXXIV, no.4, 1982, pp.162–99; Roman Laba stresses the links between the 1970–71 strikes of the Baltic coast; for him Solidarity owed its birth to the workers, and he minimizes the influence of the KOR intellectuals and the links they had developed with the working class since 1976: see Roman Laba, *Worker Roots of Solidarity: A Political Sociology of Poland's Working Class Democratization*, Princeton, NJ, 1991.

29 See M. Jagielski's statement at the first negotiating session in A. Kemp-Welch (trans.), *The Birth of Solidarity: The Gdańsk Negotiations, 1980*, London, 1983, pp.40–43; also T. Kowalik, 'Experts and the Working Group', ibid., p.145.

30 Ibid., pp.168–79.

31 Leslie Holmes, *Politics in the Communist World*, Oxford, 1986, p.309.

32 Kania, op. cit., pp.20–21, 26, 38–9; also Politburo protocols 27 (28 August 1980) and 28 (29 August 1980) in Włodek, op. cit., pp.78–90.

had the most profound effect on society, including the PZPR itself. It released reserves of energy, enthusiasm, excitement and optimism. Over 90 per cent of the population supported the Gdańsk Agreement.[33] The rapid expansion of membership to over nine million, one million of whom were also party members, reflected this wide-ranging support. Economic issues were primary, underpinned by sentiments of egalitarianism and social justice, with little support among Solidarity members or the population at large for fundamental political change. This was consonant with Solidarity's formal acceptance of the parameters of the existing system, including the leading role of the PZPR and the international alliance with the USSR.[34]

Solidarity endured as a trade union *cum* social movement for sixteen months, ended by the declaration of martial law on 13 December 1981.[35] Its strengths lay in its size, its enthusiasm, its commitment to participatory democracy and its discipline. Its weaknesses lay in its inability to generate a set of clear strategic priorities, especially given the breadth and vagueness of much of the Gdańsk Agreement. This in turn was a product of the many different interests which Solidarity embodied, as well as its inexperience. Not surprisingly, the decentralized regional structure which suited the breadth of the movement generated tensions between local activists and the national leadership under Lech Wałęsa. There were distinct regional emphases.[36] Divisions also developed within the National Commission itself. The adoption of a formal programme based on the central theme of 'a self-managing republic' at the Solidarity Congress of September 1981 did little to clarify its position on major issues. Different pictures of Solidarity have emerged, depending on the perspective of the observer. Thus Solidarity was essentially anarcho-syndicalist,[37]

33 David S. Mason, *Public Opinion and Political Change in Poland, 1980–1982*, Cambridge, 1985, p.93.
34 Ibid., especially pp.119–22.
35 The literature on Solidarity is vast and some of it will be cited below. The most vivid accounts are still those of Neal Ascherson, *The Polish August: The Self-Limiting Revolution*, London, 1981; and Timothy Garton Ash, *The Polish Revolution: Solidarity 1980–82*, London, 1983.
36 Alain Touraine *et al.*, *Solidarity: The Analysis of a Social Movement*, Cambridge, 1983, especially pp.156–78.
37 Raymond Taras, *Poland: Socialist State, Rebellious Nation*, London, 1986, p.65.

stumbling inexorably towards corporatism,[38] a 'revolution of the soul',[39] a synthesis of trade unionist, democratic and nationalist elements,[40] a 'workers' movement *sui generis*,[41] a 'case of emancipatory praxis'.[42]

The PZPR leadership, however, came increasingly to see Solidarity as dominated by 'anti-socialist elements' bent on power. This is why one can see a primary weakness in Solidarity's failure to construct an alliance with the party's reformist elements. The hardliners for their part had an interest in seeing Solidarity depicted as rampantly radical. Already in June 1981 the secret police were reportedly engaged in defacing monuments commemorating the USSR's wartime role, thus giving credence to the view that anti-socialist elements were gaining the upper hand.[43] In the final analysis it was the triumph of this view of Solidarity as a clear and present danger to socialism and the inability of the party (*qua* party) to counter it which led to the party's abdication of control to the military through the proclamation of martial law on 13 December 1981 and the forming of the Military Council of National Salvation (WRON).

With the Gdańsk Agreement the regime had yielded to demands which it was incapable of meeting in the short term and which many of its own supporters opposed. August 1980 marked the beginning of a process of change in the PZPR's own structure and functions. It now faced a confident society organized in two institutional structures, Solidarity and the Catholic Church, whose own mutual relationship was closely interwoven, if at times uneasily.[44] The party's rank and file had proved highly responsive to Solidarity's appeal, and they generated pressure for genuine internal democratization, promised so often before. Although Gierek was replaced as leader of the PZPR by Kania, a representative of the conciliatory line, the party leadership

38   Ost, op. cit., p.133 and especially Chapter 6.
39   Ash, op. cit., p.280.
40   Touraine *et al.*, especially p.174.
41   Oliver Macdonald, 'The Polish Vortex: Solidarity and Socialism', *New Left Review* 139, 1983, p.14.
42   Michael D. Kennedy, *Professionals, Power and Solidarity in Poland*, Cambridge, 1991, p.84.
43   Stanislaw Starski, *Class Struggles in Classless Poland*, Boston, MA, 1982, p.124.
44   Macdonald, op. cit., pp.26–9.

remained divided over how best to respond to Solidarity's challenge; its provincial bureaucratic apparatus remained conservative and apprehensive.[45] The most notable example of spontaneous change from within the party was the 'horizontal movement', which sought to establish links among party cells and between local party bodies and the trade union(s). Traditionally, communist parties stressed only vertical lines of communication, to and from the centre. Even some of the party's reform wing found these horizontal links intolerable, threatening the party with disintegration.[46] The leaders made concessions, including (at the Extraordinary Party Congress of July 1981) the first competitively elected Politburo and Central Committee in the communist world, but they could not resolve the crisis within the PZPR.[47]

The decision to introduce martial law is still a subject of passionate controversy.[48] Many remain convinced that the party was never committed to reform, merely biding its time for a suitable moment to seize the offensive. In October 1981 Kania was replaced by Jaruzelski, who thus combined the key posts of Prime Minister, party leader, and Minister of Defence. Jaruzelski was the key figure in the decision to impose martial law. His own justification at the time rested on the overt danger of civil strife and the more veiled, oblique argument that Soviet intervention was imminent. His recent memoirs, and those of Stanisław Kania, stress the latter. Certainly there was relentless (and public)[49] Soviet pressure on the Polish leaders, whom the Soviet side regarded as soft and inept. The USSR resisted the idea of invasion but

45 Paul G. Lewis, *Political Authority and Party Secretaries in Poland 1975–1986*, Cambridge, 1989, p.284.

46 Wijciech Jaruzelski, *Stan wojenny DLACZEGO ...*, Warsaw, 1992, p.203.

47 George Kolankiewicz, 'Renewal, Reform or Retreat: The Polish Communist Party after the Extraordinary Ninth Congress', *The World Today*, vol.37, no.10, 1981, pp.369–75; Z.A. Kruszewski, 'The Communist Party during the 1980–81 Democratization of Poland' in Jack Bielasiak and Maurice Simon (eds), *Polish Politics: Edge of the Abyss*, New York, 1984, pp.241–59.

48 Jack Bielasiak, 'Solidarity and the State: Strategies of Social Reconstruction' in B. Misztal (ed.), *Poland after Solidarity*, Oxford, 1985, pp.19–38, summarizes some of the various explanations; the contemporary political debate is discussed in later chapters.

49 See Roger E. Kanet, 'The Polish Crisis and Poland's "Allies": The Soviet and East European Response to Events in Poland' in Bielasiak and Simon, op. cit., especially pp.322–33.

prepared the Warsaw Pact for that eventuality. The preferred Soviet option was that of martial law, a scenario for which the PZPR certainly made long-standing contingency preparations.[50] The party leaders were constantly reminded of the invasion of Czechoslovakia and they had long experience of the capacity of the USSR for ruthless removal of awkward allies. Jaruzelski recounts how, on departing with Kania for a secret meeting in Brest in April 1981 with representatives of the Soviet leadership, he set in order his personal affairs and instructed his closest aide to care for his family should he fail to return.[51]

The Politburo's view of Solidarity became increasingly apocalyptic. By early December the tone was one of inevitable confrontation; the counter-revolutionary forces had made their intentions clear and the party was paralysed and frightened. The 'insurrectionary atmosphere', the stockpiling of weapons, the rejection of a National Accord (*porozumienie*), the dominance of 'extremists' ready to seize power and hang all communists from nearby lamp-posts – this is a picture which vividly confirms the gulf between the ruling elites and the Polish population;[52] it is also clearly belied by the lack of preparations made by Solidarity for the eventuality of the repressive option.

MARTIAL LAW AND ITS AFTERMATH

The declaration of martial law (the 'state of war', *stan wojenny*) on 13 December 1981 came as an immense shock. The element of surprise, the severing of telecommunications and the mass internment of

---

50 The possibility of martial law was raised at the Politburo meeting of 29 August 1980; the protocol is published in *Polityka* 48, 30 November 1991. The Polish defector Ryszard Kukliński revealed detailed planning for intervention in 'Wojna z narodem', *Krytyka*, vol.4, no.475 (reprinted separately in April 1987); Polish party documents specifying preparations for internment were published in *Polityka* 45, 10 November 1990; for reports of some Soviet Politburo meetings in 1980 and 1981 see *Rzeczpospolita* 292, 12–13 December 1992; public statements made by participants, such as Soviet General Dobrynin, have affirmed preparations for a Soviet invasion: see *The Guardian*, 14 March 1992.

51 Jaruzelski, op. cit., p.96.

52 Politburo Protocol 18 (5 December 1981), *Polityka* 49, 7 December 1991; Jaruzelski, op. cit., pp.367ff.

Solidarity activists were sufficient to prevent organized national opposition. Local resistance was widespread but quickly quelled. Miners' protests, notably the pitched battle with anti-riot squads at the Wujek mine near Katowice where seven miners died, became a symbol of defiance; but the regime had little difficulty in maintaining order. The mines and other strategic industries were militarized and their workers brought under military regulations. Civil rights were suspended, including the right of association; only the Church was now a legitimate meeting place. Thousands of Solidarity members lost their jobs, while the military also embarked on a new 'cleansing' process to rid the country of corruption.[53]

Martial law under the new Military Council of National Salvation lasted formally until 22 July 1983.[54] It is generally regarded as mild in comparison with the many examples of military governments wreaking atrocities on their own people; but it left a deep imprint on Polish society, not only because of its repressive methods but also because it was widely experienced as a national betrayal. Jaruzelski spoke of the imminent catastrophe of civil war, but he had caused the blood of his countryfolk to be shed. He spoke of continuing the reform process, but he had attempted to destroy the main engine of change, Solidarity itself. He talked of a social contract, but he was to dictate its terms and conditions.

Of course some did welcome martial law as the restoration of order out of anarchy and some accepted the moral force of Jaruzelski's argument that his choice was the 'lesser evil'. Solidarity's popularity had declined, not least because of an unremitting government propaganda offensive: this attributed blame for economic deterioration to Solidarity's strike action and economic demands.[55] It would be misleading to suggest that the whole nation was united against Jaruzelski and the nucleus of close associates who became the locus of decision-making in the 1980s.

The period of maximum repression lasted for about a year,

53 George Malcher, *Poland's Politicized Army: Communists in Uniform*, New York, 1984, pp.204–8.
54 On this period see George Sanford, *Military Rule in Poland: The Rebuilding of Communist Power 1981–1983*, London, 1986a, and Malcher, op. cit.
55 David S. Mason, 'Solidarity, the Regime and the Public', *Soviet Studies*, vol. XXV, no. 4, October 1983, pp.533–45.

although coercion, imprisonments and harassment continued throughout the decade. In the summer of 1984 some 31,000 persons were released from prison under the first amnesty, but any resultant good will was eradicated by the murder of Father Jerzy Popiełuszko in October by three officers of the Interior Ministry. The murder reinforced distrust of the regime, which could not be overcome by official disavowal of responsibility and the public trial of the perpetrators.[56] At the same time Jaruzelski embarked on a strategy of controlled participation and political innovation under a restored and rejuvenated Communist Party. This new 'social contract' would also enlist popular support for vital economic reform. Jaruzelski failed on all counts.

The party itself was ideologically bankrupt and institutionally weak. It not only remained a conservative institution after its purge by the military leadership; it resembled a (considerably militarized) head at odds with its body, the provincial *apparat*,[57] and with ossified limbs reaching to the grass roots: local party organizations were inactive, unable to respond to initiatives from the centre and unable to recruit new members. The party's functions were being eroded and confused and its relationship with society at large remained one of estrangement. Nor was the attempt to create regime-sponsored but theoretically autonomous social organizations a success. These new consultative bodies included PRON, the Patriotic Movement for National Renewal; the OPZZ or National Trade Union Accord; and the Social Economic Council. These bodies themselves faced a dilemma. If they proved craven and subordinate to the authorities, they would be dismissed by the population, which was in any event inclined to see them as merely another party tool in different guise. If they made demands perceived as too radical or non-conformist, they would lose credibility with the regime. None escaped this dilemma. PRON, although often critical of government, never succeeded in transcending the public ridicule which greeted its inception. The OPZZ was not supine either and gained members more rapidly than expected; but the parlous state

---

56 The Deputy Minister of the Interior in the Mazowiecki government, Jan Widacki, quotes numerous documents and intelligence reports to show the parallel strategy of disinformation, infiltration and provocation against the opposition, including the Church: see Jan Widacki, *Czego nie powiedział Generał Kiszczak*, Warsaw, 1992.
57 Lewis, op. cit., pp.218–52.

of the economy meant that the government had little to offer in order to make it a credible trade union movement.

Nor could the government do better in its attempts to co-opt elements of the dissident intelligentsia, through its Consultative Council, some weakening of censorship,[58] erratic tolerance of the wide and growing network of underground literature, indeed of a political counter-culture, fostered by underground Solidarity.[59] The advantages of cooperation could not outweigh the stigma of collaboration with a regime which had introduced martial law.

Political institutional innovations were greeted with equal suspicion, whether the Civil Rights Ombudsman, the Tribunal of State, the referendum, or changes in the electoral system to produce more choice. The rhetoric of renewal and democratization had been repeated too many times before. None of these mechanisms proved effective and some, like PRON and the November 1987 referendum, proved counter-productive; the latter failed to endorse the leadership's economic strategy. Broadly the policies constituted 'a vastly asymmetrical process with an active state courting a passive population';[60] nor were they uniformly supported by the party itself.[61]

The Jaruzelski leadership also embarked on a strategy of economic reform. It made some progress in reducing subsidies through progressive price rises, but like its predecessors it proved incapable of transforming the planning mechanism. The heavy industrial lobby proved well able to protect its fiefdom, while economic policy combined an uneasy and contradictory farrago of market elements and the plan.

The failure of the regime to win support for 'socialist renewal' was not due solely to a generalized mistrust of party-government initiatives or to preoccupation with the daily struggle to acquire goods and

58 Alexander Remmer, 'A Note on Post-Publication Censorship in Poland', *Soviet Studies*, vol.XLI, no.3, 1989, pp.415–25.
59 Sabrina P. Ramet, *Social Currents in Eastern Europe*, London, 1991, pp.64–74, 87–98.
60 George Kolankiewicz, 'Poland and the Politics of Permissible Pluralism', *East European Politics and Societies*, vol.2, no.1, 1988, p.157.
61 For different approaches to the nature and type of factions within the PZPR see Jadwiga Staniszkis, 'Patterns of Change in Eastern Europe', *East European Politics and Societies*, vol.4, no.1, 1990, pp.77–97; Ewa Morawska, 'On Barriers to Pluralism in Pluralist Poland', *Slavic Review*, vol.47, no.4, 1988, pp.626–36; Werner Hahn, *Democracy in a Communist Party*, New York, 1987, pp.247–62.

services: it was also a result of alternative focuses of loyalty, notably Solidarity and the Roman Catholic Church. The memory of Solidarity remained very strong even though the institution was in practice very weak. Underground Solidarity had neither the depth of social support it had once enjoyed, nor the cohesion of its leadership, nor even the breadth of shared values.

Still, Solidarity remained sufficiently active in the 1980s to provide a tangible reminder of the gulf between the rulers and the ruled. The nucleus of a Solidarity underground continued to operate under the leadership of Zbigniew Bujak, who headed a provisional national executive until his arrest in May 1986. Although it was now a very different Solidarity,[62] it did provide for the continuity of the Solidarity myth. Its activities, including demonstrations, protests, boycotts, and above all the maintenance of a thriving underground press, never took on a mass character, but they provided a constant thorn in the side of the government. Solidarity formed a major barrier to the regime's strategy of controlled participation. It offered an ethical alternative to collaboration and a source of moral opprobrium directed against those willing to cooperate with the regime.

The Church had provided a reservoir of alternative values as well as non-communist interpretations of Polish history and culture[63] throughout the post-war period. Moreover, it had not fallen prey to secularization: rather, there had been an increase in religious practice. Church leaders maintained links with leading opposition intellectuals, while numerous local priests provided a haven for underground activities. They also maintained their long-standing practice of cultivating good relations with the regime. The Church, assisted by both Catholic and non-Catholic intellectuals, assiduously fostered the myth of a link between Catholicism and Polish nationhood stretching back more than a thousand years.[64]

---

62 See Jerzy Holzer and Krzysztof Leski, *Solidarność w podziemiu*, Łódź, 1990.

63 V. Chrypinski, 'Church and Nationality in Post-War Poland' in Pedro Ramet (ed.), *Religion and Nationalism in Soviet and East European Politics*, London, 1989, pp.246–51.

64 See Muryjane Osa, 'Resistance, Persistence and Change: The Transformation of the Catholic Church in Poland', *East European Politics and Societies*, vol.3, no.2, 1989, pp.268–99 for a critique of the traditional arguments linking Catholicism and Polish national identity.

However, it was not Solidarity which directly inaugurated the process leading to the final collapse of the regime but a new generation of young militant workers whose demands included the legal restoration of Solidarity. Signs of unrest had been apparent since January 1988. In May strikes began in the Gdańsk region. The regime's response was typically ambivalent, combining repressive measures with concessions. Yet there were also oblique signs that it was recognizing the exhaustion of options for change within the existing framework, while leading Solidarity intellectuals also broached again the notion of a broadly-based anti-crisis pact.[65] Wałęsa was still a powerful influence on the working class, and the regime may have hoped that he could restrain this new activism. None the less, the political leaders were not yet fully committed to a strategy of negotiated settlement with the opposition. Repression of strikers and harassment of opposition members continued, along with further efforts to co-opt elements of the intelligentsia.

The acceptance of negotiation received a strong new impetus from strikes which swept Silesia and the Dąbrowski Basin in September. The deep wound of political alienation was revealed anew, and the regime's appeal to the Church and Solidarity to act as intermediaries appeared to be an act of humiliating desperation. In retrospect it was also the first hesitant step towards solutions which were to prove more far-reaching than any of the participants imagined. The developments of September 1988 inaugurated the Round Table negotiations between the communist government and the illegal opposition movement; their culmination was the installing of Tadeusz Mazowiecki as the first modern non-communist prime minister in Eastern Europe.

THE LEGACY OF THE COMMUNIST REGIME

The experience of the communist regime in Poland has left an enduring legacy in all spheres, political, economic, social, cultural and psychological. The factors which make up these various subsystems may be analytically extracted and distinguished, but empirically they are

---

65 Holzer and Leski, op. cit., p.153.

dynamic, inter-linked, and interdependent; changes in one area generate change in others. None the less, as a starting-point we can essay some generalizations about factors which are likely to have an enduring effect on the evolution of the post-communist system. Some are characteristic features of the communist states; some result from the specific Polish experience; still others are themselves a product of the interaction between the two.

Socio-Economic Features

The socio-economic structures of the former communist states are distinctive when compared with the capitalist democracies to which they now aspire. Poland and all the former communist states have a large agrarian sector and a large working class, concentrated in large-scale heavy industry, much of which is based on obsolete technology. Their service sectors are undeveloped and their quaternary or knowledge-based sectors are at best incipient. Capitalist states have small agricultural populations, a shrinking manual working class, a hugely expanded white-collar sector, and a strong middle class, both entrepreneurial and professional. If the restructuring of the East European economies is to follow this capitalist path, there will need to be a further mass exodus out of agriculture and a transformation of the working class into a new technocratic, white-collar stratum, and the birth of a class of capitalist entrepreneurs as well.

In Poland the working class centres on the vast industrial fiefdoms of heavy industry which are a direct consequence of the Stalinist model of industrialization. There is little likelihood that many of these enterprises can compete successfully in a world economy already showing reduced demand for the steel, armaments, chemicals or ships which were the showcases of economic success in the 1950s. In developed areas of light industry such as textiles the prospects of successful competition against low-wage economies also seem remote. The planned economy was notorious for its production of inferior goods using outdated machinery; the captive markets of the Soviet bloc absorbed what was offered, regardless of quality.

At the same time, the Polish working class has been notable for its assertiveness and self-confidence. The years of workers' protest, 1956,

1970, 1976, 1980 and 1988, have major symbolic status as milestones in resistance to oppression, crowned with ultimate triumph. Solidarity was strongest in the very bastions of heavy industry now most threatened by the reshaping of the economy. There is a strong tradition of faith in workers' self-management solutions[66] and use of the strike weapon for both political and economic gains. This is the experience of challenging authority, rather than seeking influence through bargaining and compromise.

There also remains a large agricultural sector, providing the potential for the reopening of tensions between town and countryside; in 1989 26 per cent of the labour force worked in agriculture, and 40 per cent of the population lived in the countryside. The distinctive Polish feature is that this class retains many traditional peasant characteristics and values. In contrast to the agricultural workers of the collective farms of their East European neighbours, Polish peasants are private owners of small-holdings (thereby unsuited to mechanization), and they are tenaciously attached to their land. They were less politically assertive under the communist regime than their working-class counterparts, and there was a strong element of distrust of state power and institutions,[67] not least because communist ideology was antagonistic to the supposed petty bourgeois instincts of the peasantry. However, the peasants were highly organized, both as a consequence of the emergence of Rural Solidarity and because of the regime's anxiety to give credibility to its satellite party, the United Peasant Party (ZSL). The peasants were accustomed to the regime's dependence on their productive capacity. They also remained the fundamental base of the power of the Roman Catholic Church.

The intelligentsia may be divided into several different categories. Some elements were directly involved in the system of state power. The swollen bureaucracy of the communist system is another element of the legacy bequeathed by the old system. Because the state assumed

---

66 See, for example, W. Morawski, 'Self-management and Economic Reform' in Jadwiga Koralewicz, Ireneusz Bialecki and Margaret Watson (eds), *Crisis and Transition: Polish Society in the 1980s*, Oxford, 1987, pp.80–110; and Włodzimierz Pańków, 'The Solidarity Movement, Management and the Political System in Poland' in ibid., pp.111–29.

67 Elzbieta Tarkowska and Jacek Tarkowski, 'Social Disintegration in Poland: Civil Society or Autonomous Familism', *Telos* 89, 1991, p.107.

such wide-ranging functions, the state administration was extremely large. To a considerable extent, the size of the administration will be a function of decisions made about the nature of the economic and welfare roles of the state; but there is a case for expecting considerable reductions. These will also affect the creative intelligentsia, which gained numerous advantages from state provision of culture and recreation. The gains in increased artistic freedom may not be a sufficient trade-off for the losses of security and finance.

All sections of the population benefited from the highly developed, although often inefficient, system of welfare benefits, and from provision for housing, education and health care. The welfare system was wider than anything provided by the capitalist welfare states,[68] since it included subsidies on basic essentials, including food and clothing, rents and heating, cultural provision and recreation and holiday facilities. Unemployment was never a problem and job security was very high; indeed, inefficient use of labour led to labour shortages and changing one's job was extremely easy. Numerous social benefits were geared to the high participation of women in the labour force.

Opinions have been very mixed about the significance of such provision. For some, these arrangements had a cumulative negative impact in fostering a dependency culture and a disinclination to hard work. For others they provided a basic, if highly bureaucratized and often unjust, system of protection and security, especially for the weaker elements of society. However, there is general agreement that certain elements of the system, such as state health care, were highly valued by the population.

Social relations also took on a specific cast under the communist system. Class conflict lacked salience and ethnic differences were submerged; Poland was a rare case of homogeneity, with no large ethnic minorities. Old community ties were dissolved by the communist governments, but new patterns of social interaction took their place. Religious worship was important, for both spiritual sustenance and political demonstration. Because of the Church's implicit challenge to official discourse, the authorities were never able to exercise

---

68 For a discussion of social policy in communist Poland see Frances Millard, 'Social Policy in Poland' in Bob Deacon *et al.*, *The New Eastern Europe*, London, 1992a, especially pp.118–28.

complete control over language. By the late 1980s the Roman Catholic Church was a confident, flourishing institution ready and anxious to place its own moral concerns on the political agenda.

Increasingly, especially in urban areas, social networks developed on the basis of mutual reciprocal assistance. Virtually everyone from shop assistants to brain surgeons provided access to goods and services for themselves and their friends or friends of friends in a vast orgy of mutual back-scratching. In a shortage economy money was a necessary but insufficient condition of obtaining the things one needed, at least for those without access to the special networks of elite shops and services. Informal relations, black marketeering and corrupt practices were a mark not of social deviance but of adaptability to the system.

The Political Legacy

The communists never succeeded in achieving anything more than fleeting periods of legitimacy for the political system of single-party rule. They enjoyed power and privilege but lacked authority. The perceived divisions between rulers and ruled, between 'us' and 'them', appeared an entrenched element of Polish political culture. Politics was equated not with the art of compromise and negotiation but with the machinations and manipulations of the PZPR. Attitudes to the state were similarly negative; after all, the party claimed the leading and guiding role *vis-à-vis* the state institutions, as well as appointment and dismissal of all key personnel through *nomenklatura*. Parliament, the state administration and the judiciary were generally held low in public esteem.

Widespread animosity to the political system was also in part a consequence of official ideological and institutional links to the USSR. The communists never succeeded in eradicating traditional anti-Russian and anti-Soviet attitudes; indeed, strong pro-American sentiments reinforced these, especially in periods of deteriorating superpower relations. The Poles developed a variety of reference points to judge their politics and economics. Western influences penetrated Poland more easily than elsewhere in Eastern Europe, through pervasive listening to external radio broadcasts, foreign travel and extensive family ties abroad, particularly in the United States, which the party increasingly came to encourage for economic reasons.

The widespread rejection of the communist political system served to mask the extent to which the interests of the population were shaped by and became bound up with the social and economic system. Stalin himself identified the process of building socialism in Poland as akin to 'saddling a cow'. That the Polish cow led the East European charge away from Soviet-style socialism came as a surprise to few. The comprehensiveness and rapidity of the process came as a surprise to almost everyone. The reins and bridle came off quickly; yet after four decades removing the saddle itself was almost bound to be shocking and painful.

2. Understanding Change

What has occurred in Poland since 1989 is widely, though not universally, regarded as a process of revolutionary change. This is revolution in the sense of process rather than event: a process of qualitative, irreversible transformation. Attempts continue to define its starting-point, its character, and its direction; to identify the pitfalls which may be encountered along the way; to learn from the experiences of other types of system transformation. There are global or systemic approaches to all these aspects, as well as approaches which seek to identify and analyse the role of particular factors. Some emphasize the continuities, others the changes. In some cases the comparative element predominates, with stress either on the importance of the similar features of communist Eastern Europe or on the significance of the specific, distinctive characteristics of individual countries. Some highlight the newness of the undertaking, others that there is nothing new under the sun.

This chapter will begin by discussing certain approaches to the nature of the communist system in Poland. This provides the basis for analysing approaches to the transfer of power from the communist elite in 1989, since explanations of why the system changed are largely also explanations of why it failed to persist. The remainder of the discussion will focus on the prospects for democracy, since that is the 'destination' desired by the emergent political elite.

THE NATURE OF POLAND'S COMMUNIST SYSTEM

Poland has always fit somewhat uneasily into the categories applied to the East European states of the former Soviet bloc. Although the term 'communist system' is now the preferred term, it does not imply that these states bore any resemblance to the communist society of Marxist thinkers. The term 'state socialism' might well be preferable, since it carries fewer normative implications. However, since 'post-communism' is widely used, it seems sensible to use the term 'communist system' to indicate similarities in political evolution and a more or less comparable point from which to assess the degree and nature of the changes that are taking place.

The Totalitarian Model of Polish Politics

Many conceptual approaches to the new post-war East European regimes took their lead from studies of the USSR. In the sphere of political analysis, as in politics itself, Eastern Europe lay in the Soviet shadow. Approaches to Soviet politics were assumed to apply also to Eastern Europe.[1] Thus the first systemic paradigm of the new Eastern European regimes after the communist consolidation of power was that of totalitarianism, derived from the study of Nazi Germany and Stalin's USSR. Because Eastern Europe was striving to become a carbon copy of the Soviet Union and rapidly adopted its political institutions and economic strategy, the application of the concept of totalitarianism appeared plausible.

The concept can be reduced to a central theme, namely that the totalitarian regime sought total control of the human activity within its ambit. In the absence of autonomous intermediate groups channelling their demands, individuals lost their capacity to influence political developments; they were not independent actors but isolated, atomized elements mobilized and manipulated by a small political elite. Within this framework, there was scope for considerable disagreement.[2] However, Friedrich and Brzezinski's approach became the most frequently cited in Western scholarly literature; it stressed the single party, usually under one leader; the use of mass terror and hence the importance of coercive institutions like the secret police; an official ideology to which all were expected to adhere; and virtual state monopoly of the means of communication, state direction of the

1   This tendency is also evident in recent discussions; for example, Leslie Holmes, *Politics in the Communist World*, Oxford, 1986, pp.379–401.
2   See Benjamin R. Barber, 'Conceptual Foundations of Totalitarianism' in Carl J. Friedrich, Michael Curtis and Benjamin R. Barber, *Totalitarianism in Perspective: Three Views*, London, 1969, pp.3–52.

economy and state control of weaponry. It was the sum of these ingredients which created a distinctive pattern or syndrome;[3] all were necessary, for the removal of any single element would change the configuration. Conceptual criticism of this model centred on its value-laden nature and its inability to cope with change; it was ahistorical, static and imbued with negative ethical judgement. Empirically, its individual elements were easy to label but difficult to measure or assess. Poland proved particularly awkward in this respect, for in the Catholic Church it retained a centre of institutional autonomy and alternative values throughout the darkest days of the Stalinist period. Marxism–Leninism was of course proclaimed officially, but much of the population did not even pretend to accept it.

Indeed, events in 1956 in both Poland and Hungary undermined the notion of a powerless society mobilized and directed by a small elite. The Poznań riots in Poland and the undoubted popularity of the new party leader Władysław Gomułka, followed by a full-blown popular uprising in Hungary, drew attention to the continuing importance of social forces and the existence of divisions within parties hitherto regarded as monoliths. Such events could not occur in a totalitarian regime; neither could the totalitarian model explain them. Change in the USSR itself also became apparent and, increasingly, attempts were made to amend the totalitarian approach to accommodate the widespread view that the post-Stalin regimes were different from their progenitors. Increasingly the concept wilted under a barrage of conceptual and empirical criticism.[4]

As Western political science moved away from the concept of totalitarianism, articulate elements of the East European opposition such as Václav Havel in Czechoslovakia and Adam Michnik in Poland were discovering it. As intellectuals, the official Marxist–Leninist claim to Truth and its requirements of distorted discourse had a par-

---

3   Carl J. Friedrich and Zbigniew K. Brzezinski, *Totalitarian Dictatorship and Autocracy*, Cambridge, MA, 1956, especially Chapter 2.

4   A.H. Brown, *Soviet Politics and Political Science*, London, 1974, pp.30–41; see also Robert D'Amico, 'The Myth of the Totally Administered Society,' *Telos* 88, 1991, pp.88–94. However, it has not wholly vanished from contemporary West European usage: see, for example, John Marks, *Fried Snowballs: Communism in Theory and Practice*, London, 1990.

ticular impact. They read George Orwell's *Nineteen Eighty-Four* and recognized their own predicament.[5] For them what was important was the fact that totalitarianism *aimed* at obliterating the private sphere; this was an ethical evaluation as much as a political analysis. The term remains in widespread use in Eastern Europe, whether to describe the old system or as a yardstick for assessing political evolution. Andrzej Walicki, for example, maintains that we should 'accept the totalitarian model as an adequate explanation of the militantly ideological phase in the development of "actually existing socialism" while ... making it clear that the further development of this system consisted in the gradual abandonment of its totalitarian features'.[6]

Comparative Communism

Gradually, in the 1960s, the study of communist regimes began to emerge as a sub-discipline of comparative politics. Gordon Skilling and Ghiţa Ionescu both made important contributions in this respect by seeking to identify not only the many common features of the East European systems, which were gradually becoming entrenched by the passing of the years and by the guardianship of the USSR; but also the distinctive national variations, which were also, if paradoxically, becoming increasingly marked.[7] These ideas were developed in subsequent textbooks[8] and comparative studies. Economists also contributed much to understanding communist systems, with regard to their economic functioning, the political interactions of the bureaucracy, and behavioural responses to the economic system.

These comparative approaches identified a number of common distinguishing features of the East European states. Firstly, the ruling

5 Jacques Rupnik, 'Totalitarianism Revisited' in J. Keane (ed.), *Civil Society and the State*, London, 1988, pp.264–71.
6 Andrzej Walicki, 'From Stalinism to Post-Communist Pluralism: The Case of Poland', *New Left Review* 185, 1991, p.94; see also David Ost, 'Towards a Corporatist Solution in Eastern Europe: The Case of Poland', *East European Politics and Societies*, vol.3, no.1, 1989, pp.152–9.
7 H. Gordon Skilling, *The Governments of Communist East Europe*, New York, 1966; Ghiţa Ionescu, *The Politics of the European Communist States*, London, 1967.
8 See, for example, Holmes, op. cit.; Stephen White, John Gardner and George Schöpflin, *Communist Political Systems: An Introduction*, London, 1982 (second edition 1987); Joni Lovenduski and Jean Woodall, *Politics and Society in Eastern Europe*, London, 1987.

parties possessed similar structures and played the dominant role in their respective societies through distinctive control mechanisms, notably the existence of a parallel party bureaucracy, whose task was to supervise the state administration, and the *nomenklatura*, whereby the party assumed control of an extraordinarily wide sphere of appointments. In every country the Party's leading bodies also retained the capacity for arbitrary intervention in the judicial process. The parties were typical 'Leninist' parties based on principles of democratic centralism.[9]

Secondly, communist systems had a single, official ideology, Marxism–Leninism. Communist elites maintained that their countries' social, political and economic development was guided by Marxism. All professed the ability of 'scientific socialism' to reveal basic laws of social development and all declared their ultimate destination to be that of a classless communist society.[10] Within the party there operated a corpus of 'agitators' and 'propagandists' with responsibility for ideological matters. The communist parties determined basic guidelines for operating the system of censorship.[11] There were mechanisms of overt socialization of the young designed to engender, among other things, an understanding of basic ideological principles and categories of analysis (whatever they happened to be at a given time).[12]

Western scholars have seen ideology as fulfilling a variety of functions in the communist systems, for the elites themselves and for the population at large. Part of the concern with ideology is obvious enough: only one world view was officially permitted, that world view was visible everywhere in the form of slogans and symbols, it was claimed to motivate policy and it laid claim to Truth and with it the ability to bring about progress.

Thirdly, communist economic systems were based on public owner-

9 See Holmes, op. cit., pp.8–9; Michael Waller, *Democratic Centralism*, Manchester, 1981.
10 Michael Waller and Bogdan Szajkowski, 'The Communist Movement: from Monolith to Polymorph', in Stephen White and Daniel N. Nelson (eds), *Communist Politics: A Reader*, London, 1986, p.23; see also Stephen White, 'What is a Communist System?', *Studies in Comparative Communism*, vol. 16, no. 4, 1983, pp.247–63.
11 For the Polish censorship guidelines see *Czarna księga cenzury PRL*, London, 1979 (2 vols).
12 On the shifts of ideological focus see Raymond Taras, *Ideology in a Socialist State: Poland 1956–1983*, London, 1984.

ship and central planning. The distinctive political economy of bureaucratic central planning, oriented above all to the development of heavy industry, generated similar economic problems. It also led to similar adaptive behaviour, not only by individuals but by institutions, the branch ministries and enterprises. Some economic problems were attributable to political decisions like investment strategy; others were a product of the planning mechanism itself.

The Soviet model of self-sufficient or autarkic development took a severe toll on the Eastern European economies, which were even less suited to the strategy of developing heavy industry than the USSR itself, with its vast size and extensive raw materials. In all cases, including that of the USSR, unbalanced development had a cumulative effect. Emphasizing heavy industry meant neglect of agriculture, consumer goods, social expenditure, infrastructural development, and environmental protection. In time the lack of development of the latter came to affect the industrial sector itself. As the economies became more developed and thus more interdependent, so they became increasingly centralized and bureaucratic. The heavy industrial ministries in particular emerged as powerful political lobbies.[13]

Because of the difficulty of gaining accurate information about the economy, the plans themselves were at best estimates of productive capacity. The characteristic concern with quantitative indices of performance had a number of consequences. It meant that enterprises and ministries tried both to understate their own capacity or to demand a maximum of inputs in order to make their task of fulfilling their plans easier. It also meant that the efficient use of inputs was of little concern to managers and labour, whose incomes and prospects depended on achieving the required quantity of output. Thus the quality and assortment of goods produced was also of secondary concern. Emphasis on output rendered the system slow to accept innovation, which was potentially disruptive of existing plan fulfilment. The emphasis on quantity was partly a result of the fact that these economies were beset by chronic shortages. At the same time the fact of shortages was itself a key factor explaining the uncertainties and

13 See Alan R. Ball and Frances Millard, *Pressure Politics in Industrial Societies*, London, 1986, pp.63–5, 72–80.

bottlenecks of the system.[14] Attempts to reform the planned economies never overcame these fundamental difficulties, even in Hungary which proved the most radical and innovative.

People adapted themselves to this system. As consumers they developed strategies for coping with shortages and long queues. They took unauthorized time from work, hoarded goods wherever possible, and bought on the black market. They built up social networks of family and friends working in different sections of the economy who would organize the provision of goods and services 'under the counter'.[15] As producers they tried to fulfil the letter of the plan, but rarely its spirit. Enterprises concentrated on those aspects of their plans which were easiest to fulfil. Managers, ministries and party officials established cosy informal relationships with one another. Workers and employees pilfered what they could, often for use in the second or parallel economy. Absenteeism was high everywhere.

Finally, the party's relationship with society was also seen as a distinctive characteristic of the communist party systems. The communist parties exerted tight control of all social organizations, blocking their development as genuine intermediate bodies. Trade unions, women's groups, and peasants' organizations existed alongside a vast number of other social and leisure organizations; but none could act as channels to express the demands of their members.

In time this view came to be qualified with the introduction of the concept of 'pressure groups' and 'interest groups' to Soviet and East European politics.[16] The theoretical underpinning of this approach lay in the notion that an increasingly complex society, with a more specialist division of labour, gives rise to the incorporation of expert elites into the policy-making process;[17] oligarchic groups of decision-makers lack the breadth of expertise necessary for efficient policy-

---

14 Janos Kornai, *Economics of Shortage*, Amsterdam, 1980 (2 vols).
15 Janine Wedel discusses the specific Polish patterns of response in 'The Ties that Bind in Polish Society' in Stanisław Gomułka and Antony Polonsky (eds), *Polish Paradoxes*, London, 1990, pp.237–60.
16 See Ball and Millard, op. cit., pp.9–13; H. Gordon Skilling, 'Interest Groups and Communist Politics', *World Politics*, vol.18, no.3, 1966, pp.118–37; Susan Gross Solomon, '"Pluralism" in Political Science: The Odyssey of a Concept' in Susan Gross Solomon (ed.), *Pluralism in the Soviet Union*, London, 1983, pp.4–36.
17 See Jerry F. Hough, '"Interest Groups" and "Pluralism" in the Soviet Union', *Soviet Union*, vol.8, no.1, 1981, pp.104–9.

making, and this encourages consultation. Modern governments cannot run modern economies on the basis of coercion, so they must develop mechanisms of consent. The identification of certain modes of interest articulation remained highly controversial, but it did provide an understanding of how various specialist interests were accommodated and helped to explain new forms of collective action as attempts to bypass the ineffective official channels of communication such as the trade unions. It was clear, however, that interest articulation depended on the terms established by the ruling parties: some were more prone to consultation than others and there were variations over time. All communist regimes certainly restricted the autonomous flourishing of 'civil society'.

The Polish Case

The communist systems, then, were widely seen as a distinct type of authoritarian political system. In respect of all these characteristics Poland provides a good example of diversity within this common framework. The Polish Communist Party (PZPR) asserted its 'leading role'. Its structures were typical: the wider rank-and-file membership, the *apparat* of full-time party officials, with the leading organs of the Central Committee, the Secretariat and the Politburo at the apex of the structure. Yet these structures did not always operate as expected. In particular, we have seen that the PZPR was periodically riven by deep divisions. Furthermore, after the introduction of martial law the party never recovered its former status, and those who exerted the greatest influence in the 1980s were professional military men.[18]

The *nomenklatura* remained a highly developed patronage system ensuring the party's control of key appointments. The list of *nomenklatura* posts grew in the 1970s[19] and again up to the middle of the 1980s, after a hiatus due to pressure from Solidarity and the demand

---

18 See George Sanford, 'Poland' in Martin McCauley and Stephen Carter (eds), *Leadership and Succession in the Soviet Union, Eastern Europe and China*, London, 1986, p.59; also Werner Hahn, *Democracy in a Communist Party*, New York, 1987, p.256.

19 A. Smolar, 'The Rich and the Powerful' in Abraham Brumberg (ed.), *Poland: Genesis of a Revolution*, New York, 1983, p.46; for an indication of the variety of *nomenklatura* posts see Denis MacShane, *Solidarity: Poland's Independent Trade Union*, Nottingham, 1981, pp.163–9.

for elections within the party itself.[20] As elsewhere, the system was seen as highly conducive to both conservatism and corruption. The PZPR worried constantly about the quality of its cadres and implicitly acknowledged 'the alienation of the provincial party apparatus from the local population, their bureaucratic isolation and inability to exercise local leadership ...'.[21] At the same time, the *nomenklatura* did not prove an insuperable obstacle to the rise of talented individuals, both party and non-party. Poland's post-communist leadership was to draw heavily on the Polish professoriat for its appointments: the future Finance Minister Leszek Balcerowicz, Prime Minister Hanna Suchocka, Foreign Minister Krzysztof Skubiszewski, Minister of Justice and then Marshal of the *Sejm* Wiesław Chrzanowski, and Minister of Education Andrzej Stelmachowski were but a few of the academics who later assumed key positions. Indeed, a 1984 report prepared for the Politburo by the Ministry of the Interior described the Polish Academy of Science as a hotbed of opposition.[22] The Catholic press, which controlled its own recruitment, often provided a haven for opposition journalists such as the future Prime Minister Tadeusz Mazowiecki.

It is difficult therefore to discuss the 'leading role' in the Polish context without qualification. The PZPR was not all-powerful, and factional struggles rather than monolithic cohesion were the norm rather than the exception; from 1956 it had to acknowledge the existence of significant social forces operating as constraints, although these varied over time.

Similar caveats apply when assessing the role of Marxism–Leninism. Ideology structured elite consciousness by providing it with a political discourse which served to justify party rule and by blocking the articulation of alternative perspectives.[23] At the same time it had a stultifying effect on elite thinking, since innovation risked condemna-

---

20 Marek Henzler, 'Najlepsi czy loyalni', *Polityka* 23, 7 June 1986.
21 Paul G. Lewis, *Political Authority and Party Secretaries in Poland, 1975–1986*, Cambridge,1989, p.289.
22 Jan Widacki, *Czego nie powiedział Generał Kiszczak*, Warsaw, 1992, pp.45, 47; the document is cited at length, pp.37–58.
23 Jan Pakulski, 'Poland: Ideology, Legitimacy and Political Domination' in Nicholas Abercrombie, Stephen Hill and Bryan S. Turner (eds), *Dominant Ideologies*, London, 1990, p.49; J. Staniszkis, 'On Some Contradictions of Socialist Society: The Case of Poland', *Soviet Studies*, vol.XXXI, no.2, April 1979, pp.178–80.

tion as 'revisionism', both from within and from the 'fraternal allies', especially the USSR.[24] Rank-and-file attitudes, however, were somewhat more problematic, not least because over 80 per cent of party members claimed to be religious believers.[25] After 1981 members also suffered the opprobrium of martial law, which sent many into the protective shell of their own closed circles; the PZPR bemoaned the ideological indifference and lack of initiative of its primary party organizations.[26] In 1988 PZPR membership fell to about eight per cent of the adult population,[27] a low figure by comparison with ruling communist parties elsewhere.

Nor did the Polish elite prove able to convince the wider population of the validity or appropriateness of Marxism–Leninism. Ideology could therefore function only to a very limited degree as a means of legitimizing the system of party rule. To some extent this was masked by people's adaptation to the system. Wnuk-Lipiński has referred to 'social dimorphism', a duality in the social life of the country, leading most people to engage in 'a continuous series of compromises between the requirements of the ideological reality to which public life is subject and the requirements of the acknowledged system of values obtaining outside public life.'[28] None the less it is an exaggeration to see the public and private realities as totally separate; in practice they were often interlinked and interdependent because of the prevalence of common idioms of euphemism, as well as informal networks. Still, by the late 1970s it was certainly plausible to see Poland as characterized by 'an open crisis of legitimation',[29] which could not be alleviated

24 See Jacques Rupnik, 'Soviet Adaptation to Change in Eastern Europe', *Journal of Communist Studies*, vol.2, no.3, 1986, p.254. For elaboration of the general point see Rachel Walker, 'Marxism-Leninism as Discourse: The Politics of the Empty Signifier and the Double Bind', *British Journal of Political Science*, vol.19, no.2, 1989, pp.161–89.

25 *Polacy '80*, cited in David S. Mason, *Public Opinion and Political Change in Poland, 1980–1982*, Cambridge, 1985, p.79.

26 This is a major theme of the *Biuletyn Komitetu Wojewódzkiego PZPR* throughout 1986.

27 Paul G. Lewis, 'The Long Good-bye: Party Rule and Political Change in Poland since Martial Law', *The Journal of Communist Studies*, vol.6, no.1, 1990, p.33.

28 Edmund Wnuk-Lipiński, 'Social Dimorphism and its Implications' in Jadwiga Koralewicz, Ireneusz Białecki and Margaret Watson (eds), *Crisis and Transition: Polish Society in the 1980s*, Oxford, 1987, p.174.

29 Maria Markus, 'Overt and Covert Modes of Legitimation in East European Societies' in T.H. Rigby and Ferenc Fehér (eds), *Political Legitimation in Communist States*,

either by improved economic performance (which could not be achieved but which was, of course, part of the promise of Marxism–Leninism) or accommodation to the values of society. The attitudes of the 'private sphere' became public for a brief period in 1980–81 with the emergence of Solidarity, which so rapidly attained a mass following, and the attendant weakening of censorship. Martial law meant a retreat to dimorphism, as conformist behaviour again predominated. However, the credibility gap between the regime and the population remained.

Even where values compatible with the ideals of 'really existing socialism' proved deeply entrenched, they were not equated with the system. Egalitarianism and a commitment to social justice and policy principles such as the desirability of public ownership (except for land) were widespread within Polish society,[30] but these general principles were not seen as embodied in the existing order. As Raymond Taras concluded in his study of ideology in Poland between 1956 and 1983, 'Dissonance between prescriptive values propagated, policy courses pursued and, most importantly, policy consequences resulting was striking'[31] throughout the whole period.

The political economy of Polish socialism also showed some distinguishing features. Agriculture remained largely in private hands after 1956. A large category of worker-peasants emerged, working in industry but retaining strong links with their family homesteads, indeed often commuting long distances to their industrial employment. In the state sector the characteristics of the planned economy were evident, but the massive debt incurred under Gierek and the need to respond to social protest gave the economy a distinctive gloss. During the second half of the 1970s the economy spiralled downwards, while the media trumpeted the 'propaganda of success'. The 'mirage of central planning [was] ... transformed into bureaucratic chaos'.[32] The effects were 'more the result of informal games than an

---

London, 1982, p.91.
30 David S. Mason, 'Solidarity and Socialism' in Jack Bielasiak and Maurice D. Simon (eds), *Polish Politics*, New York, 1984, pp.118–37; Pakulski, op. cit., p.42; Włodzimierz Pańków, 'Transformations in the Polish Social Environment in the 1980s', *Journal of Communist Studies*, vol.6, no.4, 1990, pp.167–71.
31 Taras, op. cit., p.251.
32 Stefan Kiesielewski, '"Planning" under Socialism', *Survey*, vol.25, Winter 1980, p.23.

expression of the will of the steering centre'.[33] The economy appeared to be 'drifting under the influence of anarchic processes, controlled neither by market nor plan'.[34] Western credits had multiplied opportunities for corruption, and elite consumption was often conspicuous. At the same time, conditions for ordinary people were worsening. In 1979 the Polish economy registered negative growth. The significance of economic factors in evoking the strikes of the 'hot summer' of 1980, culminating in the emergence of Solidarity, can hardly be overestimated.

Economic reform was thus high on the agenda of the Jaruzelski regime in the 1980s; yet once again the reform measures proved inadequate to the task. The intention to introduce elements of the market mechanism had little practical import, other than a series of price rises which further alienated the population. The state bureaucracy and the party *apparat* resisted decentralization. The 'essential relationships within the hierarchy and towards the centre remained unchanged'.[35] The 'second phase' of reform, beginning in 1986, was similarly fruitless. Thus the 'command economy' in Poland did not function as the commanders intended. Explanations need to combine both the systemic features of central planning, elite incompetence, and the imperatives of the world economic system, which was rapidly demonstrating the growing technology gap between East and West.

Poland was also distinctive in the matter of elite–society relations. The ability of society to protect the Church (as well as the other way around) made itself felt in the early days of Polish Stalinism. In 1956 the inadequacy of trade unions as a vehicle for expressing workers' concerns led to street protests and the development of workers' councils. By the late 1970s elements of the working class and the intelligentsia were nurturing a thriving counter-community which bypassed

33 Jadwiga Staniszkis, 'On Remodelling of the Polish Economic System', *Soviet Studies*, vol.XXX, no.4, 1978, p.549.
34 Włodzimierz Brus, quoted in George Blazyca, 'The Degeneration of Central Planning in Poland', in Jean Woodall (ed.), *Policy and Politics in Contemporary Poland*, London, 1982, p.117.
35 Martin Myant, 'Poland – The Permanent Crisis?' in Roger A. Clarke (ed.), *Poland: The Economy in the 1980s*, London, 1989, pp.9–10; see also D. Rosati, 'Poland: Systemic Reforms and Economic Policy in the 1990s' in George Blazyca and Ryszard Rapacki (eds), *Poland into the 1990s: Economy and Society in Transition*, London, 1991, pp.24–5.

official channels. With Solidarity this counter-community became a mass social movement which affected the PZPR's own internal structures and processes.

The banning of Solidarity did not erase its influence, while the Church's influence increased in the 1980s with its assumption of a mediating role between regime and society. Even Jaruzelski's new trade unions, which developed after 1982, could not function as the old state-sponsored unions had done.[36] There is a certain irony in the fact that it was the OPZZ which triggered the government's resignation in September 1988 by threatening a vote of no confidence. The blurring of the distinction between the establishment and the 'opposition', however, should not blind us to the fact that most opposition activity was illegal, including the extensive network of clandestine organizations disseminating 'unofficial' literature. At the same time one can note how 'domestic society, benefiting from the more restrained and inclusive strategies of the party–state, grew ... and slowly colonized all aspects of official institutional relations'.[37]

Poland and the Concept of Civil Society

It was with the birth of Solidarity that the concept of 'civil society' made a strong reappearance in political analysis. The concepts of 'interest groups' and 'strategic elites', of 'limited pluralism' or 'quasi-pluralism' were inadequate to describe the growing dissident movement in Poland in the late 1970s. The term 'civil society' appeared to capture certain of its elements and to reflect the theorizing behind it, especially in the writings of Adam Michnik.[38] In effect, it embodied the notion that collective action could create a genuine sphere of autonomy separate from the state. Solidarity's mass appeal and its theory of a 'self-governing republic' reinforced the concept and gave it credence.[39]

36　On the 'new' trade unions of the 1980s see Frances Millard, 'Trade Unions and Economic Crisis in Poland' in William Brierley (ed.), *Trade Unions and the Economic Crisis of the 1980s*, Aldershot, 1987, pp.87–100; David S. Mason, 'Poland's New Trade Unions' *Soviet Studies*, vol.XXXIX, no.3, 1987, pp.489–508.

37　Grzegorz Ekiert, 'Democratization Processes in East Central Europe: A Theoretical Reconsideration', *British Journal of Political Science*, vol.21, no.3, 1991, p.303.

38　David Ost, *Solidarity and the Politics of Anti-Politics*, Philadelphia, 1990, pp.55–74.

39　The inspirational work was Andrew Arato, 'Civil Society Against the State', *Telos* 47,

However, the idea of civil society was not always easy to distinguish either from the general notion of democracy (based, after all, on the concept of a society of citizens) or from the liberal view of a genuine arena of social autonomy separate from that of the state. It also seemed to suggest an overriding unity and common set of interests, ignoring both diversity of interests (for example, of class and gender) and conflicts of values (for example, religious and secular). What it did do was to draw attention firmly to social forces, modes of participation and the concept of citizenship itself.[40]

Poland, then, possessed many distinctive features. It is hard to conceive of it as a 'typical' communist state, if indeed such existed. Rothschild has argued that the East European experience since 1956 is a 'return to [the] diversity' stifled by the Stalinist mode.[41] Yet that diversity remained to a considerable extent confined to a common framework of authoritarian practices and comparable institutions. We need both dimensions to explore the causes of change in the communist world.

EXPLAINING THE DOWNFALL OF COMMUNISM

The Causes of Change

Views of a systemic crisis of communism[42] gained strength as changes in Poland and Hungary during the summer of 1989 produced a domino effect throughout Eastern Europe and accelerated the disintegration of the USSR. The Polish case seemed a striking vindication

---

1981, pp.23–47. A romantic view of Solidarity in this context is Jeffrey Goldfarb, *Beyond Glasnost: The Post-Totalitarian Mind*, Chicago, 1989, pp.131–42; see also the various essays in John Keane (ed.), *Civil Society and the State*, London, 1988 and especially Z. Pelczynski, 'Solidarity and the "Rebirth of Civil Society", 1976–81', ibid., pp.361–80. For a critical assessment of the concept see Ellen Meiksins Wood, 'The Uses and Abuses of "Civil Society"', *Socialist Register 1990*, London, 1990, pp.60–84.

40 See Edward Shils, 'The Virtue of Civil Society', *Government and Opposition*, vol.26, no.1, 1991, pp.3–20.

41 Joseph Rothschild, *Return to Diversity*, Oxford, 1989.

42 Zbigniew Brzezinski, *The Grand Failure: The Birth and Death of Communism in the Twentieth Century*, London, 1990.

of such arguments. From 1956 onwards the terms 'crisis' and 'contradiction' cropped up with increasing frequency. It is tempting, therefore, to see 1989 as resulting from the cumulative impact of coincidental crises: political crises, legitimation crises, economic crises, and social crises, themselves the product of interdependent and overlapping contradictions of elements of the Polish communist system.

Indeed, the situation in 1980 was already being analysed in terms of multiple crises. Korboński identified a series of developmental crises: in the political sphere the impotence of the existing structures and institutions in ensuring compliance, which generated a crisis of penetration evident by 1976; a participation crisis resulting from the absence of structures of interest articulation; and a legitimation crisis; and also a socio-economic crisis of distribution.[43] Lamentowicz analysed a series of structural contradictions and the resultant shaping of bureaucratic behaviour as mechanisms preventing the system's adaptive evolution.[44] Even the PZPR's own post-mortem contained elements of the systemic critique.[45]

It is not surprising, therefore, that similar arguments emerged with greater force and wider applicability after 1989. Bartłomiej Kamiński analysed the system as inherently flawed from the outset, since it rested on 'a base of direct coercion' and lacked the capacity to 'channel self-interested behaviour into socially beneficial performance'; the fusion of polity and economy meant that there was no dynamic of adaptation or innovation.[46] Grzegorz Ekiert argued that previous crises *in* state socialism were transformed in the 1980s into a crisis *of* state socialism, which unfolded at different rates and with different degrees of intensity in different countries. The identity crisis of the ruling party, the disintegration of its ancillary organizations, the failure of the planned economy and the emergence of a thriving second economy, a new, independent political society, and the relaxation

---

43 Andrzej Korbonski, 'Dissent in Poland, 1956–76' in Jane L. Curry (ed.), *Dissent in Eastern Europe*, New York, 1983, pp.29–39.

44 Wojciech Lamentowicz, 'Adaptation through Political Crisis in Post-War Poland', *Journal of Peace Research*, vol.XIX, no.2, 1982, pp.117–31; also Staniszkis, 'Contradictions', op. cit., pp.172–8.

45 'The Kubiak Report', *Survey*, vol.26, no.3, 1982, pp.87–107.

46 Bartłomiej Kamiński, *The Collapse of State Socialism*, Princeton, 1991, p.3.

of geopolitical constraints were the interconnected features of this period.[47] Yet we should be cautious not to impute a determinism to this process of deepening systemic crisis. After all, change requires not only the objective conditions for change but also agents of change.[48] The argument that the system was capable of reform or adaptation looks weak in retrospect;[49] however, it draws attention to key actors in the process, to ways in which elements of change were already being nurtured in the womb of the old system, and to the limited nature of the changes achieved in the early stages of post-communism. The system did not collapse in violent upheaval: there was initially merely a transfer of power to a different (or reshaped) political elite, which in turn embarked on a process of system transformation. Let us focus on these three elements in turn.

The Agents of Change

Elite decomposition
Mono-causal explanations of complex processes are rare and mostly unsatisfying, but it is appropriate and plausible to rank certain explanatory variables. Of these, the most powerful focuses on the condition of the Communist Party. The crumbling of elite unity is one of the oldest explanations of political change. If elites maintain cohesion, they can withstand enormous pressures for change over quite a long period of time, not least because they retain the coercive option. Jaruzelski had already demonstrated the ease with which he gained control of Polish society through martial law in 1981; it is not difficult to cow unarmed people with tanks. However, he also learned the limits of coercion, especially for dealing with economic crisis. In Poland and Hungary (and indeed the USSR) the process of change was elite-led, a reformist strategy with (unintended) revolutionary consequences. This is an illustration of authoritarian power holders' attempting 'to relieve pressure on themselves while at the same time

---

47 Ekiert, op. cit., pp.285–313.
48 However, Staniszkis's use of the term 'chance' seems an unfortunate choice: see Jadwiga Staniszkis, *The Dynamics of Breakthrough in Eastern Europe*, Oxford, 1992.
49 See, for example, Arato, op. cit., p.26; Ost, 'Corporatism', op. cit.

preserving as many of their interests as possible'.[50]

In Poland the June 1989 election was the mechanism which brought about the peaceful withdrawal of the communists from power. The communists themselves negotiated its terms at the 'Round Table' (see Chapter 3). Clearly this was not a revolution in the ordinary sense of the term. There was no violence, no mass outburst of spontaneous collective action; no new social groups mounting a challenge to the system. Finding itself helpless in an economic and political maelstrom, the elite moved to more radical solutions than hitherto: 'Crisis creates an environment in which elites seek alternatives to existing norms that have been discredited by events.'[51] The Polish elite had apparently exhausted all alternatives and reluctantly agreed to move to a genuine power-sharing arrangement with the opposition. Bronisław Geremek, one of the key figures in the Round Table negotiations, referred to 'a certain sense of helplessness within the ruling elite'[52]. Obviously, neither splits in the elite nor an elite learning process can provide the whole explanation for the decision to recognize Solidarity. Authoritarian regimes cannot seek a partner in society unless there is one available.

At the same time it is important to reaffirm the significance of a parallel reform strategy continuing in the USSR under Gorbachev (although lagging considerably behind the changes in Poland and Hungary). Jaruzelski's reformism had become the new bloc 'norm'; Soviet pressure, albeit more discreetly than before, was now on the orthodox regimes of East Germany and Czechoslovakia (itself 'normalized' Brezhnev-style after the Warsaw Pact invasion put paid to the reformism of the 1968 Prague Spring). Gorbachev's main significance was that the so-called hardliners in Eastern Europe now had no external buttress on which to rely in their internal party battles.

50 A. Stepan, 'Paths toward Redemocratization: Theoretical and Comparative Considerations' in Guillermo O'Donnell, Philippe Schmitter, and Laurence Whitehead (eds), *Transitions from Authoritarian Rule*, London, 1986, p.65; the distinction between democratization and re-democratization does not seem essential here.
51 G.J. Ikenberry and C.A. Kupchan, 'Socialization and Hegemonic Power', *International Organization*, vol.44, 1990, p.284, quoted in James Clay Moltz, 'Divergent Learning and the Failed Politics of Soviet Economic Reform', *World Politics*, vol.45, January 1993, p.301.
52 Bronisław Geremek, 'Between Hope and Despair', *Daedalus*, vol.119, no.1, 1990, p.103.

The opposition was alert to internal changes in the USSR but remained constrained by the uncertainty surrounding the Soviet position *vis-à-vis* Eastern Europe. It is easy to put too much emphasis on the 'Gorbachev factor', although obviously it should not be ignored (see Chapter 8). However, Kumar's argument that 'By confining Soviet troops to their barracks ... Gorbachev effectively disarmed the rulers of the East European states'[53] appears to ignore the objective difficulties of Soviet intervention in Eastern Europe as well as the existence of domestic military forces.

Jaruzelski did not accept the result of the June 1989 election *because* Gorbachev refused to intervene. What was more important for the ultimate loss of power by the Polish communists (specifically their weakness within the Solidarity-led coalition and their inability to exploit their control of the presidency) was the accelerating effect that developments in Poland and Hungary had on East Germany and Czechoslovakia; there the Soviet Union's refusal to provide support for the communist leaders was surely decisive for the weakening and disorientation of the elites. The result of this tangle of interrelated developments was the disintegration of the whole bloc and far greater freedom of manoeuvre for the post-communist governments.

The role of the populace

It has been quite common for the changes in Eastern Europe to be subsumed under a general notion of popular rebellion; added to this one finds the argument that the regimes were naked in their unpopularity because of the removal of the Soviet cloak: '... deprived of the Soviet Kalashnikov crutch, those elites did not have another leg to stand on',[54] says Ash. Rose has used the concept of 'near absolute dissatisfaction' with the communist regimes.[55] Tarrow has spoken of a 'wave of mobilization' in Eastern Europe, with 'mass outbreaks of collective action ... best understood as the collective responses of

---

53 Krishan Kumar, 'The Revolutions of 1989: Socialism, Capitalism and Democracy', *Theory and Society*, vol. 21, no. 3, 1992, p.323.

54 Timothy Garton Ash, *We the People*, Cambridge, 1990, p.141.

55 Richard Rose, 'Escaping from Absolute Dissatisfaction: A Trial-and-Error Model of Change in Eastern Europe', *Journal of Theoretical Politics*, vol.4, no.4, 1992, pp.371–93.

citizens, groups and elites to an expanding structure of political opportunities.[56]

The regimes' fall cannot be explained, however, in terms of levels of popular dissatisfaction or manifestations of 'popular power'. Poland had experienced numerous examples of collective action which did not bring down the regime. It is only when the power structures are being eroded that discontent can be effective.[57] This is not to deny the importance of mass protests in Czechoslovakia and East Germany as mechanisms further undermining the confidence of their ruling elites. The strikes of May and August 1988 played a similar role in Poland, even though they were relatively limited; but mass discontent cannot function as a primary explanation of change.[58]

In the Polish case coercive measures against striking workers in 1988 were far from absent, but the strikes gave credibility to an alternative elite strategy, that of a pact with the opposition, of which the main architect was the Minister of the Interior, Kiszczak. The Round Table negotiations, however, were confined to a narrow stratum; representatives of the ruling elite sat down with a self-selected group of opposition activists. Of course, the shape of the opposition owed much to the mass mobilization of 1980. However, the point here is that the public manifested little sign of interest in the Round Table. Mobilization was far greater when it became clear that the June election would actually provide opportunities to challenge the communists, and the rapid resurgence of Solidarity surprised even its own activists. However, it would be very misleading to see the changes in Polish politics as the product of a mass anti-communist outpouring. Even the crucial June election saw a rather low turnout of 62 per cent. It is precisely the form of political change (peaceful, non-confrontational) that helps to explain why the initial changes left intact so much of the structure (and process) of communist rule.

56 Sidney Tarrow, '"Aiming at a Moving Target": Social Science and the Recent Rebellions in Eastern Europe', *PS: Political Science and Politics*, vol. 24, 1991, p.13.
57 See Kumar, op. cit., pp.320–21.
58 See Jane L. Curry, 'The Psychological Barriers to Reform in Poland', *East European Politics and Societies*, vol.2, no.3, 1988, pp.484–509.

CONTINUITY AND CHANGE

The focus on change directs attention to the decay and crumbling of the old system and the build-up of pressures for something to happen. It would be a pity to forget Marx's lesson that the old system often nurtures incipient structures which presage a new stage of social development or to leave to historians the analysis of the continuities which will inevitably persist. In Poland changes already apparent in the economy had both social and political consequences in the 1980s. The legal private sector began to grow substantially and the illegal (but tolerated) second economy continued to thrive on the system's persistent shortages. In Rostowski's view the expansion was so great as to be irreversible, thus changing the quality of the system from a socialist one to an emerging 'mixed' economy.[59] These developments helped to change the structure of employment and made additional sources of income more important, including work abroad; indeed, the US dollar began to function as an alternative currency. As a result there was a 'general decrease in direct economic dependence on the state as the sole source of employment, income and security, both in the objective sense and in the subjective sense of the reduced psychological feeling of dependence'.[60]

These changes also marked the beginning of the transformation of elements of the *nomenklatura* from a group merely controlling the means of production to actually owning them, which was potentially more lucrative. There emerged 'a peculiar fusion of the power elite of the *ancien régime* and private economy, as some members of this elite started to enter private enterprises or form various cooperatives using their channels and influences to protect and develop their economic activities.'[61] This form of 'political capitalism' or *nomenklatura* capitalism, parasitic on the state sector, was clearly evident in Poland by

59 Jacek Rostowski, 'The Decay of Socialism and the Growth of Private Enterprise in Poland', *Soviet Studies*, vol.XLI, no.2, 1989, p.194.
60 Marek Ziółkowski, 'Social Structure, Interests and Consciousness: The Crisis and Transformation of the System of "Real Socialism" in Poland', *Acta Sociologica*, vol.33, no.4, 1990, p.297.
61 Ibid., pp.295–6; also Włodzimierz Panków, 'Transformations in the Polish Social Environment in the 1980s', *Journal of Communist Studies*, vol.6, no.4, December 1990, p.172.

1987,[62] although it is an exaggeration to see it as 'the creation of an economic class'.[63]

Changes in social values and attitudes were also becoming evident before the communist loss of power. The evidence of sociological surveys in the 1980s shows increasingly positive attitudes to certain characteristics of the (abstract) market economy: competition, 'the laws of the market', private ownership, privatization, often with simultaneous commitment to the values of egalitarianism, job security and welfare.[64] These were more marked in urban areas; the rural sector retained many characteristics of the peasant culture.

It is also useful in this context to note again how the opposition counter-culture itself influenced and penetrated official or political society. Ekiert notes how 'domestic society ... grew in strength and slowly colonized all aspects of official institutional relations'.[65] This meant that there existed a cohesive counter-elite, albeit an inexperienced one, ready to assume office. It is paradoxical that the new incumbents too wished to bring about radical transformation of the polity, society, and the economy, if in the reverse direction to that sought by their predecessors. It was not necessarily the case, however, that the factors which had nurtured or effected this transfer of power would similarly facilitate the development of the changes which they desired.

PROSPECTS FOR DEMOCRACY

Most discussions of the future of Eastern Europe have centred on the issue of democracy and its bedfellow, capitalism. This is because of the overwhelming commitment of the new political elite precisely to

---

62 Staniszkis notes that eighty *nomenklatura* companies could be identified by 1987; Jadwiga Staniszkis, '"Political Capitalism" in Poland', *East European Politics and Societies*, vol.5, no.1, 1991, p.128.

63 Staniszkis, *Breakthrough*, op. cit., p.8.

64 The Polish Academy of Science's series of reports by Adamski's team is the major source here: Władysław Adamski *et al.*, *Polacy '80*, Warsaw, 1981; and *Polacy '84*, 1986 (2 vols); *Polacy '88*, 1989; and *Polacy '90*, 1991; Lena Kolarska-Bobińska summarizes some of this material in 'The Myth of the Market and the Reality of Reform' in Gomułka and Polonsky (eds), op. cit., pp.160–79.

65 Ekiert, op. cit., p.303; compare Elemér Hankiss, 'The "Second Society": Is There an Alternative Social Model Emerging in Contemporary Hungary?', *Social Research*, vol.55, nos 1–2, 1988, pp.39–42.

the twin goals of 'democracy' and the 'market economy'. In some instances it may also reflect the conviction that the 'transition' in Eastern Europe will indeed entail a democratic capitalist outcome (perhaps because socialism is dead and a third way 'a mirage'[66] or because the march of historical forces has led us to the 'end of history'[67]), but that is not a necessary assumption. 'Transition' implies change from one state to another, qualitatively different one; it implies fluidity and process, but it does not suggest a predetermined outcome.

If we lay out the balance sheet, the prospects for Polish democracy seem grim, since the list of positive factors is far shorter than the list of possible obstacles and barriers. Still, we should remember that there is no fixed 'essence' of democracy that is attained, consolidated, and then maintained for ever. Most of the world's democratic systems retain substantial 'undemocratic' features, whether in the form of widespread corruption, violations of civil liberties, the alienation or exclusion of sections of the population. The predominant form is liberal democracy, with strong elitist elements mixing uneasily with a commitment to mass participation. Such states experience periodic strains, sometimes lesser, sometimes profound.

Democracy, then, is not a self-equilibrating end-state. Empirically, it takes many forms. This does not mean we cannot identify some common core of meaning. The rule of law is paramount, and so is the notion of a private sphere reserved to individuals and groups, where the state may not legitimately intrude. Both the rule of law and the commitment to civil liberties are part of the liberal heritage of the eighteenth-century Enlightenment. Participatory mechanisms are also essential, whether yielding representative institutions or entailing procedures for direct involvement of citizens, or both. The dominant liberal variant thus combines the two elements of civic participation and respect for human rights; democracy is not simply a matter of counting heads (majority rule) but of respect for the views of others

---

66 Ralf Dahrendorf, *Reflections on the Revolution in Europe*, London, 1990, pp.37ff.
67 Francis Fukuyama, *The End of History and the Last Man*, London, 1992; for a discussion of elements of the debate surrounding Fukuyama's thesis see Kumar, op. cit., pp.313–17; also Fred Halliday, 'An Encounter with Fukuyama', *New Left Review* 193, 1992, pp.89–95; M. Rustin, 'No Exit from Capitalism', ibid., pp.96–107; Ralph Miliband, 'Fukuyama and the Socialist Alternative', ibid., pp.108–13.

(minority rights). In a democratic political system conflicts are resolved peacefully through accepted institutional arrangements.

The concept of capitalism is just as varied in practice as that of liberal democracy. There are various mixes of private and public ownership, varying degrees of state intervention. The new Polish elites are no more precise about their vision of capitalism than they are about their concept of a democratic polity. The choice of the goals of capitalism and democracy is more a result of the demonstration effect than of philosophical choice. It has been widely observed that the East European revolutions lacked a theory or vision.[68] Instead, Western Europe served as the major reference point: it is affluent and permits freedom to its citizens; the wealth is a result of capitalism and the freedom a consequence of democracy. None the less, we should note the powerful historical argument for associating the two, namely that of their reciprocal evolution: all states acknowledged to be 'democratic' are also capitalist. This is not a simple causal relationship, for the converse is not true; it is plausible to envisage the emergence of a form of capitalism in Eastern Europe, but without the entrenching or stabilizing of democratic institutions. In this sense, then, assessing the advantages and disadvantages faced in consolidating a (more or less) stable, democratic system may be misleading, for the possible variants of political and economic relationships are very considerable and the 'end product' (or temporary resting stations) will surely be as distinctive as the Italian, Swedish or Mexican.

The Balance Sheet of Prospects

The balance sheet is negative, but not entirely so. Poland has a number of characteristics which seem beneficial to bringing about or supporting a democratic polity. The Poles have a strong sense of national community and common culture; the country is largely homogeneous in terms of religion and ethnicity. There are tensions to be sure, but there is little sign of an integration crisis or uncertainty about who belongs to the community of citizens. In addition, the population is

68 Claus Offe, 'Capitalism by Democratic Design? Democratic Theory Facing the Triple Transition in East Central Europe', *Social Research*, vol.58, no.4, 1991, p.866; Jurgen Habermas, 'What Does Socialism Mean Today? The Rectifying Revolution and the Need for New Thinking on the Left', *New Left Review* 183, 1990, p.5.

not just literate but educated in a wider sense. There is a national press and television to provide effective political communication.

The Polish communist regime (like the Hungarian) had provided a partial foundation on which to build because of its 'liberalization' (the 'process in which the ruling elite gradually widens the sphere of things permitted ... but ... without granting the rights, or without tolerating the assertion of rights, that would guarantee these new opportunities and liberties'[69]). There was experience of mutual accommodation of differences of outlook (the Church was a major factor here). There was a formal commitment to the rule of law and 'socialist' democracy.[70] The 'soft law' constraint was apparent; violations of economic and planning law were tolerated because the system could not have functioned otherwise; officials often enjoyed immunity for their illegal behaviour; civil rights were defined vaguely and hedged with 'responsibilities'. Yet people had absorbed enough of the rhetoric to detect the system's hypocrisy, and there were institutions to build on, such as a 'sovereign' parliament.

The issue of elite commitment to democracy is also significant here. Those who took over the reins of power from the communists moved immediately to undermine despised elements of the old system and thereby to institutionalize certain democratic features. They altered the constitutional framework; eliminated prior censorship and the agencies of communist control of the media; dismantled the secret police; held free elections; re-established property rights. Formal, procedural mechanisms are necessary, if insufficient, conditions of democratic development.

The final factor facilitating democratic development is that of geographical location. Western Europe has economic, political and strategic interests in the emergence of a stable, democratic and prosperous Eastern Europe. The European Community in particular is formally committed to assisting change. The post-communist governments of Poland, Hungary and Czechoslovakia immediately expressed a desire to join the EC. It is by now clear that a vast gesture such as that provided by the United States to Western Europe after the Second

---

69 Elemér Hankiss, 'In Search of a Paradigm', *Daedalus*, vol.119, no.1, p.195.
70 Jack Bielasiak and Barbara Hicks, 'Solidarity's Self-Organization: The Crisis of Rationality and Legitimacy in Poland, 1980–81', *East European Politics and Societies*, vol.4, no.3, pp.489–512, attribute this to the impact of Solidarity in 1980–81.

World War, a new 'Marshall Plan', is unlikely to materialize. Nor is there a mechanism for the imposition or monitoring of democratic structures as there was for the defeated powers of Germany and Japan. Still, Western Europe does not want a cauldron of boiling tensions on its doorstep. In the most optimistic variant, the 'international system will provide generous support'[71] whenever extremes threaten.

What, then, of the obstacles to democratic development and how are they related to capitalist development? They are international, political, economic, social, and cultural. They are intermingled, interdependent and reciprocally related; each has the potential to influence the others. Let us try to unravel some of the key arguments. My assumption here is based on Marx: individuals make history but they do not make it in circumstances of their own choosing. It is impatient of determinist notions of impersonal global forces or the idea that 'history goes on without anyone ever doing anything.'[72]

The first major obstacle is the magnitude of the task. This is not merely a transformation of one aspect but a multi-dimensional transformation. How multi-dimensional is unclear, but at the least it is simultaneous economic and political change which is being sought. This is very different from other instances of democratization, for example in Southern Europe, which have left intact the (capitalist) structure of the economy.[73] Transforming the economy changes the class structure and generates new patterns of inequality and new social conflicts, which need to be addressed by the political system. However, redistributive measures may be resisted on the grounds that this would divert resources from essential economic investment. The likelihood of resistance to redistribution is increased by the external constraints on decision-makers arising from high levels of debt and the dependent or peripheral character of the emerging capitalism.[74]

71 Emanuel Richter, 'Upheavals in the East and Turmoil in Political Theory: Comments on Offe's "Capitalism by Democratic Design?"', *Social Research*, vol.58, no.4, 1991, p.901; see also Attila Agh, 'The Transition to Democracy in Central Europe: A Comparative View', *Journal of Public Policy*, vol.11, no.2, 1991, pp.146–7.

72 Adam Przeworski, *Democracy and the Market*, Cambridge, 1991, p.96.

73 Offe, op. cit., pp.867–8; Bill Lomax, 'Internal (and External) Impediments to Democratization', Paper presented at the Workshop on Regime Change, Charles University, Prague, September 1992, pp.9–10.

74 Andre Gunder Frank, 'Economic Ironies in Europe: A World Economic Interpretation of East–West European Politics', *International Social Science Journal* 131, 1992, esp.

Discussions of class play a great role in evaluating prospects for democratization. The close link historically between the rise of the bourgeoisie and demands for liberal reforms, especially guarantees of property rights and contractual relationships,[75] has led to a focus on the link between the concept of 'interests' and democracy. Given the presence of only an incipient bourgeoisie, what social forces can be conceived as objectively 'interested' in democratic development (or by extension the market economy). The answer appears to be 'not many': the 'immediate short-term interests of industrial workers, peasants and members of the intelligentsia are still linked with the old mechanism'.[76]

The argument here is that a successful transformation programme requires the 'creation of its social base'. At the same time, social dislocations and the fluidity of the class structure combined with democratic political institutions provide opportunities for the emergence and articulation of the interests of 'backlash movements and ... a significant anti-reform coalition'.[77] Accommodation of these interests could threaten capitalism, while lack of accommodation could endanger democracy, with support for populist or authoritarian politics.[78]

Nor does it require the concept of 'interests' to observe the absence of popular consensus regarding the proposed direction of change. Poland lacks a strong democratic tradition, and there is widespread uncertainty surrounding the concept of democracy itself. In recent surveys about one-third of respondents felt the polity to be in a state of transition but they could not identify its nature; only twenty per cent felt that democracy would emerge, while nineteen per cent thought nothing had changed ('the old elite continued to rule behind the veil of Solidarity').[79] Values fundamental to the workings of

pp.48–54, is the strongest version of this argument; see also Bob Deacon, 'The Impact of Supranational and Global Agencies on Central European National Social Policy', Workshop on Social Responses to Political and Economic Transformation, Prague, May 1992 (unpublished paper); Lomax, op. cit., pp.16–17.

75 C.B. Macpherson, *Democratic Theory: Essays in Retrieval*, Oxford, 1973.

76 Ziółkowski, op. cit., p.302; see also Edmund Mokrzycki, 'Eastern Europe after Communism', *Telos* 90, 1991–92, p.135.

77 Paul G. Lewis, 'Democratization in Eastern Europe', *Coexistence*, vol.27, no.4, 1990, p.263.

78 Offe, op. cit., pp.886–7; also Ekiert, op. cit., p.313; Staniszkis, *Breakthrough*, op. cit., p.177.

79 A. Rychard, 'Stare i nowe instytucje życia publicznego', *Polacy '90*, op. cit., p.48.

democracy, such as tolerance and compromise, are not deeply entrenched; they may well be strained as the enthusiasm generated by the removal of the communists wanes. If politicians cannot deliver, attachment to the new institutions is likely to weaken and disillusionment set in. For many, the above considerations lead to a gloomy prognosis.[80] Capitalism may develop, but it may well be unrestrained capitalism; democracy may develop, but it may prove to be deformed democracy. Much therefore will depend on the educative capacity of the elites, their skill, their probity. The real battle, however, is likely to take place over the economy and the ameliorative or redistributive issues (or both). Capitalism by definition creates winners and losers.

80 See, for example, Jerzy Szacki, 'Polish Democracy: Dreams and Reality', *Social Research*, vol.58, no.4, 1991, pp.711–22.

3. Unsaddling the Socialist Cow: the Round Table and Its Consequences

We have seen how, throughout the years of communist domination in Eastern Europe, Poland had enjoyed a reputation for its distinctive adaptations of the communist system. It had a thriving religious life, an assertive working class, a peasantry based on the private ownership of land, a vigorous critical intelligentsia. It had a Communist Party which had variously tried to rule through dialogue and concession; through mobilizing the sentiments of patriotism; and through repression and coercion, culminating in the abdication of the party to the military establishment during the brief period of martial law (1981–83). After martial law the party never regained its previous position; the 'leading role', still the vital explanatory variable for communist politics elsewhere, in Poland remained largely rhetorical.

Poland was also distinctive in its final rejection of the communist system. It was the first country in contemporary Eastern Europe to install a non-communist prime minister; this fact alone stimulated and accelerated the processes of change elsewhere in the region. Poland was also the first to apply shock therapy to its sluggish, crisis-ridden economy under its controversial Minister of Finance Leszek Balcerowicz. The Balcerowicz programme generated debates on the economic lessons of transition within Poland, in other former countries of the so-called Soviet bloc, and later in the Soviet successor states.

The Round Table negotiations of winter 1989 and the subsequent election of June 1989 marked the turning-point for Polish political developments in the post-war period: they marked the formal end of the communist system, if not its final interment. Reform 'from above' was sabotaged by the triumph of Solidarity in the Round Table election, as those 'below' refused to be manipulated by the old practices; they marched to a different drum in a different direction.

The period of Mazowiecki's tenure was one in which evolutionary change assumed the quality of irreversibility in the processes of transformation. It is a period which began with the forces of change in a mood of cautious optimism. This gave way to heady excitement blended with anxiety as Solidarity took control of the government, backed by strong nationwide popular support. Gradually, however, this consensus eroded, both within the political institutions and within the country at large. The election of Lech Wałęsa to the presidency and Mazowiecki's subsequent resignation marked the beginning of a new phase in post-communist development.

THE GENESIS OF THE ROUND TABLE AND THE ELECTION OF 1989

The Round Table

We have examined in Chapter 2 a number of arguments adduced to explain the failure of communist regimes generally and of the Polish communist regime in particular. The Round Table may be seen as the final attempt by Polish reform communists to transform the system while maintaining control of the process of change. Its formal initiation came on 26 August 1989 when the Minister of the Interior General Czesław Kiszczak announced the PZPR's endorsement of his proposal for embarking on 'round table' discussions with representatives of social and political organizations, including Solidarity. Kiszczak had a long record of informal contacts with members of the Church hierarchy, which supported the initiative; in the spring of 1988 he had set up indirect contacts with the opposition.[1]

The Round Table, expected to convene in the autumn, finally assembled in February 1989. This delay was a product both of the suspicion and hostility aroused by the proposal in both camps and of disputes over particular issues. Neither was surprising: those co-opted have genuine cause to fear their neutralization, while the co-opters

---

1 Witold Bereś and Jerzy Skoczylas (eds), *Generał Kiszczak mówi ... prawie wszystko*, Warsaw, 1991, p.261; Bronisław Geremek and Jacek Żakowski, *Rok 1989. Bronisław Geremek Opowiada: Jacek Żakowski Pyta*, Warsaw, 1990, pp.10 15.

similarly fear the polluting effects of their opponents. In addition, there were in fact thorny issues to resolve prior to the negotiations.

Lech Wałęsa's responsiveness to Kiszczak encountered hostility within Solidarity as he threw the weight of his authority behind the proposals and, in consequence of an undertaking to Kiszczak, against the strikes which had finally pushed the party to take its last stand. Criticism directed against Wałęsa was based on deep suspicion of the government's intentions, given the absence of prior guarantees and continuing repression against the strikers as well as continuing anti-Solidarity propaganda issuing from radio and television.[2] Some had already viewed the initial strike wave in May as a government provocation.[3] Wałęsa also faced criticism from radical opposition groupings. Some, such as Fighting Solidarity and Solidarity '80, claimed to be the true heirs of Solidarity. Others, like the Confederation for Independent Poland (KPN), pre-dated Solidarity and had maintained a separate existence. For such groups compromise with the regime was seen as a betrayal,[4] and this view was not absent from Solidarity itself. Those who supported Wałęsa recognized the risk.[5]

At the same time important elements within the party, both at national level and in the provincial party apparatus, remained committed to a hardline approach based on repression. Furthermore, the regime's trade union ally the OPZZ, whose chairman Miodowicz was also a member of the Politburo, remained adamantly opposed to the concept of trade union pluralism and distanced itself from the regime by proposing a parliamentary vote of no confidence in the government of Zbigniew Messner.

The situation appeared one of considerable disarray on all sides when preparatory meetings convened in Warsaw on 15–16 September.[6] Jaruzelski and Kiszczak were clearly prepared not only to talk to Solidarity but to concede its legalization, but they faced opposition

2 Jerzy Holzer and Krzysztof Leski, *Solidarność w podziemiu*, Łódź, 1990, pp.159–61.
3 *Tygodnik Mazowsze* 253, 1 June 1988.
4 J. Dziadul, 'Opozycja w opozycji', *Polityka* 9, 4 March 1989.
5 Geremek and Żakowski, op. cit., p.18.
6 An extensive transcript of his notes, including numerous verbatim recordings of Kiszczak's remarks, is provided for the informal meetings and working groups of the Round Table from 16 September 1988 to 5 April 1989 by Krzysztof Dubiński, *Magdalenka: Transakcja Epoki*, Warsaw, 1990.

with the party. The government of Messner was unpopular and threatened by its own supporters in the OPZZ and in parliament. On 19 September the government duly resigned after a lengthy televised parliamentary debate in which few participants had a positive word to say about its record or its prospects. This was the first time that a communist regime had conceded the destruction of a government which was in effect its own creature.

On 27 September Mieczysław Rakowski was confirmed as the new prime minister, promising to form a broad-based government of reconciliation. Rakowski, whose previous incarnations had included a respected role as editor of *Polityka* and a less highly regarded role as a defender of martial law in 1981 (when he had been Minister for Trade Unions), was extremely unpopular with Solidarity. Not surprisingly, the Solidarity intellectuals Andrzej Micewski, Andrzej Paszyński and Witold Trzeciakowski refused to join Rakowski's government, both because of a reluctance to be associated with him and to take co-responsibility for government policies; but also so as not to pre-empt any decisions of the Round Table. At the same time (accurate) rumours were flying about, centring on government objections to the composition of the Solidarity delegation (particularly the inclusion of the regime's greatest *bêtes noires*, Jacek Kuroń and Adam Michnik[7]). Solidarity was also incensed by the sudden decision of the Rakowski government to close the Lenin Shipyard in Gdańsk, ostensibly on economic grounds but perceived as a political act against the birthplace of Solidarity. These disputes, added to by threats of resignation from the party by a majority of provincial party first secretaries,[8] led to a hiatus in the informal negotiations, which reconvened on 18 November as a result of pressure on both sides from the Roman Catholic Church.

While many elements of Solidarity were equivocal, uneasy or opposed to a conciliatory stance, Wałęsa pushed ahead with preparations. He was well briefed for his triumphal performance in the famous television debate with OPZZ leader Miodowicz on 30 November. On 18 December he formalized his extensive circle of advisers to form

---

7   Wojciech Jaruzelski, *Stan wojenny DLACZEGO...*, Warsaw, 1992, p.216; Bereś and Skoczylas, op. cit., p.263.
8   Holzer and Leski, op. cit., p.166.

the Citizens' Committee under (*przy*) the Chairman of Solidarity, generally known as Wałęsa's Citizens' Committee. A broad range of subgroups began to prepare for negotiations. The party by contrast was ill prepared. Formally still uncommitted and wracked with division, it took until the end of January for Jaruzelski to secure endorsement of the new strategy.

The crucial tenth plenum of the Central Committee of the PZPR was conducted in two sessions, on 20–21 December 1988 and 16 January 1989. Extensive personnel changes made in December in the Politburo were probably necessary to secure assent to the Round Table, by removing key opponents and bringing in individuals more receptive to the need for change. Both Rakowski and Geremek note the particular significance of Professor Janusz Reykowski.[9] The new Politburo threw its weight behind the inner core of generals, Jaruzelski, Kiszczak, and Siwicki. Prime Minister Rakowski himself in a speech to the plenum put the following arguments: Solidarity was gaining in popularity and should be drawn in to share responsibility; this would become more significant in coming months, for difficult economic decisions lay ahead and with them a threat of renewed social unrest.[10] However, when the plenum reconvened, hostility to the Round Table remained. After two days' intense discussion the Politburo presented itself for a collective vote of confidence which passed without opposition. On 18 January 1989 the leadership's 'Position' (*Stanowisko*) 'on the question of political and trade union pluralism' was also endorsed by 143 votes to 32, with 14 abstentions, a success attributed by Rakowski to the shock of Jaruzelski's proffered resignation: 'Jaruzelski was criticized, but it was also recognized that he was the only politician reckoned with by the opposition, the Church and politicians abroad.'[11]

The plenum, then, marked the adoption by the Communist Party of the new strategy of negotiated power-sharing with the opposition. Clearly the strategy was perceived within the party as new and radical,

9   Miecysław Rakowski, *Jak to się stało*, Warsaw, 1991, p.169; Geremek and Żakowski, op. cit., p.31.
10   Rakowski, op. cit., p.171.
11   Ibid., p.176; see also K. Janowski, 'From Monopoly to Death-Throes: The PZPR in the Process of Political Transformation' in George Sanford (ed.), *Democratization in Poland 1988–90*, London, 1992, pp.165–7.

for the party apparatus reacted vigorously against the proposals. There was a section of the *apparat* which loathed Solidarity and viewed it as an insidious anti-socialist cancer eating away at society. However, it should also be noted that popular front approaches have a long tradition in the communist movement, which has historically (often wrongly) remained convinced of its ability to manipulate its allies. The communists fully expected the arrangement to benefit them; they expected to continue to control the state even while relinquishing some of their previous mechanisms of rule. Solidarity expected this too, but while the communists saw a deal as presenting the possibility of peaceful transformation within the system, Solidarity saw it as the first phase of the transmutation of the system. Solidarity was correct because it understood the depths of rejection felt by the population and the regime did not: indeed the party leaders thought that the Rakowski government was gaining in popularity and that the party would reap the credit for the Round Table.[12] However, the party's general strategic miscalculation was also accompanied by a number of tactical errors as well as some uncomfortable behaviour by its own allies.

The quasi-official trade union movement was the first to assert its independence. The OPZZ feared (wrongly as it happened) that the re-legalization of Solidarity would lose it members, perhaps rendering it unviable. Its leaders set about proving their commitment to the working class by a sustained and successful campaign for extensive wage rises. Strikes (often with the cooperation of not-yet-legal Solidarity factory committees) engulfed the textile industry, transport, mining, health, and numerous other sectors. The OPZZ gained separate representation at the Round Table despite Solidarity's opposition.

The Round Table convened its first session on 6 February 1989 and its last on 5 April. The achievement of agreement was by no means assured and at the last the outcome still hung in the balance.[13] Negotiations were conducted in a number of working groups or committees (*zespoły*), with separate sub-committees and working parties. The most important were the Committee for Political Reform, co-chaired by Geremek and Reykowski, the Committee for Economic and Social

---

12 Jerzy Urban, *Jajakobyły*, Warsaw, c.1992, p.169.
13 Geremek and Żakowski, op. cit., pp.133–4.

Affairs (Władysław Baka and Witold Trzeciakowski), and the Committee on Trade Union Pluralism (Tadeusz Mazowiecki, Aleksander Kwaśniewski and Romuald Sosnowski of the OPZZ). Ten sub-groups convened on issues such as health, education, judicial reform and the environment.

The crucial decisions were those reached in the dialogue on political reform (although the agreed re-legalization of Solidarity, which finally occurred on 17 April, was a *sine qua non* of political change). The *Sejm* would retain its legislative superiority but its composition would be altered by a new type of quasi-competitive election. The communists and their allies – the United Peasant Party (ZSL), the Democratic Party (SD), and 'loyal' religious groupings – would be assured of 65 per cent of the seats, although within this global arrangement 35 uncontested seats would be reserved for 'eminent' candidates of the so-called National List (a system which had operated since 1985), while in the remainder communist would compete against communist, Peasant against Peasant and so on. The other seats (35 per cent of the total) were reserved to non-party candidates nominated by groups of at least 3,000 citizens, who would also compete freely against one another.

A new Senate, with powers of legislative initiative, deliberation and delay, was to be freely contested. There would be 100 senators, two each from 47 provinces and three from the largest urban provincial conurbations, Warsaw and Katowice. Although the prime minister would remain responsible to the *Sejm*, both houses of the National Assembly (the *Sejm* and the Senate) would jointly elect a new president for a six-year term.

These changes in the electoral mechanism were portrayed as interim ones, providing a gradual, evolutionary path to full parliamentary democracy. Ironically, it was not Solidarity but the official regime delegation which insisted that the initial changes should focus on the central structures of government, including cutting short the term of the current parliament and holding early, 'non-confrontational' elections. Solidarity preferred a strategy focusing on developing guaranteed civil liberties, the independence of the judiciary and autonomous local government.[14] The official camp was in a state of confusion over the proposals for institutional reform: there were elements of strategic thinking and unplanned, spontaneous, *ad hoc* responses. The most significant of these was Kwaśniewski's sudden proposal that the Senate be freely elected.[15] The position of candidates on the National List was not reconsidered after Solidarity's refusal to include candidates; it was assumed that it would succeed (in uncontested elections a negative vote requires deletion of the candidate's name; this had never happened on a massive scale and candidates easily achieved the required absolute majority of votes). Stanisław Gebethner, an academic adviser to the government side, confirms the 'triumph of (misplaced) political instinct' over 'academic knowledge' and an overwhelming 'lack of political imagination'.[16] The former party press spokesman Jerzy Urban viewed the Round Table as a strategic error, enabling Solidarity to mount a massive public propaganda campaign.[17]

The Round Table agreement has frequently been referred to as a 'conspiracy' between the regime and elements of Solidarity, an argument which became common in political rhetoric after the public emergence of divisions within Solidarity in the spring of 1990. The evidence offered relies on the fact that elements of the Round Table met informally whenever the negotiations appeared deadlocked. The case against this view is far stronger: the *ad hoc* and inadequate preparations, divisions within the government coalition negotiating team, the reports of participants, and – most telling of all – the failure of the 'official' team to realize its aims of incorporating and thus neutralizing Solidarity, coupled with achievements by Solidarity wildly exceeding its most optimistic aspirations. The election of June 1989 was the direct cause of this respective defeat and success.

14 The fullext of the agreed Round Table protocols was published in *Rzeczpospolita* 82, 7 April 1989.
15 See Rakowski, op. cit., p.196, p. 200; Geremek, op. cit., p.90.
16 Stanisław Gebethner, 'Political Reform in the Process of Round Table Negotiations' in Sanford, op. cit., p.63.
17 Urban, op. cit., p.156.

The June 1989 Election

The election did not arouse great public excitement. Opinion polls showed that people were more preoccupied with economic matters, especially inflation, than political ones. Solidarity was not confident of a sweeping victory; it was anxious that there was too little time for organizing the campaign, too little money, and too little access to the mass media. It was widely felt that the government had deliberately forced the acceleration of elections for precisely this reason. By mid-May, when the nationwide campaign structure of citizens' electoral committees (*komitety obywatelskie*) was firmly in place, Solidarity announced that it would be pleased with a majority of the independent sector of the *Sejm* (161 seats in total) and about half the Senate.

The communist leadership, however, was anxious. Jaruzelski acknowledged that there was neither a sense of danger nor a spirit of battle within the party.[18] However, some optimistic assessments were received in April from the provincial committees, leading some to expect that the party would take a majority of Senate seats.[19] By mid-May, however, Rakowski was writing in his diary, 'Things are bad ... the Party is still on the defensive ... internal party discipline is weakening'.[20] Certainly the party ran a lacklustre campaign and Solidarity a dynamic one. Solidarity rapidly mobilized its lists of candidates, often with the help of the Church in areas where its local organization was lacking.[21] Candidates had individual photographs taken with Wałęsa and Solidarity ran an effective and highly visible poster campaign, while communist literature was notable for its relative absence. Some communist leaders appeared surprised that there was a campaign at all: after all, the Round Table had agreed to 'non-confrontational' elections. The atmosphere intensified when it became clear that Solidarity was not only campaigning for itself but also against the communists. The lively new Solidarity daily *Gazeta Wyborcza* (Election Gazette), edited by Adam Michnik, catalogued the errors and sins of the past 40 years. Leading Solidarity activists urged the electorate to

18 Rakowski, op. cit., p.213.
19 Gebethner, op. cit., p.63; Rakowski, op. cit., p.220.
20 Rakowski, op. cit., p.223.
21 Geremek and Żakowski, op. cit., p.157.

delete all the names on the National List. There were some reports of harassment of opposition candidates and attempts to manipulate the campaign,[22] although generally the election was regarded as fair. With hindsight Solidarity's victory looks unproblematic, but it did not appear so at the time. Solidarity ran an intelligent and well-organized campaign ('a festival of national improvisation'[23]) and it rode to victory on the shoulders of the disillusioned, angry and frustrated. It established a nationwide network of regional and local 'citizens' committees' to coordinate the campaign with the National Citizens' Committee. It also benefited from strikes and street demonstrations by young radicals, often with anti-Soviet banners at their head. The establishment's cause was not helped by fighting between police and demonstrators protesting against a Warsaw court's refusal to register the independent students' union, whose reinstatement (alongside Solidarity and Rural Solidarity) had been an element of the Round Table agreement.

To win a seat on the first ballot a candidate needed an absolute majority of votes cast, i.e. 50 per cent plus one vote. After the first ballot Solidarity had won 92 of the 100 Senate seats and 160 of the 161 'independent' seats in the *Sejm*. A second ballot was needed for 262 unfilled seats: only three establishment candidates won in the contested seats of the coalition. Worse still from the PZPR's point of view was the defeat of all but two of the National List, both of whose names had been placed at the bottom of the ballot's two columns. Many voters simply struck through the names with a large cross (according to some observers, failing accidentally to include the last two names). However, others clearly discriminated: the candidates on the National List received from 38.7 per cent to 50.8 per cent of the vote across the country.[24]

Solidarity's success not only generated turmoil and recriminations in the PZPR but created a constitutional dilemma as well. No provi-

---

22 Paul G. Lewis, 'Non-competitive Elections and Regime Change: Poland 1989', *Parliamentary Affairs*, vol.43, no.1, 1990a, p.96; Jerzy Baczyński and Władysław Władyka, 'Kampania majowa', *Polityka* 23, 10 June 1989.
23 Timothy Garton Ash, *We the People*, Cambridge, 1990, p.25.
24 Voting behaviour in the 1989 election, including a discussion of regional differences, is analysed in Barbara Heyns and Ireneusz Białecki, 'Solidarność: Reluctant Vanguard or Makeshift Coalition', *American Political Science Review*, vol.85, no.2, 1991, pp.351–70.

sion had been made to fill the seats of candidates defeated in the National List. The implication was not only that the *Sejm* would be short of its constitutionally defined number of 460 deputies but also that the establishment coalition would command 60 per cent of the *Sejm* rather than the agreed formula of 65 per cent. Given Solidarity's victory in the Senate, this could also mean the inability of the coalition to ensure the election (by both houses) of its candidate for the presidency – an unwritten clause of the Round Table 'contract'.

Solidarity repeated its assurances that it would abide by the Round Table agreement, that it did not seek either to form a government or to enter a coalition. Although Solidarity preferred that the 33 seats should remain temporarily vacant, to await a decision by the new parliament, it was anxious not to be seen to betray the Round Table (on the eve of the first ballot Wałęsa had even announced his support for 'all but one' of the National List candidates, and *Gazeta Wyborcza* had urged its readers to read each name and make individual decisions about them). The Round Table reconvened, and the Solidarity delegation finally agreed to endorse a supplementary decree by the Council of State, providing for a fresh election for the 33 vacant seats. Previous candidates would not stand, and two candidates from the coalition parties would compete on a first-past-the-post basis in each seat. Critics argued that amending the electoral law by decree was illegal. More important, there were strong arguments that the population itself had abrogated the Round Table agreement.

Table 3.1 Sejm *deputies by Party Affiliation*

PZPR (Communist)	ZSL (Peasant)	SD (Democrat)	Catholic	Solidarity
173 (38%)	76 (17%)	27 (6%)	23 (5%)	161 (35%)

In the second round voters showed a marked lack of interest in choosing between competing official candidates. Average turnout was 25.9 per cent, considerably higher (43 per cent) in constituencies where there was a run-off for the Senate, and slightly higher (26.5 per cent) in constituencies where Solidarity had endorsed a 'reform' candidate. Formally, despite Solidarity's success in winning all 161 of the non-party sector of the *Sejm* and all but one of the 100 seats in the Senate (one went to a wealthy private businessman, Henryk Stoklosa), the Round Table agreement remained intact. The establishment coalition controlled 65 per cent of the politically dominant lower house (see Table 3.1).

Yet the picture was less clear-cut than the figures indicate. Subsequent propaganda would emphasize the continuing dominance of the communists. In fact, communist influence was less than 38 per cent, for a number of communist deputies were overtly sympathetic to Solidarity and the election débâcle further weakened their partisan allegiance; some of these had been elected with Solidarity support in the second round. It was estimated that 25–30 deputies would broadly support the opposition.

Nor were the other partners likely to prove more reliable. Most of their leaders were absent, having been defeated in the National List. The new deputies were less bound by the old conventions and some also owed their election to Solidarity support. At least three Peasant Party deputies were Solidarity members, plus an indeterminate number of sympathizers. A number of the Democratic Party's deputies also owed their mandates to Solidarity endorsement,[25] while the Catholic groupings had always been opportunist. This uncertainty was to impede the process of government formation; it meant that for the first time in a communist political system parliament would actually play a key role in the creation of the executive. The result was, of course, the appointment of a non-communist prime minister.

Before continuing the discussion, however, it would be useful to assess the successes and failures of the respective contenders, notably the PZPR and Solidarity. The communists could and should have won, given the undemocratic nature of the Round Table agreement. They made serious strategic and tactical blunders which reinforce the judgement that despite the conversion to reformist politics of the top leadership, the party as a whole (including its leaders) was caught in a time warp, unable to depart from old habits and perceptions, and fun-

25 P. Winczorek, 'The Internal Evolution and Changing Policies of the Democratic Party' in Sanford, op. cit., p.187.

damentally uncomprehending of the gulf which existed between it and the society it had ruled for more than 40 years. The PZPR proved itself incapable of competing in a partly competitive election. First of all, the Communist Party appeared to think that Solidarity would not fight the election because it was described as 'non-confrontational'. Yet a competitive election is by its nature a confrontation of programmes, personalities or both. Although it was commonplace to speak of 35 per cent of the *Sejm* as 'reserved' for the opposition, this did not mean that Solidarity was automatically going to win them. Other groups put forward candidates for the non-party sector: trade unionists from the OPZZ and a myriad of individual candidates together with those from other (non-Solidarity) opposition groups stood for the *Sejm*, while in addition to such candidates, communists also ran for the Senate. Contests occurred between members of the opposition. In the Warsaw suburb of Żoliborz, for example, Jacek Kuroń's main rival was the well-known lawyer Władysław Siła-Nowicki. Siła-Nowicki's dissident credentials and long-standing opposition role (he had left Solidarity after a rift with Wałęsa) had been somewhat marred by his decision to join Jaruzelski's Consultative Council in 1986; but Siła, received warmly by Cardinal Glemp on the eve of the election, played the religious card against Kuroń. It was not a foregone conclusion that the untidy ex-Marxist would win Żoliborz. In the event Kuroń won 65.9 per cent of the vote and Siła-Nowicki 21.1 per cent (there were three other candidates).

The casual approach to the campaign also reflected a deep underlying misconception of the relationship between rulers and ruled. Senior party and government officials believed that the party would reap credit for its inauguration of the reform process. Rakowski also pointed optimistically to opinion polls showing the government gaining in popularity and to a rather favourable economic assessment by the World Bank. (Data processed later from the Academy of Science showed that from the spring of 1988 to the spring of 1989 there had been 'a sudden collapse of attitudes supporting the monocentric order, accompanied by an intensification of protest attitudes and a further opening of hitherto passive social groups to political stimuli ...' and strongly negative attitudes to the Communist Party, the linchpin of the system[26].) The inaccuracy of the PZPR's assessment was revealed most starkly in the débâcle of the National List.

The National List was clearly a catastrophic mistake, committed despite warnings from the party's own ranks that things could go dreadfully wrong. A number of arguments were put forward to support it. One stemmed from the expectation that many new deputies would be elected; thus the presence of experienced politicians would ensure some continuity, as well as a core of guarantors of the Round Table settlement. Fundamentally, however, it appears that the party suffered from the assumption that things would continue as they had done in the past, that is, that putting a name on the List was tantamount to electing that person. No measures were taken to ensure election (for example, by including more names than places and specifying that the first 35 would be elected). Nor was the issue of what would happen if all or part of the National List failed to win election ever seriously contemplated – hence the failure to provide for such an eventuality.

Although the National List was clearly a major error, forcing the absence from the *Sejm* of the elite corps of the PZPR and its allies and permitting Solidarity to support reform candidates in the second round, it was not the only one. The PZPR also failed to control its own processes of candidate selection. Instead of limiting the number of candidates for each contested *Sejm* seat to two, the party exercised no discipline from the centre, thus permitting any party members who could gather the requisite 3,000 signatures to contest the election. With a majoritarian second-ballot system, a high number of candidates reduces the chance of electing a candidate on the first ballot. In some *Sejm* constituencies there were eight or nine candidates from the same party competing against one another, while in Senate contests the Communist Party allowed its own vote to be split, in one case seventeen ways. Of course, one could take the argument back a stage and argue that using a majoritarian system itself was an error: a different electoral system might have saved the PZPR the psychological trauma and demoralization of the first-round defeat.

---

26 Krzysztof Jasiewicz, 'Election Behavior in Light of Studies from the Series "Poles"', Paper presented at the Annual Conference of the Political Studies Association, University of Durham, April 1990, p.7.

Does this mean that communist incompetence, arrogance, traditional modes of thinking (or a combination of all three factors) were entirely responsible for their defeat? It seems rash to assume that all would have been well for the PZPR if it had pressed for different technical solutions. The political context was changing rapidly, and divisions within the party would certainly have continued to plague the leadership. Equally important, a different electoral system might have led to the smooth embodiment of the Round Table agreement, but the communists would still have faced a major problem of ensuring the support of the hitherto satellite parties. For this was another miscalculation: the Communist Party's leaders assumed the stability of the coalition,[27] even as others were observing the fragility of the alliance. Jacek Kuroń had noted in March 1989 that a guaranteed majority for the coalition 'does not mean a majority for the Communist Party, since the other coalition partners are beginning to come to life ...'.[28]

Neither the United Peasant Party nor the Democratic Party was immune from tensions and disputes over the nature and extent of reform. A number of Solidarity sympathizers were elected as deputies from their ranks (it has been noted that Solidarity could have done more to encourage and support the nomination and election of reform candidates from both the coalition partners and the religious groupings[29]). The willingness of the two coalition parties to shift their allegiance was to be of major importance in the election of the president and the formation of the new government.

THE NEW EXECUTIVE

The President

Following the Round Table election the paramount issue was how the new government would be constituted. In the politicking of subse-

---

27 Rakowski, op. cit., p.229; Urban, op. cit., p.171.
28 Translated from *Tygodnik Mazowsze* 8 March 1989 in *East European Reporter*, vol.3, no.4, Spring–Summer 1989, p.33; see also Winczorek, op. cit., p.184.
29 For example Baczyński and Władyka, op. cit.

quent weeks the question of the two key executive posts of president and prime minister became inextricably linked. However, before a government could be formed, the question of the presidency had to be addressed (among the president's functions was the nomination of the prime minister). Under the constitutional amendments resulting from the Round Table the president would be elected jointly by the two chambers of parliament. The unspoken assumption of the Round Table was that Jaruzelski would become president. However, developments during the election campaign coupled with the PZPR's defeat led him to withdraw his candidacy on 29 June. Jaruzelski had been the focus of personal attacks and protest demonstrations condemning him as the man responsible for the introduction of martial law. The coalition partners and members of the Church hierarchy were also expressing doubts as to whether he was the appropriate choice.[30] Yet Jaruzelski's preference for his close friend and ally Kiszczak presented no fewer problems: it would be no solution to replace one general responsible for martial law with another, equally culpable – Kiszczak had served as Interior Minister since July 1981. After lengthy discussions with party leaders, Solidarity representatives and members of the parliamentary clubs, and following a public statement by Lech Wałęsa that Solidarity would accept him as president, Jaruzelski reconsidered and announced his candidacy on 18 July.

The election of the president required an absolute majority of valid votes cast. In the event Jaruzelski won by the lowest possible margin of one vote. The outcome was by no means a foregone conclusion, since Jaruzelski could not count on (and did not receive) all the votes of the establishment coalition. This created a dilemma for Solidarity, which wanted a Jaruzelski presidency without voting for it: a positive vote 'would have meant the acceptance of martial law', yet geopolitical constraints (that is, Poland's position at the 'heart of the [Soviet] empire') required a communist president.[31] The dilemma was apparently resolved by *ad hoc* calculations by some Solidarity representatives. One actually voted for Jaruzelski, while 36 absented themselves, spoiled their ballots, or abstained (see Table 3.2).

---

30 Rakowski, op. cit., p.236.
31 Jacek Kuroń, *Moja zupa*, Warsaw, 1991, p.11.

Table 3.2   The Vote for Wojciech Jaruzelski

	For	Against	Abstain	Invalid	Absent
PZPR	171	1	–	–	1
ZSL	54	6	13	–	3
SD	20	4	3	–	–
Catholic	23	–	–	–	–
Independent (Stoklosa)	1	–	–	–	–
Citizens' (Solidarity)	1	222	18	7	11
Total	270	233	34	7	15

The Prime Minister

Jaruzelski's suggestion that Solidarity should participate in a broad coalition, in effect a national government, was immediately rejected; but the question of whether Solidarity should take part had been pursued privately since the results of the first round of voting had become known[32] and was conveyed to the public with Adam Michnik's famous and controversial article of 3 July 1989 in *Gazeta Wyborcza* under the headline 'Your President – Our Premier'. Michnik and Kuroń represented the minority view of the time that Solidarity should assume responsibility for forming the government, with Mazowiecki and Andrzej Wielowieyski firmly opposed. Wałęsa and Geremek overtly supported neither side, but the ferment of discussions and negotiations continued within Solidarity and with the former satellite parties.[33]

Michnik's view gained currency after 2 August, when the *Sejm* approved Jaruzelski's nomination of Kiszczak as prime minister. Jaruzelski's continuing support for Kiszczak can be explained only by loyalty, friendship and respect; politically it was another mistake. Solidarity could not have tolerated the kind of musical chairs being proposed at the top: to win an election and then to see the two gener-

32   Ibid., pp. 10–15.
33   Ibid., p.13; Geremek and Żakowski, op. cit., pp.227–37.

als occupy the key positions of state (and with Rakowski now First Secretary of the PZPR following Jaruzelski's resignation to become a 'non-partisan' head of state) was unthinkable.

Wałęsa spoke forcefully against the notion of a Kiszczak government and mooted the idea of a government coalition composed of Solidarity, the ZSL and the SD. Talks and informal soundings continued with the parliamentary clubs, with the party leaderships, with members of the Church hierarchy and with Jaruzelski. The PZPR reacted angrily to the notion of a three-party coalition and condemned it as a betrayal of the Round Table; but it rapidly became clear that Kiszczak could not form a government. On 14 August he announced his intention to resign, suggesting that the Peasant Party leader Malinowski might lead a coalition. This suggestion undoubtedly came too late; Wałęsa rejected it, and momentum was gathering for a Solidarity-led coalition. Malinowski was regarded within his own party as an element of the *nomenklatura*. Jarosław Kaczyński, acting as Wałęsa's emissary, had aroused the wrath of the parliamentary clubs by discussing matters with the leaders of the ZSL and SD rather than with their elected deputies.[34]

On 17 August, after discussions with Malinowski and the Democrats' leader Jóźwiak, the idea of a 'government of national responsibility' was accepted, but with a Solidarity prime minister. Wałęsa, expected by the Solidarity deputies to lead the government, announced three possible nominees, Mazowiecki, Geremek and Kuroń. The Solidarity leader also affirmed a commitment to the Warsaw Pact, and it was clearly recognized that the communists would retain the key ministries of Interior and Defence. After further discussions with Solidarity, the ZSL and SD, Jaruzelski formally nominated Mazowiecki. The *Sejm* approved the appointment by a huge margin on 24 August, and Mazowiecki addressed himself to the task of forming his government.

In the new government Solidarity had the premiership and eleven ministries, the Democratic Party two ministries, while the United Peasant Party and the PZPR each had three. In addition, Solidarity had two deputy prime ministers and the other parties one each. The

---

34 Kuroń, op. cit., p.14; Geremek and Żakowski, op. cit., pp.240–41; cf. Jarosław Kaczyński, *Odwrotna strona medalu*, Warsaw, 1991, pp.38–9.

communists, with threat and bluff and bombast, had attempted to exact more, but their bargaining power was virtually non-existent, especially after Soviet assurances that the new government was a Polish internal affair (the Soviet Ambassador Vladimir Brovikov had also noted pointedly that the PZPR 'will have to adjust to the new conditions'[35]). Rural Solidarity, incensed at the offer of the agricultural portfolio to the ZSL, albeit to Janicki, who was a member of both, achieved an additional agricultural ministry (for development).

The formation of the government brought to an end the period of communist rule in Poland. Almost overnight the leading role of the Communist Party had disappeared. However, at the time the position did not appear so clear-cut. The arguments raging within Solidarity over whether to participate in government appeared just as valid as they had done in June.[36] The prime fear was that of responsibility without power. The communists retained control of the key ministries of Defence and the Interior. Communist *nomenklatura* appointees remained in place, not only in the state bureaucracy but also in the provincial administrations. Indeed, only the communists possessed experienced middle-ranking cadres. The communist-inspired union, the OPZZ, remained numerically stronger than the trade union wing of Solidarity. The USSR was still viewed as a constraint in foreign policy, although the nature of that constraint was far from clear.

The political drama of July and August was played out against a backcloth of declining government authority and continuing public protest. There was widespread anxiety over the political uncertainty, as well as the rapidly deteriorating economic situation, with mounting inflation and increasingly acute shortages. Indeed, as Mazowiecki was conducting negotiations over the composition of the future government, Rakowski instituted a measure which he later recognized as a powerful hostage to fortune and which he in retrospect found 'inexplicable'.[37] This was the decision to free agricultural prices, that is, to eliminate the extensive retail price subsidies long enjoyed on basic foodstuffs. As a result of this decision, the peasant farmers kept

35 *The Guardian*, 19 August 1989.
36 Kuroń, op. cit., p.11.
37 Rakowski, op. cit., p.243.

their products from the market in anticipation of higher prices. Shortage of many goods gave way to virtual absence; most shops displayed empty shelves during late August. The government had increased subsidies and permitted wages to rise very rapidly in the period of the Round Table and election campaign. Freeing agricultural prices gave a huge boost to inflation.

Thus although Mazowiecki's new government was able to attribute much responsibility for the economy to its communist predecessor, it inherited an economic situation even worse than originally foreseen. Nor could it be sure just how long its legitimacy and credibility would endure, especially given the continuing presence of prominent communists in the government. It would be a mistake, however, to ignore the excitement of these months among the former activists of the opposition. As the window of opportunity opened ever more widely, optimism increased regarding the potential for sweeping, fundamental transformation of the existing system.

THE MAZOWIECKI GOVERNMENT

The government of Tadeusz Mazowiecki lasted from September 1989 until Mazowiecki's defeat in the first ballot of the presidential election in November 1990. In July 1990 most of the communist elements of the government were removed, and Mazowiecki to all intents and purposes headed a Solidarity government. During this relatively brief period in office Mazowiecki initiated fundamental changes to inaugurate the process of transforming Poland into a capitalist liberal democracy.

From the outset the Solidarity ministers played the key role in the coalition. Garton Ash noted that 'Having fought each other for nearly a decade, Solidarity and party leaders now worked side-by-side with little more rancour than you would find between the players of two rival football teams'.[38] Mazowiecki himself was a mild-mannered Catholic intellectual journalist with a reputation for listening to all sides of an argument. He lacked administrative experience, although he had served as a Catholic deputy in parliament in the 1960s and as a

38 Ash, op. cit., p.44.

key adviser to Lech Wałęsa since 1980. The crucial members of the government were its economic team, led by Minister of Finance Leszek Balcerowicz and Industry Minister Tadeusz Syryjczyk, both vigorously committed to a free market economy and privatization. Aleksander Paszyński, Minister of Housing, was also a firm advocate of reducing the role of the state and leaving major decisions to the market.

Generally Solidarity's ministers were of a liberal (and academic) cast, both economically and politically, rather than possessing a social democratic, trade unionist orientation as might have been expected. The trade union element of Solidarity had maintained a certain distance from the election, and this was symbolized by Wałęsa's own disinclination to stand for parliament. Solidarity in its trade union guise bestowed neither its name nor its financial support on the parliamentary club, which called itself the Citizens' Parliamentary Club (OKP). The government also expressed this divergence. Even the flamboyant proponent of self-management Jacek Kuroń, who took the portfolio of Labour and Social Policy, became convinced of the need for the programme of economic liberalism promoted by Balcerowicz and encouraged by the International Monetary Fund and foreign advisers such as Jeffrey Sachs. Sachs proved influential in gaining the acceptance by Solidarity intellectuals of the government's economic programme.[39] The political liberalism (notably an emphasis on the rule of law and the protection of minority rights) was reflected in the painstaking preparation of the legal ground for further change and the refusal to engage in witch-hunts against former opponents. Economic liberalism was manifest in a preference for private entrepreneurial capitalism (in contrast to workers' self-management) and in the decision to apply the short sharp shock treatment to the thorny problem of removing subsidies and eliminating the black market. Generally – although not always – when the two liberalisms collided, the political won: privatization, for example, was not to be inaugurated until the legal bases of ownership were clearly established.

Although Mazowiecki himself was hugely popular in the country at large, tensions emerged almost immediately between the various insti-

---

39 Kuroń, op. cit., p.12.

tutional strands of the Solidarity movement. Wałęsa, reportedly 'incensed over the new Prime Minister's spirit of independence in forming the government',[40] filled Mazowiecki's old job, personally appointing the new editor of the *Solidarity Weekly* (*Tygodnik Solidarność*) without consulting Mazowiecki. Geremek, now leader of the Solidarity parliamentary club the OKP, openly criticized the government for excessive secrecy and an inadequate information policy. We shall see later how these tensions intensified and led to new ones, resulting in the break-up of Solidarity.

For the moment, however, incipient tensions were kept in check by personal friendships and a common dedication to the 'Solidarity ethos', as well as the commitment to a government that was now 'ours', not 'theirs'. The government worked quickly and within a fortnight had presented the IMF, the World Bank and the European Community with a draft programme, intended to 'transform the Polish economy into a market economy, with an ownership structure of that found in the advanced industrial economies'.[41] The government also moved quickly on the political front, taking advantage of the broadly-based consensus regarding the need for change.

Developments in the Political Sphere

Constitutional amendments in December 1989 and March 1990 (see Chapter 5) deprived the PZPR of its 'leading role' and its ideological monopoly. The state was no longer a socialist state but a democratic one, based on the rule of law. The Polish People's Republic became the Polish Republic, and the old symbol of the crowned eagle was restored. A number of institutions were abolished, among them the Office of the Censor and the Bureau of Religious Affairs. Other aspects of the dismantling of communist power took more time and needed more preparation.

In the speech which followed his nomination to the premiership on 24 August 1989 Mazowiecki stated his determination to draw a thick

40 Konstanty Gebert, 'The Polish Press since the Round Table Accord', *East European Reporter*, vol.4, no.1, Winter 1989–90, p.77; see also Geremek and Żakowski, op. cit., p.281.
41 For the English text of the government's 'Memorandum on the Economic Reform Programme in Poland...' see *East European Reporter*, vol.4, no.1, 1989–90, pp.66–9.

line (*gruba linia*) separating his government's responsibility from that of the previous regime.[42] However, the new government could not altogether avoid the issues of recent history, if only to reassure the public that this was genuinely to be a new system. This meant bringing to book those who had committed crimes which had been ignored, if not instigated, by the previous political authorities. One of the first acts of the new *Sejm* was the establishment of a commission to investigate the activities of the Interior Ministry since December 1981, that is, after the declaration of martial law. A number of cases were singled out for special investigation, notably the murder of Father Popiełuszko.

It was also deemed vital to ensure a compliant civil service capable of serving new ministers. The recognition of bureaucratic power, and the 'lessons' drawn from the Chilean experience of the 1970s, had been highlighted by leading Solidarity intellectuals as a major obstacle to change. How could one ensure that decisions would be carried out by an administration staffed by communists? Even worse, how could one begin this process in the key ministries of Defence and the Interior, still controlled by communist generals?

The Mazowiecki government took the view that skill and experience should be utilized; no one should be barred from a job simply because he or she had been a member of the Communist Party or because the appointment had come through the *nomenklatura*. Of course, senior posts in the bureaucracy saw a rapid changeover, but changes were much slower for middle-ranging officials. The government was concerned, in its own words, to avoid witch-hunts. In most areas the new ministers were given considerable discretion with regard to their own administrators. Not surprisingly, many older personnel opted for retirement. Some left after the ban on civil servants' participation in joint stock companies (*spółki*) in August 1990. For the police force – including previous employees of the notorious secret police, which was abolished and replaced with a new Office of State Defence (*Urząd Obrony Państwa*) – verification commissions were set up to examine the records of individuals.

Communist privileges also needed to be removed. The first step was

42 Mazowiecki's speech is reproduced in Zbigniew Domarańczyk, *100 dni Mazowieckiego*, Warsaw, 1990, pp.106–8.

the removal of the vast network of subsidies, tax exemptions and bank credits from the PZPR, its auxiliary organizations and its previous coalition partners (in 1989 the state budget envisaged 37,600 million zloties for subsidies alone).[43] The second step was the confiscation of communist ^-sets; the PZPR was busy creating an economic empire from its property by leasing buildings for new economic ventures and transferring elements of its media empire to new private firms organized by party members. By the end of January 1990 a government commission had been established to assess the legal title of the old ruling parties to the buildings they occupied.

The PZPR had also controlled the official media, largely through the massive RSW empire, which monopolized production, distribution and retail sales of virtually the entire press. Given its entrenchment, abolishing censorship and lifting all prohibitions against establishing new newspapers and journals were a necessary but insufficient condition of ensuring diverse, independent media. A second commission had the task of submitting proposals for dismantling RSW's paper mills, printing presses, publishing houses, press agencies and distribution network. New appointments were also made to state radio and television.

The issue of *nomenklatura* capitalism also surfaced quickly. The transfer of public assets to private individuals or companies had begun in 1987. Profitable elements of large enterprises were hived off or leased to these new private firms. The Mazowiecki government introduced regulations to prevent private firms exploiting state assets, but it opposed retrospective legislation. Although it was prepared to act against firms which had been established illegally according to the existing law, it was extremely difficult to find hard evidence of such practice. The legalistic approach of the government was bitterly attacked by its opponents for complicity in *nomenklatura* exploitation of public assets.

In July 1990 Mazowiecki responded to pressure from Wałęsa to deal more vigorously with the communists. Most importantly, he removed Kiszczak from the Interior Ministry and Siwicki from Defence. President Jaruzelski remained as the last symbol of commu-

43 Louisa Vinton, 'The Politics of Property: Divesting the Polish Communist Party of its Assets', *RFE/RL Report on Eastern Europe*, vol.1, no.17, 27 April 1990, p.18.

nist rule. In the event, Jaruzelski resigned quietly in the autumn to permit an early presidential election. A constitutional amendment introduced the new principle of direct election to the presidency.

We can see, then, that the process of eliminating the sources of communist power was linked to a number of positive steps designed to further the establishment of a democratic framework. However, the precepts and values of the old regime were also embedded in legislation. The legal question was a thorny one. Legislation could not be drafted hastily – and when this happened, it usually proved to be full of loopholes and inadequacies – but the government's view that existing (communist) law must be obeyed until new legislation was in place led to considerable resentment. *Nomenklatura* capitalism incensed the Solidarity trade union, for example. So too did the government's insistence on the need to obey existing law regulating strike action.

Economic Policy

In Chapter 1 we identified the major problems of the communist system of central planning and the specific policies which had led to enduring economic failure. By the autumn of 1989 the new government faced an intensification of these problems along with new ones, namely a situation of near hyper-inflation (partly because of the freeing of agricultural prices in August) and – as a result – a severe budget deficit. The government's programme envisaged that the twin goals of stabilizing the economy and altering its basic structure must be pursued simultaneously. The method chosen was the 'big bang' or the short sharp shock, on the principle that 'you can't cross an abyss with small steps'. To the surprise of many, the *Sejm* quickly approved a package of new legislation.

The main measures for stabilizing the economy were introduced on 1 January 1990. They were intended to lead to a situation where prices would find the 'proper' level, that is, they would result from the interplay of supply and demand and would serve as a genuine reflection of scarcities in the economy. At the same time opening trade to world markets would create domestic competition as well as affecting the price structure. Most prices were immediately freed from bureaucratic interference, while the government also dramatically reduced the level of consumer subsidies, especially in energy. Internal convertibility of the zloty at a rate roughly equivalent to the black market rate followed, and nominal interest rates were increased substantially to bring about positive rates in real terms. To prevent a wage–price spiral the government limited wage increases to a small fraction of price inflation through a tax-based income indexation policy (the *popiwek*). Foreign trade restrictions were relaxed and many of the complex rules regulating the private sector were removed. The government initiated preliminary measures for breaking up existing monopolies in order to permit competition; but most of the structural reform programme needed careful preparation, especially the privatization of large-scale enterprises; modernization and development of the banking and financial sector, and reform of the tax system, and measures to encourage foreign investment.

Despite the shock to the population of the massive price increases they experienced in January, and with inflation higher than predicted, the government was optimistic in the initial stages of its programme. The black market disappeared overnight and queues vanished; shops and street bazaars were full; exotic imported goods were easily available. Other positive aspects emerged in the coming months, including a healthy budget surplus and a strong foreign trade performance. Initial assessments were favourable.[44] However, it became evident that inflation would continue to be far higher than expected, while the resulting recession would be deeper. Real incomes fell and domestic demand collapsed, while enterprises showed little of the postulated restructuring. Industry responded by reducing production, putting workers on short time or sending them on holiday. Large-scale bankruptcies were avoided, but mainly by the expedient of accumulating debts. Uncertainty and insecurity increased as unemployment rose far more rapidly than expected: 400,000 by the spring and nearly 1.2 million by the end of 1990. A measure of fiscal and monetary relaxation in June 1990 permitted some wage increases, but discontent was spreading. Social problems intensified and became more visible: increased crime, prostitution, and drug abuse caused anxiety; home-

---

44 See, for example, Jeffrey Sachs and David Lipton, 'Poland's Economic Reform', *Foreign Affairs*, vol.69, no.3, 1990, pp.47–66.

lessness was formally acknowledged. Mazowiecki's standing declined and abuse of Balcerowicz became a national sport. The political situation became increasingly fraught.

The conflict within Solidarity intensified from the summer of 1990 (see Chapter 5) and began to be played out during the presidential election of November–December. Mazowiecki campaigned on the achievements of his government and resigned following his ignominious defeat. Although several members of his team continued in their posts under the new prime minister, engendering a considerable degree of continuity, Mazowiecki's resignation marked the end of the beginning of post-communist politics in Poland.

POLITICAL CHANGE IN 1989–90

The Round Table formula gave the reform wing of the PZPR the illusion that it could retain political power through the incorporation and neutralization of Solidarity, but the illusion was to prove short-lived. This is not to suggest that the outcome was pre-determined, quite the contrary, for the pact was negotiated by individuals making real choices and taking genuine political risks. Solidarity benefited from basic errors of judgement by the communists in framing the settlement and in the electoral process itself. Once the election had been lost, the situation became even more uncertain.

Solidarity leaders have frequently remarked on their own perceptions of the communists as a potentially duplicitous partner capable of instant and insidious betrayal. The suppression of the Chinese student protests in Tiananmen Square spoke eloquently. However, the PZPR's acceptance of the election result should not really be surprising.[45] It is difficult to conceive of Jaruzelski, so personally scarred by the experience of martial law, as reaching again for a coercive option which had clearly failed before. It is equally difficult to imagine Gorbachev's sanctioning such a move, given his own domestic political turmoil,

---

45 See, for example, Janusz Ziolkowski, 'The roots, branches and blossoms of Solidarność' in Gwyn Prins (ed.), *Spring in Winter: The 1989 Revolutions*, Manchester, 1990, p.60, who finds it 'most remarkable ... that the Communist Party accepted the defeat.'

economic crisis and determination to nurture good relations with the West. After all, it was the politically weak Senate which was the great triumph for Solidarity; to all appearances the PZPR would still have the resources to dominate the political process. What set the seal on the communist defeat was the chain reaction against the communist system which spread throughout Eastern Europe. This gave Mazowiecki increasing freedom of manoeuvre, although at times he appeared slow to take advantage of it.

By the time of his departure Mazowiecki's government had lost much of the public confidence which had greeted its inauguration, and a high level of emotional rhetoric characterized public life. The achievements of the transition appeared to be soon forgotten or taken for granted. The government's slow, legalist approach generated frustration and anxiety, as unemployment rose, recession deepened and the standard of living dropped. Within parliament there was little effective debate surrounding possible alternative approaches, and the government proved itself unwilling or unable to communicate effectively with the population. It had placed too much faith in the rhetoric of market liberalism on the one hand and of civil society on the other. Spontaneous regeneration failed to take place in the economy and the capacity of society for self-organization and self-emancipation proved similarly chimerical. Nor should we ignore longer-term factors, which would persist with successive governments. Political and administrative inexperience, the dire economic legacy, inflated popular expectations, a lack of structures linking the citizenry to the polity, and personality conflicts all took their toll.

The achievements, however, were profound. By a process of peaceful negotiation through formal parliamentary institutions and procedures the old political system was dismantled. The Mazowiecki government demonstrated its commitment to the rule of law, the ethos of reconciliation, tolerance of diverse viewpoints, and the government's electoral accountability. It could not guarantee that its successors would continue along the route it had marked out; but there was clearly no possibility of going back to a polity based on the hegemony of a Leninist party.

4. Polish Governments after the Presidential Election

Wałęsa's victory in the presidential election of 1990 meant that Solidarity now controlled the executive branch of government. His great personal authority temporarily lifted the public mood, for he had campaigned on promises to accelerate the reform process while mitigating its hardship. At the outset of his term Wałęsa found himself floundering. He did not understand the institutional framework in which he had to operate. He was estranged from the close advisers who had served him throughout the 1980s, for most of them had supported Mazowiecki in the 'war at the top' which split Solidarity into the two camps which vied for the presidency (see Chapter 5). Although Wałęsa had won decisively on the second ballot, taking 74 per cent of the vote, his political base was inchoate and bedevilled by internal contradictions. The new president found the task of learning his new job difficult, demanding and frustrating. He did not move his family to Warsaw and took every opportunity to visit them in Gdańsk. What appeared to surprise Wałęsa most was the lack of autonomous power vested in the office of president and the need to negotiate and compromise with other political actors. As the wounds of the 'war at the top' began to heal, new ones opened. Further fissiparous tendencies emerged in Solidarity as parliamentary elections approached. The 1991 election generated a highly fragmented parliament, with no obvious centre of gravity around which to construct a stable coalition government. Its defeat on a vote of confidence in May 1993 left it in a caretaker capacity until the September 1993 election.

In his first two years as president Wałęsa formally nominated four prime ministers. The process of government-formation proved complex, and this raised fears of political paralysis and instability. However, three of these four, all claiming Solidarity provenance, did prove able to form a government. The first, from January to December 1991, was headed by the liberal economist Jan Krzysztof Bielecki.

Jan Olszewski led the second, formed in December 1991 after the indecisive result of the first fully competitive parliamentary elections in October. Olszewski, of right-wing Christian Democratic persuasion, fell at the beginning of June 1992 after five turbulent months ended in a parliamentary vote of no confidence. Waldemar Pawlak of the Polish Peasant Party (PSL) received presidential and parliamentary endorsement; but Pawlak could not mobilize sufficient parliamentary support to form a government. In July 1992 Hanna Suchocka became the first Polish woman premier, leading a complex seven-party coalition whose constituents included the parties of two former prime ministers, Mazowiecki and Bielecki, and also the clerical nationalist ZChN, the linchpin of the Olszewski government. It was frequently described as a government of 'fire and water', but it surprised many by its relative durability.

Gradually the new politicians began to acquire experience. A nucleus of ministers emerged who had served in more than one government. The institutional framework took shape, culminating in the acceptance of a 'Little Constitution' which facilitated the survival of the Suchocka government. However, the problems of political communication remained; the population was generally ill-informed and uninvolved in the process of political reconstruction. The political institutions were singularly unsuccessful in generating public trust and prestige. Wałęsa's popularity waned. Parliament proved ineffective as a link between public and polity. In 1991 the *Sejm* remained outwardly unchanged. It was still the 'contract parliament' elected as a result of the Round Table agreement. After the election of 1991 both chambers were highly fragmented, with numerous small parties lacking strong social roots. The pressure group universe remained small, with only the trade unions, peasant movements and the Catholic Church able to give voice to their demands. Generally the public mood grew more sombre after the presidential election, although ebbs, flows and eddies could be plotted against political and economic developments.

THE GOVERNMENT OF JAN KRZYSZTOF BIELECKI

It was clear that the presidential election would resolve none of the crucial political, economic and social problems which were accumulating in the summer of 1990. Indeed, in some respects it exacerbated them. Mazowiecki, correctly interpreting his defeat as a massive vote of no confidence in his government, resigned immediately following the first ballot.

As Wałęsa began the process of seeking a new prime minister, his first choice was the lawyer Jan Olszewski. However, Olszewski abandoned his consultations 'in the face of important differences between the president-elect and me over the shape of the government'.[1] Wałęsa then pursued two further possibilities: first, that Mazowiecki's government remain in office until after parliamentary elections in the spring; or, second, that a new government be formed and elections delayed: 'No responsible person', said the official statement 'would undertake such a major task for a period of three months.'[2] The first proposal obviously depended on Mazowiecki's willingness to serve as a 'disposable prime minister'[3] of a government rejected by the people under a president whose criticism had been his undoing. The second proved feasible, albeit entailing the continuation of the Round Table parliament. The *Sejm* itself was not averse to delaying elections; most deputies could not look forward to being re-elected.

On 4 January 1991 the immediate problem appeared to be resolved when the *Sejm* approved the nomination of Jan Krzysztof Bielecki as the new prime minister. Bielecki, an economist and entrepreneur, was a member of the Liberal Democratic Congress (KLD), a small political party based in Gdańsk and enjoying good relations with the Centrum, the party which had spearheaded Wałęsa's bid for the presidency. Bielecki was a member of that wing of Solidarity most closely associated with liberal, free market economics. He promised a 'government of experts' and rapid privatization of the economy. Most of his ministers, however, came from tiny, incipient political parties.

---

1   *The Independent*, 19 December 1990.
2   *Rzeczpospolita* 297, 21 December 1990.
3   Adam Krzemiński, 'Trzeci wariant', *Polityka* 52, 29 December 1990.

It soon became clear that the government would provide neither the 'turning-point' nor the 'acceleration' urged by Wałęsa during the election but rather a government of continuity. Bielecki's economic inclinations were broadly similar to those of the Mazowiecki government, and this was reflected in the person of Leszek Balcerowicz, who remained Minister of Finance and also became Deputy Prime Minister. Several other ministers kept their posts, notably Foreign Minister Skubiszewski and Defence Minister Kołodziejczyk, a former communist. Bielecki's close associate Janusz Lewandowski, for a time leader of the Liberals, became Minister of Property Transformation. The leader of the right-wing Christian National Union (ZChN), Wiesław Chrzanowski, became Minister of Justice. Adam Głąpiński, Jerzy Eysymontt and Krzysztof Zabiński of the Centrum also received ministerial posts. Although the government was broadly of centre–right persuasion, the new Minister of Labour Michał Boni had been the chief Solidarity negotiator with his predecessor Jacek Kuroń, another poacher-turned-gamekeeper (indeed, Boni later joined Bielecki's KLD).

The substantial support within the *Sejm* for Bielecki (only the deputies of the Polish Peasant Party [PSL] voted against him) proved a false dawn, both for the new prime minister and also for the president; Bielecki's relationship with Wałęsa was not an easy one at the start. The political and administrative inexperience of the new team took its toll. However, the executive's main problem was the absence of a reliable majority in the *Sejm*. Bielecki's government was seen as a short-term expedient lasting only until parliamentary elections could be held. Neither Wałęsa nor Bielecki had a coherent political base; both underestimated the significance of this factor.

The president refused to associate himself directly with the Centrum, though he brought several of its members into his office, the presidential Chancellery, which was headed by the Centrum's leader Jarosław Kaczyński. The government no longer enjoyed the luxury of almost effortlessly commanding support. The Left Parliamentary Club still represented most former communists, although the PZPR had ceased to exist from January 1990. Then its members still saw themselves as bound by the Round Table agreement and had supported Mazowiecki, albeit uneasily and critically; now they went formally into opposition. The main peasant party, the PSL, had been in opposition since the autumn of 1990, when it withdrew from Mazowiecki's government in protest over agricultural policy. Mazowiecki's own supporters split from the Citizens' Parliamentary Club (the OKP) in the *Sejm* to form a parliamentary club of the Democratic Union (UD). The deep divisions and personal animosities towards the supporters of Wałęsa continued to fester after his electoral victory, although the UD did not consistently vote against the government. Tensions between government and parliament quickly emerged as the main focus of political conflict.

The government had some early successes, particularly in foreign policy. Skubiszewski brought to completion his negotiations with Germany. Poland's international position appeared strengthened; in March the Paris Club of official creditors announced that they were (under strict conditions) writing off 50 per cent of Polish debt owed to them, and the IMF also announced a three-year adjustment loan. Negotiations with the USSR over troop removals proved more complex and difficult, as the Soviet leadership, concerned to placate its conservative elements, shifted to the right in 1991; still, there was progress under a canopy of invective. The president made numerous forays abroad, with state visits to the USA, Britain, France, the EC and Moscow in the first months of his presidency.

Wałęsa, although undoubtedly distressed by the economic hardships facing the population, appeared finally convinced of the necessity to continue on the course set by Balcerowicz. It was clear that the Deputy Prime Minister had the support of the United States, the IMF and the World Bank. A much heralded conference of economists called together by Wałęsa in May 1991 fizzled out, with no consensus on alternatives to the harsh Balcerowicz medicine, made worse by the impact of the Gulf crisis and the virtual collapse of the Soviet market from the start of the year. Despite tensions within the government, notably between Balcerowicz at Finance and Eysymontt in the Central Planning Office, it maintained anti-inflationary policies as the centrepiece of its economic measures. The privatization of small-scale retailing and service establishments proceeded apace, and the number of new private businesses (and the now ubiquitous street traders) expanded rapidly. However, mass privatization, strongly supported by the president and the Minister of Ownership Transformation, made little progress.

The state sector continued to dominate the economy, and there was still little sign of the fundamental enterprise restructuring which government economists had anticipated as a result of external competition and new financial discipline. Continuing accumulation of debts and systematic sales of assets became the preferred (if short-sighted) management tactics. Furthermore, new investment in modern equipment was made difficult by punitive interest rates, part of the wider programme of macro-economic stabilization. Yet it was only in the summer of 1991 that the government was partially converted to the need for an industrial strategy, symbolized by the appointment of Henryka Bochniarz as Minister for Trade and Industry.

The trade unions' tolerance was also reaching its limits. Immediately following Wałęsa's inauguration strikes broke out, directed mainly against the hated *popiwek*, the indexation system designed to curtail wage increases. The phased removal of price subsidies continued to erode the standard of living. In the first six months of 1991 industrial production fell by 9.3 per cent compared with the first half of 1990. Unemployment continued to rise, exceeding 1.57 million by the end of June.[4] Discontent increased and on 23 May the Solidarity trade union, now under the leadership of Marian Krzaklewski, mobilized its members for a day of protest against the government's economic policy. Strikes and protests became frequent occurrences, although lack of union funds meant they were usually of short duration.

The government was unresponsive to trade union demands. It complained that parliamentary obstruction was thwarting the economic initiatives which were necessary to improve the situation. Bielecki confronted the *Sejm* with a deadline of 15 June for passing the measures needed for the so-called 'leap into capitalism'; otherwise the government would resign. On 12 June Wałęsa requested that the government be given the power to issue economic legislation by decree. The president's tone became more and more strident. He was embroiled in controversy with the *Sejm* over the new electoral law,

---

4   1.57 million was the official figure for registered unemployed: 'Statystyka Polski' no.8, *Rzeczpospolita*, 29 July 1991.

and he attacked it bitterly as an illegitimate remnant of the now defunct Round Table agreement. His popularity continued to decline. Both Wałęsa and Bielecki showed signs of increasing frustration. In a meeting with Solidarity trade union leaders Wałęsa's comments suggested a willingness to search for authoritarian solutions: '... they say "You must be tough", but when I talk tough they say "Obey the law". But obeying the law I can do nothing. If they take to the streets, if there are brawls, I won't have any choice. I will have to throw brothers at brothers'.[5]

The *Sejm* was unreceptive to demands for increased government powers, but it did agree to the establishment of a legislative 'fast track' for urgent measures. At the same time the *Sejm* failed to override the presidential veto of the new electoral law. However, it also rejected Wałęsa's own proposals, embodied in a law approved by the Senate. The president embarked on a series of factory visits to try to demonstrate popular support for dissolving the *Sejm*, although he was clearly torn between the desire to act regardless of the Constitution (which permitted dissolution only in tightly defined circumstances) and the desire to act in accordance with the law. The president's public reception was at best mixed and on occasion downright hostile. When the *Sejm* overrode a second presidential veto, with only a hundred deputies voting in Wałęsa's favour, he backed down and signed the new electoral law.

A temporary truce appeared to hold in July, when a government spokesman confirmed that 'the communist-dominated parliament' was no longer blocking its reforms. Seven significant economic reform bills had been passed in recent weeks. The appointment of Bochniarz appeared to signal a greater sensitivity to the problems of industrial restructuring, and she announced plans for identifying and assisting troubled enterprises and improving the flow of government information. Yet the truce did not provide a respite for the beleaguered government. Negotiations with the European Community were proving difficult and unrewarding. Polish negotiators expressed public anger at the failure of the EC to honour promises to open its market to Polish agriculture, textiles and steel. Wałęsa was once again manifesting unease over the government's economic programme. Reports surfaced

5   *The Independent*, 18 June 1991, provided an edited transcript of Wałęsa's comments.

that he had requested the IMF to sanction the dismissal of Balcerowicz and the introduction of a state of emergency.[6] Prime Minister Bielecki for his part delayed until 30 August submitting the government's resignation after the *Sejm* refused to pass deep cuts in the state budget. A massive budget deficit threatened, a product of the erosion of the tax base through recession and widespread tax evasion.[7] Bielecki's task was unenviable. The wheels of parliament ground exceeding slow, despite the creation of the 'fast lane' to speed urgent legislation. Industrial unrest and peasant protest punctuated the summer months, and a number of giant industrial firms, including the Ursus agricultural machinery plant, tottered on the edge of bankruptcy. The government aroused the hostility of public sector employees by suspending the index-linking of their pay to average wages in the industrial sector.

The Bielecki government also found itself under attack as a series of corruption scandals became public. These cast doubt on the integrity and competence of the banking system and the probity of customs and excise officials. Several had their origins in the earlier period of Mazowiecki's government,[8] but they reflected generally on the post-communist Solidarity governments and became a useful source of demagogic rhetoric during the election campaign. The alcohol affair, the cigarette affair and the television affair involved manipulation of import duties and customs regulations. The Art-B scandal, which broke in August, was particularly damaging. The Art-B conglomerate had been able to exploit the inadequacies of the banking system by opening an account and then flying around the country to open new accounts with cheques from the first. Cheques took time to clear in the slow and clumsy postal system, while interest payments started immediately a cheque was deposited: the same money was accruing interest several times over. It also transpired that the banks had lavishly provided Art-B with unsecured loans and credit guarantees.[9] On the heels of the Art-B revelations other arrests followed in connection with suspected embezzlement of the Foreign Debt

6 *The Guardian*, 29 July 1991.
7 Joanna Solska, 'Z lewej kieszeni', *Polityka* 48, 30 November 1991.
8 See P. Tarnowski, 'W oparach spirytusu', *Polityka* 32, 11 August 1990, on the alcohol affair.
9 Jerzy Andrzejczak *et al.*, *Art–B Bluff*, Warsaw, 1991, pp.99–121.

Servicing Fund (FOZZ), set up by the communists in 1989. The Deputy Finance Minister lost his job over FOZZ, while the former chairman of the National Bank was arrested in connection with Art-B.[10]

By the summer of 1991 the political parties were embarking on the first stages of the election campaign, for which they needed above all to establish public recognition. The parties attempted to reap capital from the government's difficulties in controlling corruption and the escalating budget deficit. The Christian National Union (ZChN) and the Confederation for Independent Poland (KPN) both based election promises on their own probity: they argued that the billions saved through eliminating corruption would permit more government spending on social service provision and economic intervention. While the Liberals and the Democratic Union broadly supported Balcerowicz, most other parties were strongly opposed. The parties mobilized professional economists in support of their respective alternative programmes. Some were closely associated with the inauguration of new parties: Professor Ryszard Bugaj of Labour Solidarity accused the government of pursuing a rigid, doctrinaire liberalism which discriminated against the state sector of the economy through its taxation policies and customs tariffs, while doing nothing to allay the insecurity and uncertainty faced by management and workers' councils.[11]

Among independent economists there was also some feeling that the government remained too complacent about the regenerative capacity of state industry. By the end of 1991 there were 2.15 million registered unemployed or 11.4 per cent of the labour force.[12] However, assessments of the government's economic policies differed widely. Jeffrey Sachs viewed the government's performance as 'excellent' and the achievements in moving to a market economy as 'splendid'.[13] A group of pro-government liberal economists criticized it, however, for excessive concentration on the problem of stabilization, resulting in a

10 The complexities of both cases meant that by the beginning of 1993 neither the accused in Art-B nor those in the FOZZ scandal had been brought to trial; see 'Niekończąca się historia', Życie Warszawy 214, 8 September 1992.
11 R. Bugaj, 'Póki nie jest za późno', Polityka 30, 27 July 1991.
12 Rzeczpospolita 13, 16 January 1992.
13 'Jest lepiej niż się wydaje', interview with Jeffrey Sachs, Polityka 37, 14 September 1991.

credit and investment squeeze on the small and medium-sized firms of the dynamic private sector and a neglect of institutional changes, particularly in the banking system. They argued for a tightly defined interventionist approach, including emergency measures to deal with state enterprises on which a local or regional economy depended, and a system of public works.[14]

Members of parliament were increasingly anticipating the election of 27 October. The cuts envisaged in the budget affected areas that were already badly underfunded, especially the police, the health service and education – areas of particular public concern. Violent crime was increasing, and the police were understaffed and lacked basic equipment. The prospect of direct health charges for patients drew attention to the plight of the elderly and the chronically ill. The *Sejm* refused to accept the government's resignation of 30 August; it also rejected a draft bill seeking authorization for the government to rule by decree. Particularly turbulent debates followed the government's new pensions bill. The Social Democrats, the heirs of the PZPR, made capital out of the pensions issue, supported by large-scale pensioners' and miners' demonstrations outside parliament. Teachers marched in Warsaw with a coffin symbolizing the death of education. Peasants protested against the burden of debt and low agricultural prices. Faced with another storm of protest, the government withdrew controversial, ill-conceived proposals to amend the system of family allowances. The situation was one of political stalemate, with no optimism that a parliamentary election could generate a government with a genuine popular mandate. Opinion polls registered deep feelings of pessimism and insecurity.

THE GOVERNMENT OF JAN OLSZEWSKI

The parliamentary elections of October 1991 brought no sign of relief. The largest party, Mazowiecki's Democratic Union, received just over 12 per cent of the vote and, to the horror of many, the former communists, now the Social Democratic Party (SDRP), came

14 Janusz Beksiak *et al.*, Open Letter to the President, 'Co zmienić w gospodarce', *Gazeta Wyborcza* 241, 15 October 1991.

a close second. The resulting composition of the *Sejm* was highly fragmented, with 27 fluid parties grouped into eighteen distinct but unstable parliamentary clubs (the parties are dealt with in Chapter 5). It took almost two months to form a government out of the havoc wreaked on the politicians by the electorate. The Democratic Union could not mobilize a parliamentary majority, and attention soon focused on the possibility of a five-party coalition of the Liberals, the Christian National Union (ZChN), the Confederation for Independent Poland (KPN), the Centrum and the Solidarity Peasant Alliance (PL). However, programmatic and personnel disputes led to the withdrawal of the Liberals and the KPN. At last Jan Olszewski constructed a three-party minority government: Olszewski's own party the Centrum, the ZChN, and the coalition of Solidarity Peasant Parties provided its main prop. Increasingly, the Polish Peasant Party (PSL) also supported the government.

Olszewski, a lawyer with a long Solidarity pedigree, enjoyed considerable personal respect as he embarked on his unenviable task as head of Poland's third post-communist government. He left office in June with his reputation badly tarnished. Certainly he faced profound problems. The first was the absence of sufficient support within the *Sejm*. This resulted from the peculiar configuration of the parties, not just the numbers represented in the *Sejm* but the incompatibility of their programmes. Even the coalition parties were divided over important issues, including that of how to try to broaden the government's parliamentary support.

However, while it benefited from *de facto* PSL support, the Olszewski government's demeanour did not assist the process of extending the coalition, although virtually every conceivable combination of alliance was proposed.[15] Jarosław Kaczyński of the Centrum, whose unremitting pressure in support of Olszewski's candidacy was widely viewed as decisive, now proved equally tireless in his efforts to broaden the government's political base, especially by including the Democratic Union (previously the chief object of the Centrum's political bile). The UD came under strain as its right-wing

---

15 See Anna Sabbat-Swidlicka, 'Poland: Weak Government, Fractious Sejm, Isolated President', *RFE/RL Research Report*, vol.1, no.15, 1992, pp.1–4, on the convoluted negotiations to extend the coalition.

faction proved more sympathetic to Olszewski than its secular, centre–left wing. However, Olszewski himself seemed unaware of the imperatives of compromise. The free hand given to his ministers in personnel matters increased political friction; for example, members of Mazowiecki's party were removed from their jobs in the ministries of Labour and Defence just when Kaczyński was trying to draw the UD into government. Olszewski appeared increasingly in thrall, not to his own party the Centrum, but to the clerical nationalist ZChN.

The political problems, then, were formidable. Olszewski headed a three-party government which lacked internal cohesion and which controlled only about one-quarter of deputies in the *Sejm*, where discipline was uncertain. The *Sejm* had accepted the Olszewski government largely in the absence of a plausible alternative. Failure to approve a government risked two unpalatable possibilities: that the president himself would take over as head of government (a constitutionally dubious proposition); or the awful prospect of fresh elections.

The situation was further complicated by Olszewski's poor relationship with Wałęsa and the deterioration in the president's relations with the Centrum. Wałęsa had steadfastly resisted the pressure to nominate Olszewski (who, it will be recalled, abandoned attempts to form a government in December 1990 because of differences between them); Wałęsa's reluctant acquiescence represented a clear political defeat, and he drew further away from his erstwhile most ardent supporters.

Wałęsa's wholesale changes in his own administration early in 1992 had led to the departure of Kaczyński and many other leading figures of the Centrum. Public denunciations of Wałęsa by his former associates came to match and exceed the bitterness expressed in the course of the 'war at the top' between Wałęsa and Mazowiecki. A six-page commentary on Wałęsa and his entourage appeared in *Gazeta Wyborcza*, criticizing the president for incompetence, incapacity for strategic planning, rudeness, laziness and superficiality; Jarosław Kaczyński accused him of 'pathological narcissism'.[16] Wałęsa was portrayed as closed off behind a wall of yes-men massaging his ego. Of these, the most important were Wałęsa's press spokesman, Andrzej Drzycimski, his personal priest, Franciszek Cybula, and above all the

16 Jarosław Kurski, 'Wódz – Przedostatni rozdział', *Gazeta Wyborcza* 95, 22 April 1992, pp.8–13.

mysterious Mieczysław Wachowski, Wałęsa's former driver. Suggestions of financial irregularities rounded off the invective directed at the Belvedere Palace.

Personal animosities tended to veil and distort the genuine constitutional ambiguities marking the presidential prerogatives (see Chapter 6). Shared executive functions between president and government had already caused friction between Wałęsa and the Bielecki government. In January 1992 Wałęsa presented parliament with a package of constitutional reform measures, later withdrawn after a critical reception. He returned to the issue later in the spring, with further proposals for strengthening presidential power, modelled on the French Constitution of the Fifth Republic. Wałęsa acknowledged his own political paralysis, attributing it to flaws in the institutional arrangements and a lack of cooperation from the government.

Olszewski's problems were, if anything, even worse than those of his predecessors because of the seriousness of the economic situation. His freedom to manoeuvre was desperately limited with regard to the economy (and pressure from the IMF was immediately forthcoming). Although the government was committed to greater involvement in the economy, it lacked a clear interventionist strategy. Olszewski and most of his ministers lacked administrative experience. Some, notably the Minister of the Interior, Antoni Macierewicz, were highly controversial figures. Others, such as Stelmachowski at the Ministry of Education, rapidly lost the good will which had greeted their appointments.

The government, identified in the prime minister's inaugural address to the *Sejm*[17] as a 'government of hope', establishing new links with society and marking the 'beginning of the end of communism', proved an egregious failure. From the outset it faced multiple, cross-cutting conflicts: within the government itself, over whether or how to broaden the coalition and over its own economic strategy; between government and president; and between government and parliament, notably the *Sejm*. The government had no clear aims, no programme, no money, and very few friends.

The budget crisis led Olszewski to rein back the high expectations engendered by the election campaign by drawing attention to the

17   *Rzeczpospolita* 298, 23 December 1991.

'serious errors' of the two previous governments. Indeed, his first tactic was to deny responsibility for the unpalatable measures bequeathed by the Bielecki government, including its provisional budget for the first quarter of 1992. Olszewski tried to carve out room for manoeuvre by presenting the outgoing government's budget figures but withholding the 'outline programme' on which they were based. The first months of 1992 saw a stream of apocalyptic rhetoric from various government departments: the economy had been virtually destroyed, national security undermined, the state administration lay in ruins.[18] If this was to prepare the ground for the government to appear as the architect of national salvation, it was notably unsuccessful.

The government finally introduced the general outline of its socio-economic programme on 15 February. The main aim was to halt the recession and to pave the way for growth by providing 'a climate for investors' and the 'aggressive promotion of exports'. In particular, exporters, agriculture and construction would find the terms of credit easier. The tax paid by state firms on their fixed assets (the notorious *dywidenda*) would be reduced, but strict wage controls would remain. The broad message, however, was one of austerity: the population could expect no real increase in either consumption or social services for about three years.

The programme had a mixed reception. Critics argued that lack of credit was not the major obstacle to industrial restructuring. Even those supporting the general economic line criticized it as unrealistic and lacking specificity. There was widespread scepticism about the government's ability to keep its projected spending under control. Olszewski's leadership abilities came into question when the Minister of Finance Karol Lutkowski resigned just as Olszewski and Eysymontt were preparing to defend their programme at a press conference. In the *Sejm* the sharpest criticism of the programme came from the government's own ranks, from the Deputy Minister of Education.[19] The *Sejm* followed Lutkowski's lead, rejecting the proposed economic strategy on 5 March.

18 See the official commentary, 'Stan państwa na przełomie lat 1991 i 1992', *Rzeczpospolita* 36, 12 February 1992.
19 *Rzeczpospolita* 48, 26 February 1992.

The *Sejm* also endorsed the Constitutional Tribunal's finding that sections of the pensions law (of the previous government) were unconstitutional. This left the Olszewski team caught in a vice between parliament, endorsing extra expenditure on pensions, and the International Monetary Fund, adamant that the planned budget deficit should not rise beyond five per cent of GNP. After four months in office the government still had no budget, and Olszewski's second Finance Minister had resigned in protest against the increased expenditure requirements of the pensions legislation. Lack of confidence in the government's economic competence virtually excluded a positive parliamentary response to government pleas for a delegated enhancement of its executive power, and in the absence of decisive action, the president finally presented his own privatization programme to the Council of Ministers.[20]

Pressure was also mounting outside parliament, notably from a new radical peasant organization, Self-Defence (*Samoobrona*), formed in January 1992 as a consequence of earlier protests in the autumn on behalf of peasant debtors. It soon attracted an estimated membership of some 300,000. In April Self-Defence occupied the Ministry of Agriculture, resulting in an agreement with the presidential Chancellery. This was expected to ameliorate the situation of peasants unable to cope with debt repayments, although it was widely noted that Wałęsa had bypassed the government and appeared to be sanctioning illegal actions; he was soon accused by Self-Defence itself of making empty promises.

The economic front was obviously central to all policy-making initiatives. However, it was not the only arena of political controversy. Stelmachowski at Education went to work with great fervour but little diplomacy. The education system was still reeling from the effects of successive budget cuts introduced by the Bielecki government. Parents were raising money to pay for books, telephones, heating and other basic requirements; their contributions were estimated at some 17 per cent of educational spending.[21] The school curriculum had been truncated in an effort to save money and virtually all extracurricular activity had ceased. Teachers' pay had plummeted to well

20 It was published in *Rzeczpospolita* 74, 27 March 1992.
21 Barbara Olszewska, 'Bez satysfakcji i pieniędzy', *Polityka* 12, 21 March 1992.

below the national average. Stelmachowski came under bitter attack, with the main teachers' union demanding his removal. In the face of teachers' strikes over poor pay and conditions and expected redundancies, the minister appeared on television waving his cane and threatening to abolish their right to strike. His introduction of compulsory ethics classes for those not taking religious instruction and his plans to abolish the Academy of Science also aroused controversy. Critics accused Stelmachowski of more concern with ideology than with education. His person became a major source of contention in the negotiations over the future government of Hanna Suchocka.[22]

As the government's public image deteriorated, Olszewski launched a concerted attack on the media for their alleged bias[23] and inaugurated changes of personnel, for example in the Polish Press Agency and in the RSW Liquidation Commission,[24] whose membership resigned *en masse* as a result of their chairman's dismissal. In May Olszewski replaced the Director of the State Committee for Radio and Television, a post which had become notorious for the brief tenure of its occupants. Olszewski's survival appeared *faute de mieux*, with parliament fearful of the consequences of a fresh election. Wałęsa dithered: on 27 April he suggested alternative candidates for the premiership, including Mazowiecki; on 20 May he declared the government's potential 'exhausted'; on 26 May he 'withdrew support' from the prime minister. It took the 'lustration' resolution, however, to force him to the decisive act of endorsing a vote of no confidence.

The Fall of the Olszewski Government

By May 1992 the Olszewski government was in a state of paralysis as regards policy-making, but it was seemingly immune to signs of its political vulnerability. On 6 May the second Minister of Finance, Andrzej Olechowski, had resigned. The Minister of Defence Jan Parys had been dismissed. Artur Balazs of PSL–Solidarity, Minister for Liaison with Political Parties, had resigned because of failure to extend the coalition; indeed, the leader of PSL–S was arguing pub-

---

22 '19 godzin dzielenia rządu', *Gazeta Wyborcza* 157, 6 July 1992; Stelmachowski defended his position in an interview in *Polityka* 17, 25 April 1992.
23 See Mariusz Janicki, 'Władza na wolnym rynku', *Polityka* 7, 15 February 1992.
24 This was the body set up to dismantle RSW, the PZPR's media empire.

licly that Olszewski should resign.[25] The government had failed to convince the *Sejm* of the merits of its broad economic programme and its specific budget proposals. It was feuding with the president. The parties of the coalition were not united and in the Centrum a split was imminent. Olszewski had clung to office largely with the support of the major peasant party, the PSL, but reports suggested that its leader Waldemar Pawlak was becoming insistent on some tangible reward. On the eve of the vote of confidence, Pawlak was already being spoken of as a possible replacement for Olszewski.

Conflict over the respective jurisdiction of the president and Minister of Defence had been a constant feature of Wałęsa's relationship with the Olszewski government. In vain Wałęsa had thrown his authority against the government's decision to retire the former Minister Piotr Kołodziejczyk; this gave rise, then and later, to suspicions that the president was soft on the old communists of the officer corps. The Minister of Defence, Jan Parys, also opposed Wałęsa's plans to reorganize the security organs. Parys favoured the concentration of defensive capability in the east, which he saw as the likeliest source of threat to Polish national security, and he openly challenged the president's jurisdiction by claiming the right to exercise effective control of the armed forces as a whole.[26]

On 6 April 1992 Parys, at a partly televised meeting of the General Staff, accused 'certain politicians' of plotting with elements of the officer corps. It quickly became apparent that these accusations were directed against the president himself, that is, against the Commander-in-Chief of the armed forces. Wałęsa requested an investigative commission and demanded Parys's resignation. Parys was sent on holiday before resigning on 18 May, but he called publicly for the formation of 'state defence committees' by 'those with clean hands' to defend Polish independence in the event of a powerless government.[27] The establishment of a National Committee for the Defence of Parys by members of the Polish Independence Party (whose former leader was Vice Minister of Defence Romuald Szeremietiew) subsequently formed the nucleus of a right-wing political formation led by Parys.

25 Balazs, quoted in *Rzeczpospolita* 114, 15 May 1992.
26 See Jan deWeydenthal, 'Political Problems Affect Security Work in Poland', *RFE/RL Research Report*, vol.1, no.16, 17 April 1992e, pp.39–42.
27 *Rzeczpospolita* 104, 4 May 1992.

The parliamentary investigative commission found Parys's accusations totally unfounded and highly damaging to the national interest. It found no evidence of attempts either to involve the army in party politics or to prepare the overthrow of democracy. It also noted that Parys had not ensured adequate coordination between the ministry and the National Security Office. Szeremietiew, hardly less controversial, replaced Parys; but Olszewski never formally disavowed his minister. Indeed, the prime minister declared the greatest achievement of his government to be the 'stabilization of the situation in the ... army and the police',[28] claims emphatically refuted by subsequent events.

The issue which finally toppled the government was that of the secret files of the Ministry of Internal Affairs. However, the government's position was insecure from the outset and had been seriously weakened by its lack of substantive achievements and its conflict with the president, symbolized by the Parys affair, which in turn reflected the intense anti-communist ethos of the government. The commitment to 'de-communization' was a major element binding the coalition parties together, and there can be no doubt that they genuinely perceived the danger of some (indeterminate) communist threat.[29] This attitude had caused a serious conflict between the president and government over the Polish–Russian Treaty of May 1992. Upon his return from Moscow, Wałęsa dispatched a letter to the *Sejm* noting his withdrawal of support from the government, whose lack of cooperation rendered him incapable of carrying out his functions. At the same time, rumours surfaced in the press that Krzysztof Skubiszewski, the highly regarded Foreign Minister, had been an agent of the communist security service.

On 28 May the *Sejm* passed a 'lustration' resolution, initiated by Janusz Korwin-Mikke of the tiny ultra-liberal Union of Political Realism. 'Lustration' means purifying or cleansing, and this resolution required Minister of the Interior Macierewicz to provide full information about current public functionaries who had cooperated with the security service in the years 1945–90. By 6 June the minister was to identify collaborators holding public positions 'of the rank of provin-

---

28 Olszewski, quoted in *Rzeczpospolita* 127, 30–31 May 1992.
29 See Jarosław Kaczyński, 'Byłem głównym rozgrywającym', *Polityka* 3, 18 January 1992; Radek Sikorski, 'Poles Apart', *The Spectator*, 27 June 1992, pp.9–12; Jan Olszewski, *Olszewski: Przerwana Premiera*, Warsaw, 1992, especially pp.28–38.

cial governor [*wojewoda*] and above'; within two months to supply the names of senators, deputies, judges, procurators and advocates; and within six months agents among the lower reaches of local government. A number of deputies expressed reservations, as did President Wałęsa himself, notably concerning the human rights implications of public revelations based on suspect files (see Chapter 7). Such discussions had been continuing for some time, for it was well known that much of the secret police archive had been destroyed and that the documentation did not take the form of individual files on named informers, agents or collaborators.[30] President Wałęsa asked Macierewicz to provide information on the manner of implementing the resolution and for assurances that an opportunity for individuals to defend themselves would be provided, for 'otherwise, that would be the greatest victory of the old Security Service'.[31]

Such arguments did not hold sway with the Interior Minister, who delivered sealed envelopes marked 'secret' to the leaders of the parliamentary clubs of the *Sejm*. After some initial confusion, it was established that the envelopes contained the names of 64 individuals whose names were drawn from the archival records of the Ministry of the Interior. A second list was circulated to a narrower circle of public officials, including the president. The lack of evidence in certain of these cases of 'collaboration' surfaced only gradually; but the revelation that the list included prominent former dissidents whose suffering under the communist regime was widely known created a strong *prima facie* case that Macierewicz had distorted his brief. These included Wiesław Chrzanowski, Speaker of the *Sejm* (and Minister of Justice under Bielecki), the intrepid anti-communist leader of the KPN, Leszek Moczulski, and a number of leading Solidarity activists such as Michał Boni. Wałęsa himself was on the second list, although Olszewski later stated that it was well known that the security police had manufactured a false file on Wałęsa. Political tensions increased when Moczulski revealed that the allegations against him had been used earlier in an attempt at moral blackmail intended to silence KPN

---

30 Witold Bereś and Krzysztof Burnetko, *Gliniarz z 'Tygodnika'. Rozmowy z byłym ministrem spraw wewnętrznych Krzysztofem Kozłowskim*, Warsaw, c.1991, pp.24–5, 47–51.
31 *Rzeczpospolita* 127, 30–31 May 1992; also J. Snopkiewicz *et al.*, *Teczki, czyli widma bezpieki*, Warsaw, 1992, pp.39–41.

criticisms of the government.[32]

The president immediately demanded a vote of no confidence, adding his authority to a motion placed on the agenda by the parties of the so-called small coalition (the Democratic Union, the Liberals and the Polish Economic Programme). Wałęsa accused the government of acting outside the law and of providing materials that were clearly fabricated. He referred to the destabilization of the polity and its political parties.[33] The vote of no confidence passed easily, by 273 votes to 119, with 33 abstentions. The acceptance of Wałęsa's nominee, Waldemar Pawlak of the PSL, as prime minister was similarly conclusive. The Liberals, most of the Democratic Union, the KPN, the Economic Programme (Big Beer), the Social Democrats and the PSL supported Pawlak. His erstwhile allies the Centrum, the ZChN and the (PL) Peasant Accord voted against, along with Solidarity and the small Christian Democratic parties. The Ministers of Defence and the Interior were immediately removed from their posts to prevent further 'destabilization'.

Arguments regarding lustration continued to dominate Polish political life. Olszewski was unrepentant. He saw himself as motivated by the highest of national ideals, the promotion of Poland's sovereignty and independence. In a televised address he stated, 'I believe that former collaborators ... could constitute a threat to the security of a free Poland ... it was no accident that a sudden proposal to bring down the government came precisely at the moment when we could finally break our links with communism.'[34] Most political parties took a clear stand on the issue. Jan Parys inaugurated a new right-wing party to counter the alleged communist resurgence, with lustration as a central plank. Radek Sikorski, Parys's former deputy, accused Wałęsa of using the old forces of military intelligence to construct a new political base.[35] Olszewski himself left the Centrum and formed a new parliamentary club, mainly drawn from the secessionist faction of the Centrum. At the Fourth Congress of Solidarity, Olszewski and Macierewicz were greeted warmly, while President Wałęsa's address received an icy reception. The Congress passed a resolution condemn-

32 *Rzeczpospolita* 132, 5 June 1992; Snopkiewicz *et al.*, op. cit., pp.44-7.
33 *Rzeczpospolita* 132, op. cit.
34 Ibid.
35 Sikorski, op. cit., p.10.

ing the 'brutal intervention of the President and post-communist forces, verging on a *coup d'état*'.[36] Leading representatives of the Centrum, the ZChN, Rural Solidarity and the PL depicted a Pawlak government as a *de facto* return to communism – despite their earlier readiness to welcome the PSL into the governing coalition. Public opinion polls showed considerable support for continuing the process of lustration (62 per cent), despite widespread acceptance of the unreliability of the ministerial archives (90 per cent).[37]

THE PAWLAK INTERLUDE

The Olszewski government had lasted for just over five months. It could claim no enduring achievements, and its legacy appeared to be a bitter divide over the lustration issue. Wałęsa's nominee for the third prime minister since Mazowiecki was Waldemar Pawlak, the young leader of the largest peasant party, the PSL. Wałęsa had for some time regarded the divisions between the Solidarity and non-Solidarity parties as ideological posturing, obstructive of pragmatic compromise (indeed, the division was increasingly blurred by the shuffle and reshuffle of political parties). He had paid highly publicized visits to the leftist weekly *Polityka* and the headquarters of the OPZZ. Pawlak was not associated with Solidarity's ten-year struggle against the old regime, nor was he thought tainted by the *apparatchik* mentality of the old PSL *nomenklatura*. He was a model of a new breed of young pragmatist (he was thirty-two years old), with an impeccable demeanour of civility and courtesy. With Pawlak the mantle of government passed, albeit only briefly, from Solidarity's hands.

However, Pawlak proved unable to form a government acceptable to the *Sejm*. The PSL was itself a successor party, still linked with the old ZSL (United Peasant Party). The coalition partners of the Olszewski government, prepared shortly before to welcome the PSL into the coalition, now found the party's historic antecedents a major obstacle to supporting it. Negotiations with the 'small coalition' (UD,

36 See the reports from the Congress in *Rzeczpospolita* 137, 11 June 1991 and *Rzeczpospolita* 140, 15 June 1992.
37 Data are from the Ośrodek Badania Opinii Publicznej (OBOP) in *Życie Warszawy* 134, 8 June 1992.

KLD and PPG) also broke down; it demanded a virtual monopoly of the economic sphere which Pawlak could not relinquish without damaging his standing with his own party.[38]

After a month of discussions attention shifted back to inter-party negotiations, mirroring those undertaken in the spring between the small coalition and the governing parties. President Wałęsa provided a powerful stimulus to success by presenting an ultimatum: if parliament were so immature that it could not generate a government, he would name his own prime minister and government team. Further developments with regard to the lustration issue also helped to bridge the gap between the parties. It was rumoured that Piotr Naimski, the head of the State Security Office (UOP), had ordered troops placed on full alert on the morning of 4 June and even that a *coup* had been planned to keep the Olszewski government in power. Macierewicz's list was found to be not only unreliable but also selective. Young, inexperienced persons had worked on the files without strict control or guidance. Acting Defence Minister Szeremietiew refused to answer questions before the parliamentary investigating commission. The ZChN expelled Macierewicz from the party. A marathon session in which Solidarity deputies played a key mediating role generated a new seven-party coalition under Hanna Suchocka of the Democratic Union.[39] Suchocka became the fourth prime minister to form a government since the Round Table election of June 1989.

THE GOVERNMENT OF HANNA SUCHOCKA

Strengths and Weaknesses of the Suchocka Government

When Hanna Suchocka became prime minister, the political situation appeared somewhat more optimistic, although she continued to face serious disadvantages. The causes of optimism were above all the existence of a government with majority support in parliament: the Pawlak interlude had concentrated minds wonderfully. Suchocka's

---

38 The PSL perspective on negotiations over the composition of a new coalition is given by Pawlak's close colleague and adviser, A. Łukczak, '33 dni Pawlaka', *Polityka* 38, 19 September 1992.

39 '19 godzin', *Gazeta Wyborcza*, op. cit.

government was a coalition of seven parties – the UD, the Liberals, and the Polish Economic Programme (the small coalition); three parties of the former government (the Christian National Union, the Peasant Alliance, the Peasant Christian Alliance); and the tiny Party of Christian Democrats. The Centrum withdrew in an argument over the allocation of posts but it was still regarded as a potential coalition partner. Solidarity, the German Minority and Christian Democracy also promised their support. This gave the government the nominal support of 233 deputies out of a total 460 (see Table 4.1). In addition, the parties had agreed that the government would not take a stand on contentious matters such as abortion; these would be left to parliament and to individual conscience. The government, said Deputy Prime Minister Henryk Goryszewski, would be a 'government of ideological peace'.[40]

Table 4.1 Government support in the Sejm *(July 1992)*

Party	Seats
Coalition parties	
Democratic Union (UD)	62
Liberal Democratic Congress (KLD)	37
Polish Economic Programme (PPG)	12
Christian National Union (ZChN)	48
Peasant Alliance (PSL–PL)	19
Peasant Christian Alliance (SChL)	10
Party of Christian Democrats (PDC)	6
Supporting parties	
Solidarity	27
German Minority	7
Christian Democracy	5
Total support	**233**

Secondly, observers drew attention to Suchocka's temperament. She seemed to many an inspired choice. Suchocka, an academic

40 Radio Zet, 6 July 1992.

lawyer from Poznań, was popular with members of all parties. She was seen as a hard-working, consensus politician, not associated with either of the UD's factions, and prone to seeking compromise solutions. Opinion polls also indicated favourable public assessments of the new (hitherto little known) prime minister. In a poll of 15–16 July 68 per cent thought Suchocka would make a good prime minister.[41] Suchocka also had the advantage of some experienced ministers, including Bielecki, now dealing with relations with the European Community; Kuroń, who regained his former post as Minister of Labour; Syryjczyk, in charge of planning the government's timetable; and Lewandowski who resumed the privatization brief. Finally, few parties were yet willing to face the population in an early parliamentary election.

Despite the existence of grounds for cautious optimism, Suchocka also faced serious potential problems. Although members of the government accepted the principle of collective responsibility, there was no guarantee that their parties could control their parliamentary deputies. The coalition brought together strange bedfellows, above all the clerical ZChN and the Democratic Union, with an influential secular wing. The peasant parties were committed to pressing for agricultural subsidies and customs barriers against food imports, while the UD and the Liberals favoured minimal interventionism. Divisions were already emerging within several of the partners and there was tension between the two factions of the prime minister's own party, the UD.

Secondly, the projections of the state budget were already proving optimistic; the deficit was worsening and the efficient collection of taxes was proving a major problem. Drought was ravaging agriculture and forest fires caused serious losses. The gravest threat of all came from the signs of growing social unrest among the peasantry and industrial workers.

Thus it appeared as though the government would need considerable luck and maximum good will to survive. That it survived for almost a year, despite growing unpopularity and increasing difficulty in mustering a majority in the *Sejm*, was due to both of these factors, but above all to the singular achievement of getting the so-called

41 *Rzeczpospolita* 168, 17–18 July 1992.

Little Constitution through parliament, despite Wałęsa's dislike of its terms. From 8 December 1992, when the new constitutional provisions came into force (see Chapter 6), the *Sejm*'s powers regarding the government were considerably weakened and the government's chances of survival increased.

The Suchocka Government

The first blush of support for Suchocka's government faded in an upsurge of unrest during the summer of 1992, but by autumn it had recouped some of its early credit, only to slump again by the end of the year. In June the radical peasant union Self-Defence had extended its ambit with the formation of a new political 'party of working people, of the impoverished, exploited and injured [*skrzywdzonych*]'. Self-Defence was led by Andrzej Lepper, known as 'the peasant Tymiński', a reference to Wałęsa's surprise opponent in the second round of the presidential election. Lepper blamed the banks, Balcerowicz and Sachs, the IMF, Western governments and the president for the situation of the peasantry. Self-Defence renewed its efforts to prevent seizure of assets from peasant debtors through direct action and demanded a debt moratorium for the whole country, as well as cheap credits for agriculture. For much of June convoys of lorries, tractors and other agricultural vehicles blockaded major roads.[42]

With the temporary muting of peasant protest, however, came increased industrial action. By mid-July 1992 strikes and protests threatened to engulf the country. Coal and copper-miners took the lead, and most of the strikes were illegal, that is, they failed to follow the 'baroque procedures' necessary prior to declaring strike action.[43] Initially wage claims formed the central plank of workers' demands. Although the government maintained that wages were a matter for negotiation with management, the unions drew attention to government policy of taxing wage increases through the hated *popiwek*. Increasingly, strikes focused more broadly on government economic policies.

---

42 Ewa Czaczkowska, 'Bojownicy', *Rzeczpospolita* 155, 3 July 1992; Krystyna Naszkowska, 'Nowy Szela', *Gazeta Wyborcza* 156, 4–5 July 1992; Witold Pawlowski, 'Bizony na Sztorc', *Polityka* 27, 4 July 1992.
43 Jerzy Baczyński, 'Duch Kuronia', *Polityka* 33, 15 August 1992.

The situation was complex, not least because of the numbers of unions represented, the variety of demands, and the position of Solidarity. Hitherto small unions had begun to capitalize on Solidarity's association with government. In the Lubin Copper Combine, a vast conglomerate with some 40,000 workers, seven major unions formed the Inter-Enterprise Inter-Union Strike Committee. The copper-miners' grievances centred on their low wages in the context of the high tax burden borne by their profitable industry. For the car-workers in Tychy the 'unfavourable deal' reached with Fiat of Italy was a key dimension. In the aircraft factory at Mielec the plant itself was at risk of bankruptcy, and it was the central role of the industry for the local economy and the rapid rate of job losses which were the major issues. At the bearings factory in Kraśnik the strike centred on the cancellation of government contracts.

The existence of genuine, deeply-felt grievances, coupled with Solidarity's ambivalent position, gave the trade unions the opportunity to test their strength in a major confrontation with the government. Solidarity's position was indeed difficult. Its parliamentary deputies had played a crucial role in the formation of Suchocka's government and were committed to its support. However, there were signs that its members would not prove amenable to control. Solidarity's National Executive found itself at odds with Sieć, representing the union in the country's major state enterprises, and also with its Warsaw and Silesian regions.

The government, while steadfastly refusing to act as a party to wage negotiations, did make concessions. On 1 August the *Sejm* welcomed its commitment to ease the *popiwek*. The government also proposed a new 'Pact for Industry',[44] involving trilateral negotiations among government, employers and unions over restructuring and privatization, wages and conditions. Solidarity and the OPZZ responded favourably to Kuroń's proposals for a new 'social contract', and gradually by late August industrial protest began to peter out as strike funds were depleted. The FSM strike at Tychy was brought to an end on 15 September after a face-saving mediating effort by the Arch-

---

44 For the draft proposals for a 'Pact on State Enterprise in the process of transformation' presented to the unions for consultation see *Przegląd Rządowy*, no.7–8, 1992, pp.51–4.

bishop of Katowice.[45]

The government appeared to have passed its first test, not only in coping with labour unrest, but also in recognizing the importance of establishing mechanisms for communicating with affected parties. The Pact for Industry was to be followed closely by a social security pact, expressly defining the responsibilities of the state, local government bodies, employers and individuals themselves. However, there were numerous concerns expressed about the role given to the trade unions by this new corporatist approach.[46] The prognosis could not be good, given the divisions in the trade union movement, the lack of knowledge of ordinary members about the economic alternatives, and the economic pressures on government. It is difficult to see how corporatist arrangements can work in a situation of economic crisis, given the impossibility of safeguarding wages and employment. In December new strikes broke out in the Silesian mines over wages and restructuring proposals. The government again stood firm, but it was far from clear that the trade unions would be able to control their members' response to agreements negotiated with government, or that the more radical unions like Solidarity '80 would decide on a strategy of partnership.

As the end of the year approached, new signs of pessimism set in, although Suchocka retained her personal popularity. The government, which had got off to a decisive start, appeared to lose its way and the coalition glue began to loosen. In August Suchocka had taken a decisive role in the decision-making process and the government started with a strong sense of direction. Within a few weeks the prime minister announced its top five priorities: privatization, agriculture, law and order, public finance and social security. It gained some credibility with its 'Pact' and at least in the interim maintained the parliamentary support of Solidarity. On 9 October it presented its 'socio-economic plan'.

The government also continued searching for new coalition partners. The combination of oddly-matched bedfellows continued to

45 See the interview with Jan Maria Rokita in *Gazeta Wyborcza* 223, 22 September 1992.
46 See, for example, R. Matyja and K. M. Ujazdowski, 'Kogo dziś reprezentują związki zawodowe', *Rzeczpospolita* 232, 2 October 1992; for more details of the Pact see Chapter 7; also Louisa Vinton, 'Polish Government Proposes Pact on State Firms', *RFE/RL Research Report*, vol.1, no.42, 1992a, pp.10–18.

worry Suchocka, especially when in September some coalition deputies deserted the government on a narrowly failing vote of no confidence in Jan Lewandowski, the minister responsible for economic transformation. However, the main candidate for inclusion in the coalition, the Centrum, demanded too high a price.[47] By the end of the year it had intensified its pursuit of alliance with Olszewski and Parys and launched new attacks on President Wałęsa, with Jarosław Kaczyński continuing allegations of past connections between Wałęsa's entourage and the communist security services[48] and his aspirations to dictatorship, and also demanding an early presidential election.

The vote on Lewandowski proved the start of a slippery slope, and the government continued on a faltering path through the autumn and into the early part of 1993. It lost key votes in the *Sejm*. Its socioeconomic programme passed by a margin of only three votes. The Democratic Union was the most loyal of the governing parties, and the departure of its centre–right faction under Aleksander Hall in September 1992 had little effect in this respect. The Liberals were frequently absent or voted against the government, for example on tax measures. The peasant parties kept up a barrage of criticism on agricultural policy. Solidarity support proved unreliable, as some deputies voted against proposals to reduce the ratio of public sector pay to that in industry and in favour of increases in retirement pensions; its parliamentary group continued to be beset by serious divisions. Calls for an early parliamentary election came from several non-governing parties.

There were some positive signs in the new year, however. The initial economic reports for 1992, although ambiguous, seemed to show signs of economic recovery; certainly the private sector was proving dynamic.[49] The rate of increase of unemployment began to slow somewhat. It was just over 2.5 million at the end of January 1993, not much changed from the previous quarter.[50] The coalition held firm

---

47 See *Życie Warszawy* 221, 16 September 1992.
48 See, for example, Jarosław Kurski and Piotr Semki, *Lewy czerwcowy*, Warsaw, 1993; but it should not be taken seriously.
49 Jerzy Baczyński and J. Mojkowski, 'Wokół zera', *Polityka* 6, 6 February 1993; *The Economist*, 23 January 1993.
50 'Statystyka Polski', *Rzeczpospolita*, 6 February 1993.

over its controversial budget proposals in February, and even some Solidarity deputies voted with the government, despite the decision of the Solidarity parliamentary club to oppose it. Key trade unions signed the Pact for Industry. Suchocka looked set to win the capacity to institute rule-by-decree in numerous areas, so long as she had the support of the president. However, dissent grew, especially within the Solidarity parliamentary club, and the government lost a vote of no confidence almost by accident (and for the lack of a single vote) on 28 May 1993. Much significant legislation, including many bills linked to the Pact for Industry, fell with the president's decision to dissolve parliament, and because of the precipitate manner of the dissolution, the prime minister had no opportunity formally to request the special powers that she sought. Although the government failed to live up to the promise of its early months, it brought some measure of temporary but welcome stability to the political system.

5. Elections and the Party System in the New Poland

Political parties are ubiquitous in modern political systems and they are significant mechanisms of democratic government. The weakness of political parties in Poland and the manner of their development have had important consequences for the political system. This chapter charts the development of the party system in Poland and the character of its parties. Between 1989 and 1993 the party system came to resemble a kaleidoscope, with numerous shifts, splits and mergers of large numbers of small parties. Few signs of stability were apparent, and the parties proved largely ineffective instruments of the democratic process.

Numerous important functions have been ascribed to political parties, which is why their weakness is so significant. Parties serve integrative functions, bringing people into the political process by providing channels of communication between society and political leaders. They bring people together by articulating certain moral or social values or a concept of the wider community. When their role is effective, the legitimacy of the political system is enhanced and the likelihood of violent social conflict is reduced.

Parties are also mechanisms of political recruitment. They select candidates for public office. Government leaders and parliamentary representatives usually achieve their positions through association with a political party. The parties 'supply' individuals who then owe loyalty to the party which has supported them. The party link provides a source of cohesion among those chosen to stand under a party's banner and between the candidates and party activists. This provides an additional mechanism of political integration and accountability. Parties also articulate and aggregate interests, that is, they express and then combine diverse demands into coherent policy proposals. They ensure that social cleavages are represented in the political process.

They actively seek to structure public choice. When in power, parties determine the priorities they will pursue.

In well-established parliamentary democracies political parties create the basis for structuring institutions. Party continuity implies a nucleus of experienced politicians operating well-understood conventions. Parliaments are structured by their party composition. Governments are similarly a party construct, whether by virtue of electoral success or through inter-party negotiations leading to coalition. In this century parties have been key structures in the political process.

The party systems of the European communist states were broadly of two types: the mono-party system (as in the USSR) where a single party existed; and the hegemonic party system (as in Poland) where ancillary parties accepted the dominance of the Communist Party. The satellite parties did spring to life and play an enhanced role from time to time, but broadly speaking communist hegemony was unquestioned. Both these types were usually subsumed as a single category of one-party or party–state systems.

The collapse of the communist regimes opened up new opportunities for the organization of political parties. Obviously, political parties could not develop instantly; still less could they begin to play the role occupied in the parliamentary democracies of their West European neighbours. A coherent party system, with stable patterns of interaction between the constituent units, would emerge only slowly and could not be guaranteed.

In Poland the election of June 1989 changed the political configuration unalterably. It set off a chain of events leading to fundamental changes to both sides in the Round Table pact. The Communist Party had, albeit increasingly ineffectually, monopolized power throughout the post-war period. Solidarity participated in the June election as a quasi-party or surrogate; it emerged rejuvenated and transformed into a genuine political organization, albeit reluctant to adopt the party format.[1] The PZPR by contrast was further discredited and soon sought to reconstitute itself.

---

1   A number of candidates in the 1989 election stressed their non-party or independent character, since the concept of party was so closely associated with careerism and opportunism; others stressed their oppositional stance: see Piotr Łukasiewicz, 'Syn legionisty' in Lena Kolarska-Bobińska, Piotr Łukasiewicz and Z. Rykowski, *Wyniki badań – wyniki wyborów: 4 czerwca 1989*, Warsaw, 1990, p.11.

Shortly after the PZPR's dissolution Solidarity also began to disintegrate. By the summer of 1990 there were two clearly identifiable axes, focused on two Solidarity presidential candidates, Tadeusz Mazowiecki and Lech Wałęsa. On the fringes were other small parties which had emerged from their clandestine existence, notably the KPN (Confederation for Independent Poland) of Leszek Moczulski. Older, 'historic' parties claimed themselves reborn and new parties formed. But parties were still unimportant in the presidential election in November 1990.

After the presidential election decomposition proceeded apace as Solidarity further fragmented and new groups saw an opportunity to gain influence through the party format. The parliamentary election of October 1991 saw the return to parliament of 29 different groupings, many claiming the party label. The move from a monocentric to a kaleidoscopic pluralist party system had taken just over two years. In the ensuing period there was little sign of stabilization as parties continued to merge and fragment. They failed to develop organizational structures and membership linking them to society. They did not represent coherent constituencies; they were based largely on personal relationships or general ideological tendencies, or a combination of the two. Politicians, perceived as self-serving and power-hungry, became increasingly unpopular.

THE BREAK-UP OF THE OLD PARTY SYSTEM

The Dissolution of the PZPR

In the early months of the Mazowiecki government it became clear that the communists would constitute no direct political threat to the changes envisaged. The PZPR emerged from the elections of June 1989 in a state of shock. Its membership continued to decline, and many used their positions within the state administration to further their own economic interests. Almost overnight the PZPR moved from monopoly to minority.

None the less, the PZPR did not move easily from its monopoly of power to become merely one political contender among others. The political context was hostile, and the PZPR was perceived as being different in two fundamental ways. First, there was the question of its current stance. Some non-communist elements accepted the sincerity of the new commitment to democracy; others saw this commitment as purely a cosmetic exercise. For the latter, the party's continuing control of the presidency and the ministries of Defence and Internal affairs, its penetration of the state administration, and the continuing presence of Soviet troops on Polish territory provided opportunities for continuing communist influence and a possible springboard for a renewed bid for power. Secondly, the PZPR was deemed responsible not only for the dire economic state of the country but also for exploiting and maltreating the population in whose name it had governed. There was political pressure for a reckoning with the past; some openly advocated revenge. These factors contributed to a major identity crisis for the PZPR. By the autumn of 1989 developments elsewhere in Eastern Europe made its search for a new credibility still less likely to fall on fertile ground.

Following the June 1989 election and Jaruzelski's elevation to the presidency, the communist leadership found itself fighting on two fronts: against hardliners angry at the perceived betrayal of socialist principles and against reformers advocating the party's dissolution. The 8th of July Movement reflected the latter view, arguing that the PZPR had exhausted all credibility; thus the forthcoming Congress should be devoted to its liquidation and to preparing for the establishment of a new democratic socialist party. This movement had close links with the PZPR's club of parliamentary deputies, who were already asserting their autonomy: about twenty of them refused to be bound by party discipline in the vote for Kiszczak as prime minister. At the Thirteenth Plenum of the Central Committee on 29 July representatives of the provincial party *apparat* openly blamed the leadership for the electoral defeat.[2] After choosing Mieczysław Rakowski (the outgoing prime minister) as the new party leader, the Central Committee elected a new Politburo and Secretariat whose composition contained elements of both the conservative 'concrete' (*beton*) and the

2   K. Janowski, 'From Monopoly to Death-Throes: the PZPR in the Process of Political Transformation' in George Sanford (ed.), *Democratization in Poland, 1988–90*, London, 1992, pp.168–9.

reformers. A few weeks later, on the day of Mazowiecki's confirmation as premier, fifteen PZPR deputies submitted a formal proposal to the *Sejm* to remove the 'leading role of the party' from the Constitution.

After an autumn of heated debates and a poll of party members, the Central Committee agreed to bring the Congress forward to January, with a new statute, programme and name firmly on the agenda. The reformers had gained the upper hand, but they already appeared to be in control of a sinking ship. The OPZZ, the quasi-autonomous trade union, set up the Movement for Working People (*Ruch Ludzi Pracy*), to establish its independence and to provide, 'if necessary', the basis for a new party of the Left, committed to economic reform and democracy. In the factories party cells were being closed down by spontaneous work-force protest. Debts needed to be paid, including a large loan from the state to finance the 1989 election; members were ceasing to pay dues and the party press was losing money. A parliamentary commission was busy assessing the party's legal title to its vast property empire.

In January 1990 the PZPR convened its final congress, from which two new parties emerged. A small group, led by Tadeusz Fiszbach and including some 25 parliamentary deputies, withdrew and established the Social Democratic Union. The Union staked its claim to the high moral ground by dissociating itself from a movement which 'continued to harbour communists' in its ranks and relinquishing all claim to the party's assets.[3] After Fiszbach's withdrawal, the Congress suspended itself. It founded a new party, Social Democracy of the Polish Republic (SDRP), then reconvened to transfer its assets to the SDRP before finally consigning the PZPR to oblivion. Rakowski did not stand for the leadership,[4] which was assumed by Aleksander Kwaśniewski, one of the new-look generation of young moderates. However, many delegates joined neither of the two new organizations, and a number of parliamentary deputies declared that they would now sit as non-party independents.

---

3   See the interview with Tadeusz Fiszbach in *Polityka* 5, 3 February 1990.
4   Rakowski discusses these events in Mieczysław Rakowski, *Zanim stanę przed Try-bunałem*, Warsaw, c.1992, pp.104–5, 142–50.

Fiszbach's Union passed quickly into obscurity. The SDRP survived, but it did not escape its past by the expedient of dissolution. It was still regarded as the Communist Party, or at least the party of former communists. The SDRP inherited both the widespread lack of confidence in the PZPR's democratic credentials and the feeling of a need to reckon with the past. The latter in particular would become a focus of major political debate.

The United Peasant Party and the Democratic Party

The communists were not alone in the search for a new identity which would dissociate them from their own post-war history. The former coalition partners, the United Peasant Party (ZSL) and the Democratic Party (SD), had changed their principles and come to the support of Solidarity; but they still bore the taint of their years of collaboration. The smaller Democratic Party, which had been officially classed as the party of the intelligentsia, had fewer members and no obvious social base. The Peasant Party, while having to face Solidarity competition for peasant support, none the less had a coherent structure penetrating the countryside, a large membership, and considerable political experience. Both, however, suffered a loss of unity and party discipline in the months following the Round Table, not least because their new deputies had won popular mandates, while the party leaders had gone down with the National List.

The United Peasant Party moved quickly to establish a new identity. It held its final congress in November 1989 and proclaimed itself 'born again'. The 'new' party adopted a cumbersome name, the Polish Peasant Party (Reborn) (*Polskie Stronnictwo Ludowe [Odrodzenie]*), but one which harked back to the pre-communist Polish Peasant Party of Stanisław Mikołajczyk. However, Kazimierz Oleśniak, its new leader, was a member of the old guard, having served as deputy premier in Rakowski's last communist government. The new arrangement was short-lived, and in May 1990 the PSL(O) merged with another of the burgeoning peasant parties, making this remodelled PSL the largest single political party.

The Democratic Party, by contrast, was faction-ridden and lacking direction. Changes of leadership did not bring greater coherence. The

SD retained a large nominal membership, and it was organized in all of the 49 provinces. Many other groups, however, were laying claim to the political centre-ground. Its long-term prospects looked less favourable than those of its erstwhile colleagues in the reborn Peasant Party[5] and it was virtually to disappear with the elections of 1991.

DIVISIONS WITHIN SOLIDARITY

Solidarity in the summer and autumn of 1989 was a *mélange* of distinct but heterogeneous, overlapping elements. It was a trade union, a diffuse political movement organized in the citizens' committees, a parliamentary body and the leading force in the government of Tadeusz Mazowiecki. Linked tenuously to the industrial trade union was Rural Solidarity, organizing individual peasant farmers. By the end of 1990, with the presidential election, these elements were being fundamentally reshuffled. Wałęsa, the main force linking them together, became a major contributor to their fission. Although most observers saw the process of disintegration as inevitable,[6] the manner of Solidarity's break-up owed much to the individual personalities involved.

After its re-legalization, Solidarity in its trade union incarnation was organized in individual enterprises linked to regional union structures, headed by the National Trade Union Executive under the leadership of Lech Wałęsa. With about two million members, Solidarity's main strength lay in the old bastions of heavy industry, especially in the Baltic shipyards and Silesian mines. Loyalty to Wałęsa and to the idea of the Solidarity tradition were powerful unifying factors, and Wałęsa's hold on the union was indisputable, keeping in check regional differences and political disagreements within the movement.

Solidarity was also a diffuse political movement, based on the autonomous citizens' committees (KOs) formed to fight the 1989 election. The KOs were vaguely linked by regional bodies to the

5   Not all were pessimistic: see Piotr Winczorek, 'The Internal Evolution and Changing Policies of the Democratic Party' in Sanford, op. cit., pp.177–94.
6   See, for example, Jadwiga Staniszkis, 'The Obsolescence of Solidarity', *Telos* 80, 1989, pp.37–50.

'Lech Wałęsa National Citizens' Committee', composed largely of intellectual advisers. The *de facto* chairman of Wałęsa's committee was Bronisław Geremek; its Secretary was Henryk Wujec. Both were members of parliament and provided a link to Solidarity's parliamentary club (the OKP), which Geremek also chaired. The OKP was united by loyalty to Solidarity but its members constituted a farrago of liberals, nationalists, Christian democrats, social democrats and agrarians. Solidarity was also the leading force in the government led by Tadeusz Mazowiecki. The Solidarity members in government were somewhat less disparate than those in the OKP. Many had close personal ties to Mazowiecki and they accepted the liberal premises of government policy. Some members of the government, like Mazowiecki himself and Aleksander Hall, had not stood for parliament in the 1989 election. Others, such as Jacek Kuroń, were also parliamentary deputies.

Thus Solidarity embraced people of disparate views masked by their common hostility to the old regime and their common commitment to democracy and a market economy. There was also a class divide between the workers of the trade union, the peasants of Rural Solidarity and (by and large) the intelligentsia of the KOs, parliament and government. Ideological differences were clearest within parliament, where they assumed an incipient organizational form.

The enthusiasm which greeted the establishment of the Mazowiecki government was reflected in the view that the trade union would serve as its major social base, holding a 'protective umbrella' over the new Solidarity politicians. A number of leading figures, including Adam Michnik and Zbigniew Bujak (former leader of underground Solidarity), hoped that it could retain its identity as a broadly-based umbrella movement, eventually transforming itself into a mass party along American lines. Certainly its election victory gave it renewed and potent legitimacy as the vanquisher of communism, and those who had experienced internment and the underground struggle had a strong emotional commitment to the 'Solidarity ethos', embracing humanism, compassion and a commitment to non-violence. The 'strategy of unity' survived for some months, but from the outset it was punctuated by bouts of dissent.

Dissent was political, organizational and, as the impact of the government's programme began to make itself felt, economic. The first conflict arose in the aftermath of the 1989 election. The trade union executive voted to dissolve the citizens' committees, on the grounds that their continuation risked a confusion of structures and jurisdiction with the union. The executive's view was that Solidarity should not become a political party but should rather strengthen itself as a trade union. The decision was met with a storm of protest. Advocates of the KOs argued that they had generated a burst of social activism and energy which should not be dissipated, that they would provide an organizational link between parliamentary deputies and their constituencies, and that they would be a school of local autonomy and self-government. These arguments were rehearsed in the Solidarity press in June.[7] Most regional bodies complied with the decision of the executive, but many local committees did not; and when the furore led to the subsequent rescinding of the decision, the KOs were soon reactivated. This was not, however, a conflict between Wałęsa and his future opponents; Władysław Frasyniuk of the Wrocław region, for example, was later to break with Wałęsa but supported him on this issue. Yet it indicated the organizational complexities of Solidarity, subsequently to be overlaid and cross-cut by personal, regional and ideological differences.

All such differences were reflected in Solidarity in parliament. New political parties had emerged just prior to or after the June election, including some whose members had been active in Solidarity from its inception. Several had received Wałęsa's endorsement in the June 1989 election. They were thus members of the Citizens' Parliamentary Club (OKP) while retaining links with their own small parties, each with a handful of deputies: the Christian National Union (*Zjedno-czenie Chrześcijańsko-Narodowe*, ZChN); the Liberal Democratic Congress (*Kongres Liberalno-Demokratyczny*, KLD), and the Polish Socialist Party (*Polska Partia Socjalistyczna*, PPS). By late 1990 organized factions were also appearing within the OKP. Its Agricultural Section included Rural Solidarity members and also members of

---

7   See for example, *Gazeta Wyborcza* 26, 13 June 1989; *GW* 31, 20 June 1989; *GW* 33, 22 June 1989; also Bronisław Geremek and Jacek Żakowski, *Rok 1989. Bronisław Geremek Opowiada. Jacek Żakowski Pyta*, Warsaw, 1990, pp.200–205.

a new Solidarity Peasant Party (PSL–Solidarity), while the Group for Defending the Interests of Working People aimed to articulate the specific needs of the working class. Increasingly, cracks began to emerge in the OKP. Even before the Mazowiecki government was constituted, elements of the Solidarity right wing had begun to attack the alleged dominance of the Solidarity 'left laity', personified by Adam Michnik and Jacek Kuroń.[8] Such attacks continued, reflecting right-wing resentment at being excluded from the new corridors of power, and they were not without impact on Wałęsa, whose role too was becoming marginalized. In October 1989 Wałęsa personally replaced the allegedly 'leftist' editor of *Tygodnik Solidarność* (Solidarity Weekly, previously edited by Mazowiecki) with his own nominee Jarosław Kaczyński.[9] The new staff of *Tygodnik Solidarność* became increasingly outspoken in their attacks on the Mazowiecki government, while Michnik's *Gazeta Wyborcza* appeared increasingly as its defender.

In November Piotr Wierzbicki wrote an influential piece[10] which analysed Solidarity in terms of three political centres: the OKP (the Family) and the government (the Retinue) in Warsaw, and Wałęsa and the union's National Executive (the Court) in Gdańsk. The Family were 'social democrats', veterans of the Workers' Defence Committee (KOR), notably Michnik, Kuroń, and Geremek. The Retinue was less homogeneous in origin, composed of Mazowiecki's cabinet, notably moderate, Catholic statesmen like Aleksander Hall. The third group, the Court, were associated with Wałęsa, pragmatists such as Kaczyński, his twin brother Leszek, and Bogdan Lis, with a 'trade union rather than political orientation' (*sic*) and close relations with the Church. Wierzbicki regarded these divisions as healthy manifestations of pluralism, not precluding cooperation (as in the person of Kuroń, Mazowiecki's Minister of Labour). However, the article gave fresh credence to the view that Michnik in particular was a dangerous

8   See, for example, Stefan Niesiołowski, 'Spór o zasady i metody', *Gazeta Wyborcza* 62, 2 August 1989.
9   This was felt by Mazowiecki as 'a clap of thunder from a clear sky': Waldemar Kuczyński, *Zwierzenia zausznika*, Warsaw, c.1992, p.185.
10 Piotr Wierzbicki, 'Familia, Świt, Dwór', *Tygodnik Solidarność* 23, 10 November 1989.

leftist. The notion that Michnik was a crypto-communist[11] became a focal point of attack for the right wing, both within and outside Solidarity.

The dissolution of the PZPR in January 1990 did not ameliorate the tensions within Solidarity; on the contrary, it intensified them. At one level the battle was over whether the unity of Solidarity could (or should) be maintained. But Walicki is surely correct that 'anti-Communist radicals, both within and outside Solidarity, felt threatened by the prospect of a post-Communist Left gaining "credibility" and forming a stable alliance with the moderate forces dominating the present government'.[12] Jan Łopuszański of the Christian National Union (ZChN) stated firmly that he and his colleagues would 'never permit an alliance between the Reds and the Pinks'.[13] Kaczyński accused the Solidarity 'left' of 'wanting to admit to power the forces of the old regime'.[14] Michnik and Geremek were openly accused of 'conspiracy ... to create from the Union a one-party system modelled on the PZPR'.[15] Mazowiecki's government itself came under increasing attack for being too lenient with the communists.

Wałęsa's own position cannot be ignored, however. It is not clear how far Wałęsa was influenced in his views by these assessments of Michnik, Geremek and Kuroń. However, Wałęsa in Gdańsk was increasingly isolated from the decision-making process. Both Kaczyński and Jarosław Kurski, Wałęsa's press officer, observed the impact of this detachment; Kurski described Wałęsa as a 'fish out of water'.[16] Mazowiecki was determined to be his own man. He did not take Wałęsa's advice over the composition of his government; he did not consult Wałęsa and gradually ceased to keep him informed of current developments.[17] Undoubtedly Mazowiecki had cause to

---

11 See Jarosław Kaczyński, *Odwrotna strona medalu*, Warsaw, 1991, pp.26–7, 34–5, 73; Wojciech Kwiatek, *Gra o wszystko*, Warsaw, 1991; cf. Jacek Kuroń, *Moja zupa*, Warsaw, 1991, p.15.

12 Andrzej Walicki, 'From Stalinism to Post-Communist Pluralism: The Case of Poland', *New Left Review* 185, 1991, p.116.

13 *Ład*, 3 April 1990.

14 Kaczyński, op. cit., p.113.

15 Kwiatek, op. cit., p.5.

16 Jarosław Kurski, *Wódz*, Warsaw, 1990, p.9.

17 Zbigniew Bujak, *Przepraszam za Solidarność*, Warsaw, 1991, p. 138; Kaczyński, op. cit., pp.60, 65; Kurski, op. cit., pp.88–91, Geremek and Żakowski, op. cit., pp.281–2.

establish his own independence. Wałęsa was used to having his own way. He excelled at playing his advisers off against one another and he enjoyed being the centre of attention.

Still, Mazowiecki's attitude to Wałęsa was a mistake, not because Mazowiecki owed his appointment to the Solidarity leader but because Wałęsa was the government's social shield in the country at large, that is, he held open the Solidarity umbrella over the government. Wałęsa was the symbol of Solidarity, regarded as the man responsible for the collapse of communism. Yet he bore the consequences of his support for the new government and his popularity declined rapidly. As the economic situation deteriorated in the early months of 1990, the government benefited from Solidarity's trade union support.[18] It did not always appear to appreciate this role, and Wałęsa became increasingly alienated, finally openly challenging the government and offering his own person as a solution: his presidential candidacy inaugurated 'the war at the top' that was to fracture Solidarity as a political movement and weaken it as a trade union.

The War at the Top

Wałęsa's admirers see his actions as necessary to prevent a new type of one-party system in Poland: he was the guardian of pluralism.[19] This was a constant theme of his own statements from early 1990 right up to the parliamentary elections of 1991. His opponents, however, cite his personal ambition, his authoritarian tendencies and his isolation from the key decision-making centres as the source of his actions in opposing the Mazowiecki camp, increasingly aligned with Geremek and elements of the OKP in parliament.

In February 1990 Wałęsa brought in Zdzisław Najder, the controversial former head of the Polish section of Radio Free Europe, to head the National Citizens' Committee. Najder's task was to prevent the integration of the OKP and the citizens' committees into a national party movement under the control of Mazowiecki.[20] This was the putative 'plan for a new monopartism'. It was hard to imagine either

18 See Kuroń, op. cit., pp.68–9.
19 Antoni Z. Kaminski and Joanna Kurczewska, 'Letter from Poland', *Government and Opposition*, vol.26, no.2, 1991, p.223.
20 Ibid.

that those who had fought so hard for democracy did so in order to generate a new single-party system, or that they could have done so if they wished. However, Wałęsa and Najder changed the balance of membership on the National KO by co-opting new members, mainly from elements of the small right-wing parties hitherto unrepresented. There is a certain irony in recalling that Mazowiecki and Hall, opposed by Wałęsa, had urged the inclusion of these elements and others of the non-Solidarity dissident movement on the list of opposition candidates in June 1989.

Also in February some Solidarity parliamentarians proposed that the parliamentary club (OKP) be reorganized as a federation of parties and groups, with proportional representation for each on the OKP executive. This proposal was directed against Geremek, leader of the OKP and a strong influence on its direction. The proponents of unity prevailed in parliament, but increasingly acrimonious debates continued outside. After a stormy meeting of Wałęsa's Citizens' Committee, Najder again expressed the differences (albeit tendentiously) as revealing 'two standpoints, one for broadening the political platform, the other for maintaining the guise of a monolith'.[21]

April brought increasingly explicit attacks on the Mazowiecki government: it was not doing enough to remove the *nomenklatura* from positions of power; its programme should be 'accelerated'. Wałęsa made his first open declaration of presidential ambition. The Round Table contract was no longer valid, he argued, with the dissolution of one of the negotiating partners. Jaruzelski should be replaced with a new president, namely President Wałęsa. Wałęsa later drew back, stating that his interest in the presidency had been but a 'metaphor', a warning to the government. He had 'stuck his finger in the fire'.[22] Although he did not announce his formal candidacy until September, everyone knew that Wałęsa wanted to be president.

The Second Solidarity (Trade Union) Congress, convening now for the first time since 1981, was overshadowed by Wałęsa's announcement. Its course was not harmonious. In his speech Wałęsa gratuitously insulted the intellectuals who had served as key advisers since the birth of Solidarity. Furthermore, the political divisions had their

21 BBC Interview, 2 April 1990.
22 Interview with Lech Wałęsa, *Rzeczpospolita* 89, 17 April 1990.

counterpart in a bout of industrial unrest. However, Wałęsa was overwhelmingly re-elected as Solidarity's leader; the support of his own grass roots was not in doubt.

The Formalization of the Split

In May 1990 Jarosław Kaczyński inaugurated the Centre Democratic Accord (*Porozumienie Demokratyczne Centrum*), a broad confederation supporting 'acceleration' and a Wałęsa presidency. The Centrum attracted numerous members of parliament, local citizens' committees and trade union branches, along with individual members of many small parties. Mazowiecki's supporters, led by Jerzy Turowicz, editor of the Catholic *Tygodnik Powszechny* (Universal Weekly), made strenuous efforts to heal the breach, but Turowicz failed to mediate between two individuals known for their stubbornness. In May 42 prominent intellectuals signed the so-called Kraków [Cracow] Accord, proclaiming a commitment to democratic, Christian and European values. Many of them were later to form the Democratic Right Forum, one of two major elements supporting Mazowiecki's candidacy for the presidency.

The mutual vituperation of 'the war at the top' intensified and in its midst came the local government elections of May 1990. Despite plans for increased powers for local authorities, they aroused little interest. Turnout was low, an average of 42.3 per cent. Solidarity's support declined: it took 43 per cent of the seats. In consolation, no other political force made a noticeable impact; but the dual effect of the war at the top and economic deterioration had clearly affected Solidarity's support.

Wałęsa kept up his bombardment of the government, and further personnel changes weakened the influence of the Mazowiecki camp outside parliament. Wujec was unceremoniously dismissed as Secretary of Wałęsa's Citizens' Committee. Wałęsa also demanded that Michnik should resign as editor of *Gazeta Wyborcza* or remove Solidarity's logo from its masthead. Michnik for his part accused Wałęsa of behaving imperiously, indeed 'like a caesar': only the Solidarity executive could make decisions regarding the logo (it was removed in September after a vote by the union executive).

Although Wałęsa's position was weakened by the vagueness of his accusations against the government and the lack of any specific alternative proposals,[23] his attacks did have an effect. On 6 July 1990 Mazowiecki dismissed former communists, including the key ministers of Defence and the Interior. Work on the privatization programme was speeded up and a package passed through the *Sejm*. The government was now truly a Solidarity government, but the movement appeared hopelessly divided into supporters and opponents of Wałęsa's candidature for the presidency.

On 16 July Mazowiecki's supporters formalized their support for the prime minister as an alternative candidate. They established ROAD, the Citizens' Movement for Democratic Action, which included most of the first generation of Solidarity advisers, including Geremek, Kuroń and Michnik, and regional union leaders Bujak and Frasyniuk. It formed an electoral alliance, the Democratic Union, with Turowicz's Democratic Right Forum on a platform of continued support for the government line. Mazowiecki himself dithered over whether to stand against Wałęsa. None the less, by late summer the gloves were off and Solidarity's divisions appeared irrevocable.

Those supporting Mazowiecki's candidacy did so because they felt that Wałęsa was unsuited to be president. Wałęsa lacked the urbanity and the skills of diplomacy, tact and compromise associated with successful heads of state. He had (to say the least) an unfortunate inability to express himself clearly and Wałęsa-isms became unflattering catchphrases, not only for the anti-Wałęsa intelligentsia: 'I am in favour, but I am even against'; 'I don't want to, but I must [be president]'. It is unfair to accuse Wałęsa's opponents of snobbery or 'an explosion of class prejudice';[24] they were certainly to be proved right about Wałęsa's personal qualities for the presidency. However, they failed to recognize the extent to which Wałęsa, whom they themselves viewed as a genuine tribune of the people with a sharply honed political instinct, would be able to mobilize support for his candidacy. Nor is it surprising that Wałęsa was deeply hurt when his friends and colleagues failed to endorse his ambitions. He was the leader of Solidar-

---

23 For a different view see Voytek Zubek, 'Wałęsa's Leadership and Poland's Transition', *Problems of Communism*, vol.XL, nos 1–2, 1991, p.78.
24 Ibid., p. 75.

ity, Nobel prize-winner, fêted abroad and visited at home by foreign statesmen. He had (as he pointed out) made Mazowiecki prime minister. Given the escalation of acrimony in the exchanges of spring and summer 1990, it is not surprising that the breach proved too wide to heal in the short term. But there was nothing inevitable about the timing of the split or its actual form: Wałęsa received warm support and assistance from many intellectuals, such as Jan Olszewski, Jadwiga Staniszkis, and Stefan Kisielewski. In this sense it is somewhat misleading to see the split as a final fracturing of the Solidarity alliance between the intelligentsia and the working class.[25] Mazowiecki was an unwilling candidate, who would have been better advised to welcome Wałęsa as an ally rather than as an adversary.

The decision to hold an early presidential election was a result of growing, though often reluctant, realization that nothing else would defuse the mounting political pressure. The electoral system was amended and Jaruzelski resigned gracefully. The election duly took place in two stages in November and December 1990. The Solidarity trade union supported Wałęsa, as did the Centrum, most of the citizens' committees and the Solidarity peasant movement.

THE PRESIDENTIAL ELECTION OF 1990

The significance of party labels in the presidential election was limited by Wałęsa's personal appeal. At the close of nominations on 25 October six candidates had gathered the necessary endorsement of 100,000 signatures: Wałęsa and Mazowiecki; Roman Bartoszcze, leader of the Polish Peasant Party (PSL) and also a former Solidarity activist; Włodzimierz Cimoszewicz, leader of the Democratic Left Parliamentary Club and formerly of the PZPR but now a 'non-party' candidate supported by the new SDRP; Leszek Moczulski of the Confederation of Independent Poland (KPN); and Stan Tymiński, an unknown Polish expatriate businessman.

The campaign was lacklustre and at times positively unpleasant, particularly the use of anti-Semitic innuendo against the government

---

25 This is the view of Miron Wolnicki, 'The New Political Economy of Central Europe', *Telos* 90, 1991–92, p.121.

camp.[26] It did give the virtually unknown non-Solidarity candidates the opportunity for public exposure and they gained ground as the campaign progressed.[27] Mazowiecki was on the defensive and he was a poor candidate, self-effacing and a weak orator. For him the campaign was a plebiscite on his government. He stood for continuity: a cautious evolutionary approach to culminate in the gradual privatization of the state enterprises which dominated the economy. Neither Wałęsa nor Tymiński offered a programmatic alternative; but both were better organized than the Mazowiecki camp.[28] Wałęsa kept promising a programme, but his main appeal was a personal, charismatic one. Tymiński, like Wałęsa, came close to promising a painless transition to the market, offering achievements 'within a month'. Tymiński criticized the government for 'treason' in its mismanagement of the economy and accused Mazowiecki of criminal activities. He too was a poor speaker; but he hammered away effectively at his single theme and made political capital of his independence from the political establishment and his personal business acumen. Bartoszcze, Cimoszewicz and Moczulski were not taken seriously; indeed, neither was Tymiński until the opinion polls revealed a late surge in his support.[29] Only then did journalists probe his background and raise doubts regarding his inexperience, the actual extent of his business empire, his alleged mystical tendencies, the appearance in his entourage of former communists and secret policemen, and even his mental stability.

The electoral system required a candidate to achieve an absolute majority of votes for outright success. The absence of a first-ballot victory would require a run-off between the top two candidates. The results of the first round on 25 November came as a shock. Wałęsa had failed to achieve the first round victory he had sought, and Tymiński, not Mazowiecki, had come second (see Table 5.1).

26 See Konstanty Gebert, 'Anti-Semitism in the 1990 Polish Presidential Election', *Social Research*, vol.58, no.4, 1991, pp.723–55.
27 Mirosława Grabowska, 'Socjologia nie skonsumowana' in Mirosława Grabowska and Ireneusz Krzemiński (eds), *Bitwa o Belweder*, Warsaw, 1991, p.91.
28 All the campaigns are discussed in Grabowska and Krzemiński, op. cit., which also includes a collection of documents.
29 On Tymiński's support in the Presidential election see R. Markowski, 'O psychologicznych "profilach" elektoratów', ibid., pp.139–44; also Tomasz Żukowski, 'Trzecia siła', *Krytyka* 37, 1991, especially pp.35–42.

Table 5.1 Presidential Election, First Ballot

	Votes	Per cent
Lech Wałęsa	6,569,889	39.96
Stan Tymiński (Independent)	3,797,605	23.10
Tadeusz Mazowiecki (Solidarity)	2,973,264	18.08
Włodzimierz Cimoszewicz (Left)	1,514,025	9.21
Roman Bartoszcze (Peasant)	1,176,175	7.15
Leszek Moczulski (KPN)	411,516	2.50

Normally, a second-ballot system would be expected to generate election alliances after the first ballot. Neither leading candidate, however, represented a political party and no political advantage could be gained from alliance with the outsider Tymiński. Indeed, the political establishment was horrified at his strong showing. Despite reservations, the Mazowiecki camp threw its support to Wałęsa. The Church too, officially neutral in the first round, urged its flock to vote for Wałęsa. In the event, on 9 December Tymiński's vote went up only slightly and Wałęsa won a mighty victory with 74.3 per cent of the vote, albeit on a reduced turnout (down from 61 per cent to 55 per cent).

The election was decided on the basis of general images of the qualities of the candidates and sets of previous attitudes (especially to Solidarity, to the Communist Party, to martial law, to the Catholic Church); there were quite significant regional differences, linked to historical factors.[30] The characteristics of the electorate proved reasonably well defined.[31] Wałęsa's supporters were largely the socially integrated, religious, pro-Solidarity workers and peasants, especially in the eastern and south-eastern parts of the country and the large

30 See Tomasz Żukowski, 'Mapa wyborcza Polski' in Grabowska and Krzemiński, op. cit., pp.119–30; J.J. Parysek *et al.*, 'Regional Differences in the Results of the 1990 Presidential Election in Poland as the First Approximation to a Political Map of the Country', *Environment and Planning*, vol.23, 1991, pp.1315–29.
31 See especially Markowski, op. cit.; Żukowski, op. cit.; Włodzimierz Daab *et al.*, *Polski wyborca '90*, Warsaw, 1991, vol.1, Chapters 5–7; Krzysztof Jasiewicz, 'Od protestów i represji do wolnych wyborów' in Władysław Adamski *et al.*, *Polacy '90. Konflikty i zmiana*, Warsaw, 1991, pp.99–122.

cities; they combined support for economic liberalism with traditional values, fervently supporting religious education in schools and opposing abortion. Mazowiecki's supporters were intellectual and entrepreneurial, with broadly liberal economic and political views, including opposition to religion in schools, to capital punishment and to a ban on abortion; they were concentrated in large cities and in the western regions. Tymiński's electorate came from the alienated and marginalized, the young and those fearful of unemployment, especially in mining areas and in the north-west. They were the most anticlerical and the most fervent advocates of the death penalty. They were more 'anti-Solidarity' than those who voted for Cimoszewicz, but there was also a 'Solidarity' element which moved to Wałęsa in the second round.[32]

The non-Solidarity vote also included the supporters of Bartoszcze, Cimoszewicz and Moczulski. We should recall that Solidarity's sweeping success in 1989 had been achieved with the support of a minority of the population. The depth of economic recession, growing insecurity regarding employment, the perceived absence of an agricultural strategy, and a deterioration in social service provision[33] provided fertile ground for mobilizing the non-Solidarity vote.

Bartoszcze, leader of the Polish Peasant Party, had a Solidarity pedigree, but it was to the class constituency that he appealed. His voters were largely from the peasantry, and he did best in the more agricultural provinces. Cimoszewicz, the candidate of the 'Left Alliance', did better than many expected, especially in Białystok province (his home territory) in the northeast, where he polled 27.2 per cent of the vote. His political base – those linked to the old system, including the OPZZ – clearly held up well. Moczulski's small vote was more evenly distributed. He appealed to radical anti-communists who believed that Solidarity was too prone to compromise.

We cannot ignore the substantial group of non-voters (almost 40 per cent of the electorate) in trying to understand Polish voting behaviour and the potential for party development. Most were traditional abstainers; they did not vote in previous elections, whether

---

32 Krzysztof Jasiewicz, 'Wyborca polski – w dziesięć lat po sierpniu', *Krytyka* 36, 1991, pp.34, 43.

33 See Frances Millard, 'Social Policy in Poland' in Bob Deacon *et al.*, *The New Eastern Europe*, London, 1992a, pp.129–43.

under the Communists, in 1989, or in the local elections of May 1990. Jasiewicz describes them as the underclass: older people, with little formal education, and largely female.[34] Solidarity's 'war at the top' had done much to undermine the public's favourable assessment of its new politicians. The implication of Wałęsa's intervention – that he could not stand by and watch while the situation deteriorated – was bound to contribute to shattering the consensus which supported the Mazowiecki government during the first months of economic shock treatment. Given Wałęsa's close relationship with Mazowiecki and Geremek in particular, their failure to build bridges and maintain strong lines of communication with Wałęsa in Gdańsk is rather surprising, especially since government policy was so potentially damaging to Wałęsa's main political base, the trade union. The government was widely criticized, by its supporters as well as its critics, for intellectual arrogance and a general failure to communicate with the population.

However, although attitudes to Solidarity were important, they were not the only factor. Class was the distinguishing feature in the electorate of Bartoszcze (the peasants) and also that of Mazowiecki (the urban professional intelligentsia). Religion also made itself felt: Tymiński's followers were the most anti-clerical element, while Mazowiecki attracted the urban secular vote. Wałęsa's support was heterogeneous in terms of class, but more unified in terms of attitudes to religion and the Church.[35] In the second round, however, many supporters of losing candidates voted for Wałęsa on the principle of the lesser evil. Thus Lech Wałęsa won the presidency on the basis of a disparate coalition. A high proportion of the population took no part in the election or expressed its alienation through support for Tymiński. The old party system had broken up, but there was as yet nothing to take its place.

PARTIES IN THE OCTOBER 1991 ELECTION

The Bielecki government, which replaced Mazowiecki's following the presidential election, was from the outset viewed as a temporary one

---

34   Jasiewicz, 'Wyborca polski', op. cit., p.41.
35   See Krzysztof Korzeniowski and Krystyna Skarzyńska, 'Wyznacziki popularności trzech głównych pretendentów w wyborach prezydenckich' in Daab et al., op. cit., pp.148–52.

in the light of expected parliamentary elections. Although the election timetable was gradually extended, not least because of controversy surrounding the electoral system (see Chapter 6), political parties prepared for the coming election. New parties mushroomed, others split, and most explored various possibilities for coalitions and alliances. On the eve of the October election, there were well over one hundred registered 'parties'. Most were tiny cadre parties or 'para-parties'[36] without social roots or public recognition; only a few could be regarded as serious contenders. These could be roughly divided into Solidarity 'pro-reform' parties wishing to continue the current economic policies, Solidarity 'anti-reform parties' arguing broadly for increased economic interventionism, the successor parties, and a heterogeneous group of small, mainly new parties testing their electoral appeal. Moczulski's KPN was distinctive: it was not linked to Solidarity, it had developed an effective organization and it bore no responsibility for policies pursued since 1989. Neither ideological nor class divisions were clear-cut; therefore most parties were competing on a diffuse and similar basis, not as representatives of interests or clear policy alternatives. Pressure groups (including the Solidarity trade union) and local organizations also fielded candidates.

The Solidarity parties were highly variegated by the autumn of 1991. The best known was Mazowiecki's Democratic Union (UD), now formally registered as a political party. In the run-up to the parliamentary elections the Democratic Union proved the most consistently popular party, attracting some 15–20 per cent of the electorate, that is, roughly the proportion which had voted for Mazowiecki in 1990. The UD retained its two wings as acknowledged factions: the right was a moderate nationalist grouping of Catholic intellectuals; the secular social-liberals placed greater stress on state intervention. The party supported the continuation of the Balcerowicz economic strategy, albeit with reservations. It did not take the notion of a continuing communist threat seriously. Its approach was rational and intellectual, self-consciously anti-demagogic and anti-populist.[37] Mazowiecki's dignity and moral integrity were an asset, but there remained much

---

36   Mirosława Grabowska, 'System partyjny – w budowie', *Krytyka* 37, 1991, p.28.
37   See the interview with Mazowiecki in *Polityka* 17, 27 April 1991.

doubt as to whether the UD could broaden its appeal beyond the urban intelligentsia who provided the core of its support.

The Liberal Democratic Congress (KLD) was virtually unknown when its leader Krzysztof Bielecki became prime minister in January 1991. The party remained small, despite attracting elements from other political groupings, for example the liberal wing of the Democratic Party. Bielecki increased its public profile, although Liberal support tended to rise and fall in line with the government's popularity. Like the Democratic Union, the KLD was restrained in its rhetoric, stressing pragmatism and professionalism. Both parties were liberal in their political and economic values, although the economic *laissez-faire* liberalism of the KLD was stronger and faith in the market greater. Bielecki was a self-styled Thatcherite. The Liberals had supported Wałęsa's presidential candidacy, but they constituted potential allies for both the Democratic Union and the Centrum, with whom they maintained good relations.

The Centrum was less unambiguously in favour of maintaining the existing direction of reform. It was broadly of a centre–right Christian democratic and pro-capitalist orientation. We have seen how its origins lay in the growing split within Solidarity. Although it spearheaded Wałęsa's electoral campaign, the president did not personally associate himself with the Centrum. However, many of his own statements regarding 'acceleration' and 'de-communization' echoed its views.

The Centrum had several ministers in the Bielecki government. Members, including its leader Jarosław Kaczyński, were also prominent among Wałęsa's presidential staff. Despite this, the Centrum was critical of the Bielecki government's performance. It was the strongest advocate of early parliamentary elections and continued bitterly to attack the 'contract parliament' of the Round Table. It had difficulty establishing a clear public image, not least because its Christian democratic emphasis was shared by numerous other parties.

The Christian National Union (ZChN) had gained a high profile because of its strong clerical advocacy; its prominent parliamentarians were outspoken, uncompromising anti-communists who also spearheaded the anti-abortion movement. The party's leader, Wiesław Chrzanowski, was Bielecki's Minister of Justice; but the party as a whole was nationalist, anti-liberal and economically interventionist. The ZChN stood in the election as part of Catholic Election Action (WAK), in which it played the dominant role. The left-wing Solidarity parties were small. Labour Solidarity (*Solidarność Pracy*) had its origins in parliament with the Group for the Defence of Workers' Interests of the OKP, associated with Ryszard Bugaj and Karol Modzelewski. Zbigniew Bujak had remained outside parliament in 1989 to concentrate (but in practice briefly) on trade union activity. Bujak was a founder member of ROAD but in April 1991 he withdrew to establish the Democratic–Social Movement (RDS). Both groups were social democratic, pro-market but strongly anti-Balcerowicz; they urged greater state interventionism and attacked the absence of a coherent industrial policy. The tiny Polish Socialist Party (PPS) fielded candidates under Labour Solidarity auspices. Bujak, convinced of his own popularity and ostentatiously rejecting developments in Solidarity after the Round Table (his memoir was entitled *I Apologise for Solidarity*[38]) entered the election contest under his own brand label.

Of the four successor parties, only the SDRP and the Peasant Party (now the PSL) retained a political base and organization. The SDRP stood for an indeterminate 'social market economy', with continuing state intervention and a strong social policy commitment. Still bearing the stigma of its past, the SDRP entered the election as the dominant element of the Democratic Left Alliance (SLD), notably with the 'old' trade unions. The PSL was the largest party, but its appeal was directed mainly to the rural population. After failing to agree a common strategy with the Solidarity peasant movement, it formed an alliance with other rural organizations. The peasants were the most disaffected section of the population, alienated and angry, especially over the high cost of credit and the issue of minimum agricultural prices.

The Polish political scene also provided a mosaic of other political parties. The largest and best known was still Moczulski's Confederation for Independent Poland (KPN). Tymiński had established Party X following his defeat in 1990. To the chagrin of aspiring professional politicians, a number of 'eccentric' parties attracted public attention.

38 Bujak, op. cit.

In the spring of 1991 opinion polls among young people showed the Friends of Beer Party (PPPP) to be the most popular. There were also various Christian democratic groups, regional and ethnic minority parties, environmentalists, and supporters of local dignitaries and pressure groups. It is little wonder that the electorate was confused and bewildered. Indeed, lack of public identification with political parties was a source of anxiety to the political elites, as opinion polls registered public ignorance and apathy.

THE 1991 ELECTION

The turnout on Sunday, 27 October, was low: a national average of 43.2 per cent. As expected, a large number of electoral lists (29) achieved representation in the *Sejm*, assisted by the highly proportional electoral system. What was unforeseen was the evenness of support for the major contenders (see Figure 5.1).

Figure 5.1 Distribution of Seats in the Sejm

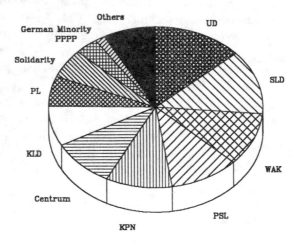

The Democratic Union, leading in the opinion polls, polled only 12 per cent, ahead of the ex-Communist Left Alliance by a hair's breadth. The first ten were national parties, followed by regional parties with a concentrated vote (that is, a low national average), and local committees.

Table 5.2 Vote for the Sejm

Party	%	Seats
Democratic Union (UD)	12.31	62
Democratic Left Alliance (SLD)	11.98	60
Catholic Election Action (WAK)	8.73	49
Centre Democratic Accord (Centrum)	8.71	44
Peasant Party–Programmatic Alliance (PSL)	8.67	48
Confederation for Independent Poland (KPN)	7.50	46
Liberal Democratic Congress (KLD)	7.48	37
Peasant Accord (PL)	5.46	28
Solidarity	5.05	27
Friends of Beer (PPPP)	3.27	16
German Minority	1.17	7
Christian Democracy	2.36	5
Polish Western Union (PZZ)	0.23	4
Party of Christian Democrats (PCD)	1.11	4
Labour Solidarity	2.05	4
Union of Political Realism (UPR)	2.25	3
Party X	0.47	3
Movement for Silesian Autonomy	0.35	2
Democratic Party (SD)	1.41	1
Democratic–Social Movement (RDS)	0.46	1
Union of Great Poles		1
Peasant Unity (PL plus PSL)		1
'Great Poland and Poland'		1
Solidarity '80		1
Piast Peasant Election Alliance (PL plus PSL)		1
Electoral Committee of Orthodox Believers		1
Kraków Coalition 'Solidarity with the President'		1
Union of Podhale		1
Women against Life's Hardships		1
Total		460

Tymiński's Party X was a regional party by default, for most of its constituency lists had been disqualified for alleged malpractice in the nomination procedure.

Results for the Senate were somewhat less fragmented (see Figure 5.2), partly because of the first-past-the-post system.

Figure 5.2 Distribution of Seats in the Senate

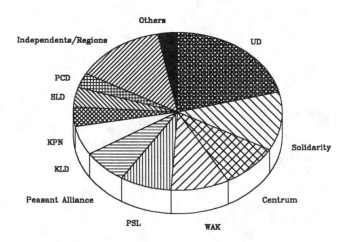

As in 1989, two senators were elected from each province, with three from Warsaw and Katowice. Each voter cast two votes (or three in the latter provinces). The Democratic Union again emerged as the largest party, with 21 per cent of the seats. The former communists, however, fared less well, with only four per cent. Of the regional parties, only the German Minority gained a seat, but independent and local candidates did well (see Table 5.3).

The immediate response of disappointed politicians was to blame the 'bad' electoral system for the results. However, the electoral system aided the fragmentation of parliament, it did not create it; nor is it clear that establishing a threshold of, say, five per cent, would have greatly simplified the process of forming a government.[39] The main

39 Stanisław Gebethner, 'Wybrane głosy w dyskusji' in Piotr Łukasiewicz and Wojciech Zaborowski, *Szanse i zagrożenia polskich przemian*, Warsaw, 1992, p.95.

problem was the inability of the parties to provide clear reference points. Most parties competed for national support, appealing through personalities rather than distinct policy alternatives. Basically, however, the election result reflected the diverse attitudes of society.

Table 5.3 Composition of the Senate by Party

Party	Number of seats
Democratic Union	21
Solidarity	12
Centrum	9
Catholic Action (WAK)	9
Peasant Party (PSL)	8
Peasant Alliance (Solidarity)	7
Liberal Democratic Congress	6
Confederation for Independent Poland (KPN)	4
Left Alliance (SLD)	4
Party of Christian Democrats	3
Christian Democracy	1
German Minority	1
Nationalist	1
Independents/Regional	14
Total	100

The campaign itself made little impact. Election meetings were few and badly publicized. Television coverage was minimal; there were no debates, interviews or reports from the campaign trail. The parties' own broadcasts were amateurish and uninformative. Few specific issues surfaced in the course of the campaign, although the government did cause outrage with an unpopular bill on retirement pensions and proposals to redistribute child benefit (soon rescinded). These issues were thought to increase support for the Democratic Left Alliance.

These general factors influenced the low turnout, as well as the pattern of voting. The campaign failed to overcome the general atmosphere of pessimism. After two years Solidarity was no longer viewed positively by the electorate; it had failed to fulfil exaggerated hopes of economic prosperity; its former leaders seemed unable to cooperate. This provided great scope for parties like the KPN, which bore no responsibility for economic deterioration or political in-fighting and which entered parliament with several satellite parties which had stood separately.

The importance of personal voting was immense. People willingly cast their Senate votes for candidates of different parties. In the *Sejm* vote lesser-known figures on party lists were pulled to success by popular colleagues. Class factors remained important for the peasant vote; but divisions within the peasant movement took their toll. The former communists did well among the working class in areas of extreme economic dislocation. The vote of the urban intelligentsia was divided between the Democratic Union, the Liberals and the Left Alliance. Religion also played a role, with the Catholic Church supporting (directly or indirectly) the Christian Democrats and the Catholic coalition WAK; the vote for the latter was higher than expected, but its chief component, the ZChN, played down its links with Solidarity. Regional differences were also apparent, with historical factors evident but also differences in the regional strength of party organization.[40]

THE PARTY SYSTEM IN 1992–93

The outcome of the unedifying political battles which followed the 1991 election have been noted in Chapter 4. Parliamentary representation gave a visibility to the parties, but their behaviour resulted in a further erosion of public confidence. New parties seemed unlikely to be able to mount an effective challenge, but the total of registered 'parties' kept increasing, to 154 in September 1992.[41] Existing parties were far from stable. There was no 'party system' of regular interactions among coherent parties. Not only was the position one of

40 For more detail see Frances Millard, 'The Polish Parliamentary Elections of October 1991', *Soviet Studies*, vol.44, no.5, 1992b, pp.837–55.
41 Some of the more unusual ones are elucidated in J. Papuga, 'Od orła do kosa', *Polityka* 37, 12 September 1992.

extreme pluralism, but the parties were scattered across the political spectrum with none strong enough to provide a clear centre of gravity. This distinguished Poland from the typical pattern of numerous parties at the birth of democratic politics, for example in Italy and Germany after the Second World War or Spain following the death of Franco. The elements of the kaleidoscopic party system continued to shatter, shift and re-form throughout 1992.

Tensions within some parties emerged immediately following the 1991 election. The Friends of Beer split, with the majority forming the new Polish Economic Programme (Big Beer). By the end of 1991 the Solidarity peasant groupings, which had campaigned jointly as the Peasant Accord (PL), split again and PSL–Solidarity left the PL parliamentary club. In February 1992 Rural Solidarity joined another PSL (*Mikołajczykowskie*) to form the PSL–PL. It may be assumed that the petty squabbling and Byzantine manoeuvring of the smaller peasant parties will continue, at least until the next parliamentary election.

The Parys affair and the fall of the Olszewski government gave rise to a more serious reshuffling of the party pack. Parys was in a weak position, without a parliamentary base; but his 'defence committees' made common cause with Olszewski and a Centrum splinter group in a federated Movement for the Republic (*Ruch dla Rzeczpospolitej* or RdR). They were joined by Szeremietiew (Parys's successor as Olszewski's Minister of Defence), Macierewicz (expelled from the ZChN over his mishandling of the lustration resolution), Bartoszcze (erstwhile leader of the PSL), and a number of tiny right-wing fringe groups in a union of 'patriotic and pro-independence forces'. The new movement excelled in anti-communist invective; it attacked the government as a corrupt kleptocracy and the president as a frontman for communist skulduggery. By the end of the year the Centrum had lost another group of deputies to the Liberals, and Kaczyński drew closer to Olszewski's camp, where he played a leading role in elaborating allegations against the president.[42]

42　Jarosław Kurski and Piotr Semki, *Lewy czerwcowy*, Warsaw, 1993, contains interviews with Kaczyński, Macierewicz, Parys, and Głąpiński detailing many allegations against the president and his close associates.

Partly in response to this development of the shrill nationalist right, Aleksander Hall and a group of the right-wing faction left the Democratic Union to build a moderate Conservative Party (*Partia Konserwatywna*) of the Christian Democratic right. Hall denounced the hysteria of the RdR, its appeal to conspiracy theories and its unwillingness to compromise. Hall had much in common with the Liberals, who had expanded their parliamentary support with converts from Big Beer and the Centrum; but a right–centrist alliance seemed likely to founder on the latter's secularism.

After Hall's departure from the UD, the Democratic Left Alliance (mainly the SDRP) became the largest party in the *Sejm*, but it continued to suffer political ostracism. Tentative moves towards a healing of the breach came in January 1993, when Labour Solidarity, Bujak's Democratic–Social Movement and representatives of other social democratic groupings formed the Union of Labour (*Unia Pracy*) under the leadership of Ryszard Bugaj. The Labour Union took few deputies from the Left Alliance, and its relationship to the SDRP was still hesitant. However, the policy differences between the two were minimal, and it seemed that with time a credible social democratic alternative could prove a major political force.

For the present, only the SDRP and Pawlak's PSL could make any claim to be mass parties genuinely linked to their constituencies. Other parties, with the partial exception of the Democratic Union and the KPN, remained little known to the public. Party programmes were largely indistinguishable, and politicians were not seen as representing people's interests but rather as arrogant, corrupt and self-serving.[43] This may be 'natural and not unexpected, in the period when a new order is emerging',[44] but lack of trust is a major obstacle to developing a democratic political culture.

The incipient Polish party system, then, was characterized in 1992 by few credible parties along with a multiplicity of small ones possessing few resources and weak organizational links. Political parties represented neither clear constituencies of interests nor coherent ideo-

---

43 See, for example, Ireneusz Krzemiński, 'Sami sobie damy radę?', *Rzeczpospolita* 283, 2 December 1992; J. Czapiński, 'Partie w (krzywym?) zwierciadle swoich zwolenników', *Rzeczpospolita* 302, 24–27 December 1992.

44 Janusz Reykowski, 'Psychologiczne problemy okresu przemian' in Łukasiewicz and Zaborowski, op. cit., p.54.

logical perspectives. Much of their rhetoric remained symbolic and emotional. Leading figures changed their political allegiance frequently as the parties split, merged and changed partners in a continuing political gavotte. The political parties were patently unable to serve as integrative mechanisms for society or as agents of conflict resolution.

The dissolution of parliament in May 1993 found most parties unprepared for the forthcoming election in September. The new electoral law, unlike its predecessor, required parties to achieve a five per cent threshold (or eight per cent for a coalition of parties). This factor stimulated a rush of electoral alliances and mergers as the parties calculated their chances of passing the threshold. Seven small right-wing groupings associated with the so-called anti-Belwedere (that is, anti-Wałęsa) campaign called for a broad 'Christian–Patriotic' bloc. These included the Centrum, its parliamentary representation now much truncated by defections; Olszewski's Movement for the Republic (RdR); Parys's Third Republic Movement; and Polish Action (Akcja Polska), formed by Macierewicz after his expulsion from the ZChN over his handling of lustration. However, the new bloc split almost as it emerged: indeed, fissiparous tendencies continued to make themselves felt in all electoral coalitions and there was no guarantee that those that survived would endure in the new parliament.

The situation was further confused by the president's attempt to retain the political initiative. After failing to persuade the parties of the Suchocka coalition to enter an electoral alliance, he announced his patronage (but not his membership) of a new political formation, the BBWR (Bezpartyjny Blok Wspierania Reform, the Non-Party Bloc to Support Reforms). Wałęsa, who disliked political parties, launched an appeal to elements of Solidarity, the business community, the peasantry and local government bodies. The parties saw the the BBWR as a genuine challenge and potential vote-winner, and responded by jealously continuing to guard their positions and seeking to achieve wider public recognition.

6. The New Political Institutions

The formal institutions of government and a Constitution regulating their relations provide the framework within which democratic political processes operate. Formal–legal arrangements coexist with and channel informal linkages. For most of the forty years of communist rule in Poland it was not the state institutions but party structures which provided the key to understanding politics. Therefore, the major task for those wishing to create a set of democratic institutions was to bring political relationships back within the framework of the state. This entailed the need to address constitutional issues.

In a stable political system institutional relationships evolve gradually. Elite consensus and the development of conventions governing the rules of the game facilitate the evolutionary process. In Poland apparent consensus on the fundamentals of a new system prevailed for a short period, but conflicts rapidly emerged over the means to these ends. Politically, they expressed themselves in institutional tensions, notably between a weak executive wishing to maximize the speed of transformation and a strong legislative body which by its nature worked more slowly. Internal conflicts within the political institutions magnified the conflicts between them. A large section of society came to view the process of institutional transformation as one designed simply to further the interests of the new politicians. This chapter will examine and analyse the workings of the new political structures and the nature and implications of the relationships among the institutions of the new state. The first stage of constitution-making took place in 1989 and concentrated on amending the communist Constitution. The promulgation of a new constitutional order proved politically impossible in 1990–92, but in December 1992 an interim 'Little Constitution' came into force.

THE CONSTITUTIONAL FRAMEWORK

In one sense the architects of the new Polish political system were fortunate. With the 1952 Constitution the communists had formally established a parliamentary system. The unicameral *Sejm* was the sovereign legislative institution, to which the executive was accountable. The main deviation from democratic principles and the source of their subversion lay in the parallel party structure and the fact that the Communist Party (Polish United Workers' Party – PZPR) itself was the key locus of power, in regard to both policy and personnel. Once these functions had been transferred to the state, the old system could be democratized by making it work according to its own professed principles. The 1989 Round Table introduced certain institutional innovations, the Senate and the presidency; but the presidency broadly replaced the collective Council of State, while the Senate's role was primarily that of legislative scrutiny.

A complete restructuring of the shape of state institutions was therefore not the most pressing issue, although constitutional amendments were necessary. After a stalemate lasting for three months, there emerged a consensus on the need for change, and the necessary two-thirds majority was mustered easily for constitutional amendments in December 1989 and March 1990.[1] 'In the course of a few hours' the director of the Senate's Legal Bureau 'prepared a draft for major constitutional amendment, which removed from the Stalin Constitution virtually all attributes of so-called real socialism'.[2] The state was no longer a 'republic of working people'; it was now identified as a 'democratic state based on the rule of law, realizing the principles of social justice' (Art. 1).[3] The Communist Party lost its 'leading role' and socialism was expunged from the Constitution, as was reference to Poland's alliance with the Soviet Union. Local government bodies were no longer merely bodies subordinate to central government administration but autonomous agents of self-government. Instead of

1 See Wojciech Sokolewicz, 'The Polish Constitution in a Time of Change', *International Journal of the Sociology of Law*, vol.20, no.1, 1992, pp.29–42.
2 Bronisław Geremek and Jacek Żakowski, *Rok 1989: Geremek Opowiada, Żakowski Pyta*, Warsaw, 1990, p.376.
3 All citations from the amended Constitution of 1952 are based on the unified version published in *Rzeczpospolita* 119, 23 May 1991.

strict limits on the private sector, economic activity was now guaranteed freedom of action without regard to type of ownership. Individual civil liberties were no longer automatically limited by the superior rights of the collective or subject to the arbitrary interference of the PZPR. The Polish People's Republic became the Polish Republic, and the old symbol of the crowned eagle was restored. Then, in the autumn of 1990, further constitutional amendment provided for direct election of the president. The old 'Stalinist' Constitution of 1952 was now unrecognizable. The constitutional framework was a liberal democratic one, safeguarded by the role of the Constitutional Tribunal, which retained the power to declare a law unconstitutional.

The Senate and the *Sejm* began work on a new constitutional settlement.[4] However, by the time the first draft proposals were ready, the parliamentary elections of 1991 were drawing near. A general feeling emerged that the Constitution should be left to the new parliament, whose legitimacy would be gained through a fully democratic electoral process. However, that parliament, in turn, was beset with internal political conflicts, rendering the necessary two-thirds majority difficult to achieve, and it was only after the inauguration of the Suchocka government in July 1992 that some progress was registered.

Thus the first stage of change was swift and almost painless not only because of the existing political consensus, but also because the communist world had been concerned to demonstrate its own democratic credentials by producing constitutions which (on paper) were strong parliamentary systems. However, removing the Communist Party from its monopoly position not only transformed the Polish system from a formally socialist to a formally liberal democratic one: it also transformed a highly executive-centred political system with a relatively passive parliament into a parliament-centred system with a relatively weak executive. Furthermore, a previously unified and disciplined political executive was now itself divided into two elements, government and president. In a time of rapid change, with perceived urgency for wide-ranging measures to be taken quickly but without the presence of developed political parties, this was a recipe for political conflict.

This conflict emerged with the election of Lech Wałęsa in Decem-

4   See Janina Zakrzewska, 'Czas konstytucji', *Krytyka* 36, 1991, pp.72–3.

ber 1990. Wałęsa found the confines of the presidency very restrictive, and his chafing at the bit was highly visible. His animosity towards the 'contract *Sejm*' and his tendency to issue statements directly counter to the policies of the Bielecki government highlighted the need to redefine the relationship of the key political institutions. Constitutional change became a key item of the parliamentary agenda. The president's supporters, especially the Centrum, favoured enhanced presidential powers, while his opponents were not displeased at the existing restraints, which they saw as effectively curbing Wałęsa's boundless ambition.

The need for a new Constitution became more pressing as the political environment became less conducive to achieving it. The relationship between the president and the *Sejm* deteriorated through the summer of 1991. Successive proposals materialized to try to mitigate the consequences of such a strong parliament. These included repeated proposals for a 'Little Constitution', a temporary measure regulating specific but limited areas pending agreement on the final shape of the politico–legal system. They also included various suggestions for granting the government the power to rule by decrees having the force of law. The *Sejm* would accede to neither. Bielecki's proposals for rule by decree failed in the summer of 1991 and his Little Constitution failed in September. The *Sejm* had determined to pass the constitutional issue to its freely elected successor.

The 1991 elections, however, simply generated further muddle. Wałęsa delayed Olszewski's confirmation as prime minister for several weeks, even though it seemed clear that Olszewski could muster a temporary majority in the *Sejm*. Wałęsa may have hoped to win support for his proposed 'Little Constitution', strengthening the president's control of government, in exchange for nominating Olszewski; but the *Sejm* proved unenthusiastic at the prospect of a government which it would be virtually unable to dismiss. After its confirmation the Olszewski government became embroiled in controversy with the president over their respective jurisdictions in foreign policy and defence. The government proved unable to build bridges with either the president or parliament, and there was no chance that its request for special powers would succeed. In the meantime the political configuration had done an acrobatic flip, as the Centrum (erstwhile supporters of a strong executive presidency) now advocated a strong parliamentary system, while Mazowiecki's Democratic Union had become more favourably inclined to a hybrid presidential–parliamentary arrangement.

After Olszewski's fall and the failure of Pawlak to construct a parliamentary majority, the political parties were shocked into a new spirit of compromise. The Suchocka government supported proposals for a Little Constitution, emerging from a parliamentary commission after four months' hard labour. On 1 August the *Sejm* gave its approval, achieving a two-thirds majority with the support of the seven coalition parties, plus the successor parties – the PSL and the Democratic Left Alliance. The Centrum and Olszewski's new Movement for the Republic constituted the bulk of the opposition, while the KPN abstained.[5] The Little Constitution returned to the *Sejm* in October, when it rejected virtually all Senate amendments. Following the president's signature, the Little Constitution came into force in December 1992.

The Little Constitution resulted from political compromise, not from abstruse principles of constitutional law. One reluctant advocate found it 'a giant rulebook', lacking vision: 'a compromise between what is and what is'.[6] Geremek agreed that it was a question of 'tit for tat'.[7] Basically it represented an attempt to find specific solutions to the problems which had emerged in the first two years of post-communist government.[8] Views were mixed as to its clarity and likely effectiveness, particularly over the vexed question of presidential power. Yet assuming the continuation of political good will, the new arrangements did assist Suchocka's survival and facilitated a more cooperative relationship between president and government. Before looking further at the provisions of the Little Constitution, however, it is pertinent to survey the workings of the key political institutions during the years 1989–92.

5	The KPN questioned the result on the grounds that its abstentions had been incorrectly counted. A recount could have been decisive since the Little Constitution passed with a margin of only seven votes, but the protest was rejected; see *Życie Warszawy* 184, 3 August 1992; *Rzeczpospolita* 181, 3 August 1992.
6	Dawid Warszawski, 'Regulamin', *Gazeta Wyborcza* 182, 4 August 1992.
7	Interview with Bronisław Geremek, *Rzeczpospolita* 187, 10 August 1992.
8	For further detail see Louisa Vinton, 'Poland's "Little Constitution" Clarifies Wałęsa's Powers', *RFE/RL Research Report*, vol.1, no.35, 1992b, pp.19–26.

THE PRESIDENCY 1989-92

The presidency was a new institution in 1989, replacing and taking over most functions of the Council of State. The president was initially elected by the two houses of parliament sitting as the National Assembly. During the Round Table negotiations the establishment side pressed for a strong presidency, reflecting the unstated assumption that Jaruzelski would be its first occupant. Solidarity preferred more modest functions; but given its acceptance that Poland would continue to be dominated by the communists (and conscious of Poland's relationship to the USSR), it did not press the point hard, although it did achieve some concessions. The president was conceived as the guarantor of the Round Table agreement. The powers granted included those of a ceremonial nature associated with the position of head of state, plus a number of politically significant ones. These included the power to dissolve parliament and call early elections in certain circumstances: if the *Sejm* failed to approve a government within three months, or to pass the state budget, also within three months; or if the *Sejm* passed legislation preventing the president from carrying out his role as 'guardian of the Polish Constitution, the protector of Poland's national sovereignty and security and the integrity of its territory; and the safeguard of its international political and military alliances' (Art. 32, para. 2). The president gained the right of legislative initiative and also the right to veto legislation and issue implementing regulations. However, the power hitherto enjoyed by the Council of State to rule by decree while parliament was not in session was removed by the expedient of eliminating parliamentary sessions. The president did gain the right to declare a state of emergency for up to three months in the event of a threat to internal security or natural disaster. The president had the power to nominate the prime minister and to express views on candidates for ministerial posts, in addition to the right to summon and chair sessions of the government (the Council of Ministers).

Not all these provisions were unambiguous and there was scope for conflict within the executive itself. The relationship between president and prime minister remained unclear and some of their functions (in foreign and defence policy and matters of internal order) were shared.

Jaruzelski and the Presidency

When General Wojciech Jaruzelski became president of Poland in July 1989 he immediately resigned as leader of the PZPR to indicate his trans-party stance. As president he was unobtrusive, a style which seemed to suit his personality but also the changing circumstances: the rapid changes elsewhere in Eastern Europe and in the USSR itself deprived him of external support. At the same time the internal disintegration followed by the dissolution of the PZPR in January 1990 deprived him of a domestic power base. His support in the military remained considerable, but the personal scars caused him by the experience of martial law in the 1980s precluded its use for political ends.

Jaruzelski developed a cooperative working relationship with Prime Minister Mazowiecki, and the powers of the presidency presented no problems for the initial reform process. There were no overt tensions in the relationship, which the prime minister always described in positive terms. Jaruzelski had some limited influence on personnel matters.[9] He was kept informed about developments within individual ministries (Kuroń later saw intelligence reports sent to Jaruzelski on his own attitude to the *nomenklatura*). However, his actions were never in doubt from a legal–constitutional point of view. In discussions of constitutional reform Jaruzelski raised several matters, but not, thought his interlocutor Geremek, 'for the purpose of bargaining'; he wished assurances, for example, that the costs and benefits of deleting friendship with the USSR had been fully considered; but reiterated his loyalty to the government.[10] Jaruzelski did not speak publicly on controversial issues. He made no use of his right of legislative initiative. He vetoed only one piece of legislation, governing the sale of state land to foreigners, in October 1990. He stated his reservations 'in a few matters', notably over the confiscation of property from the PZPR and the removal of some retirement benefits from former notables, but without success; on minor matters the *Sejm*

9   Witold Bereś and Jerzy Skoczylas (eds), *Generał Kiszczak mówi ... prawie wszystko*, Warsaw, 1991, p. 277; W. Bereś and K. Burnetko, *Gliniarz z 'Tygodnika': Rozmowy z byłym ministrem spraw wewnętrznych Krzysztofem Kozłowskim*, Warsaw, c.1991, pp.26–7.
10   Geremek and Żakowski, op. cit., pp.378–9.

accepted the president's views.[11]

However, Jaruzelski constituted a powerful symbol of the old system and he became the centre of attention after Wałęsa revealed his own presidential ambitions. Wałęsa criticized the Jaruzelski presidency (unjustly) as a destabilizing factor in Polish political life. The Marshal of the *Sejm* of that time, Mikołaj Kozakiewicz, refers to the 'decidedly unpleasant atmosphere' surrounding the pressure on Jaruzelski to resign.[12] Jaruzelski for his part had anticipated a shortened term of office. He accepted new provisions for direct election of the president, now limited to two five-year terms. His resignation came after just over one year of his (then six-year) term; it was, he said, a decision taken in the national interest; the time had come to take the 'next step in the democratization of the state'.[13] The departure of Jaruzelski and the election of Lech Wałęsa brought to the fore new issues of presidential power and the relationship of the president to the government on the one hand and parliament on the other.

The Wałęsa Presidency in 1991

Lech Wałęsa's presidential inauguration took place on 22 December 1990. Wałęsa demonstratively chose to receive the presidential insignia not from Jaruzelski but from the émigré Polish President Ryszard Kaczorowski. 'It was not,' commented Walicki, 'an act of national reconciliation but a triumphalist gesture'.[14] Nor was national reconciliation to be a notable characteristic of Wałęsa's first months in office.

Lech Wałęsa clearly expected to be a strong president. He used tough imagery. He would 'knock heads together'. He would 'cast brother against brother'. He would be a 'Flying Dutchman' travelling around the country to sort things out. He personally 'did not want to be president', but someone must represent the nation and get things moving. Equally clearly, Wałęsa found it difficult to understand the

---

11 Mikołaj Kozakiewicz, *Byłem marszałkiem kontraktowego ...*, Warsaw, c.1991, pp.44–5.
12 Ibid., p.45.
13 Interview in *Rzeczpospolita* 232, 5 October 1990.
14 Andrzej Walicki, 'From Stalinism to Post-Communist Pluralism: The Case of Poland', *New Left Review* 185, 1991, p.121.

nature of the presidency and the political framework within which it operated. This lack of awareness, reflected in his numerous interviews, made for an inconsistent approach. Often Wałęsa would announce his intentions, only to withdraw again as he encountered legal or political constraints. Introducing direct elections had given the president an independent legitimacy; but there had been no addition to the presidential powers agreed by the Round Table. Wałęsa needed the cooperation of government and parliament; yet he had no political base of his own and few powers of patronage.

The first problem arose with the appointment of Mazowiecki's successor as prime minister. Jan Olszewski found Wałęsa unwilling to give him a free hand in forming a government. They disagreed over matters of policy and personnel. Olszewski's nomination was never put to the *Sejm*, while Mazowiecki also refused to resume the post after his resounding public vote of no confidence. Wałęsa announced publicly that he could find no one prepared to act as prime minister for a short period; it would thus be necessary to defer parliamentary elections (later he rescinded this acceptance and attacked the *Sejm* for delay). Krzysztof Bielecki proved acceptable to both the president and parliament; yet his appointment marked a departure from Wałęsa's repeated commitment to 'acceleration' in favour of a government of continuity, keeping to the broad approach of Mazowiecki.

An early indication of difficulties to come was the controversy over the president's staff. Wałęsa proposed a new, 200-member Political Council (*Rada Polityczna*); it was construed as an attempt to create a 'super-government' or a 'super-parliament' (or both). In the face of a political storm, Wałęsa settled for a Presidential Advisory Committee, which itself generated controversy (February 1991) by advising the abolition of the *popiwek*, the mechanism for taxing wage increases above the accepted norm. This was an attack on a central plank of the government's anti-inflation policy. When the committee called a gathering of economists, this in turn was construed as an attempt to bring down the Bielecki government. In August 1991 the committee caused another stir by expressing the view that Wałęsa should not act as 'President of all Poles' but should stand unequivocally for the forces of independence and democracy (a phrase interpreted as meaning the Centrum and its allies). Wałęsa resisted such suggestions. However, the linking of his advisers and staff with prominent party leaders (especially from the Centrum) who also remained serving members of parliament created considerable confusion of roles, as well as conflict with both government and the *Sejm*. The presidential staff, organized in the Chancellery, was headed by Jarosław Kaczyński, Senator, editor of *Tygodnik Solidarność* and leader of the Centrum. His twin brother Leszek later became the president's Minister of State for National Security (confusingly, the title of minister can apply either to a government post or to an office of the presidency); several other Centrum activists also held important positions. As parliamentary deputies they pushed hard for constitutional solutions to increase presidential power and joined in Wałęsa's battles against the detested 'contract *Sejm*'. However, in the late summer and autumn, prior to the October elections, Wałęsa became increasingly isolated. He publicly criticized his own staff in the Chancellery and continued to express deep frustration at his perceived political impotence.

Wałęsa and the Bielecki Government

Bielecki took office with neither a strong party base nor a cohesive, reliable coalition of support. His government consisted of ministers from different parties, including his own Liberal Democratic Congress; but the parties were tiny, with only a handful of members each in the *Sejm* and no recognition in the country. He owed his position to Wałęsa, whose officials often bypassed the proper ministerial channels and issued direct instructions to ministerial personnel.[15] Wałęsa also advocated economic policies contrary to those of government ministers. For example, in April 1991 Lewandowski, Minister of Property Transformation, presented the government's views on reprivatization (namely, the restoration of property to its previous owners). The government declared itself in favour of limited reprivatization of property which had been illegally confiscated, with compensation in the form of capital shares. The next day Wałęsa's representative presented a draft document proposing the physical return of all possible property with few exceptions, while industrial enterprises would secure 20 per cent of shares to their workers. The government had

15 See, for example, Bereś and Burnetko, op. cit., p.110.

rejected such an approach as impractical and too costly. Right up to the parliamentary elections in October Wałęsa continued to return to his own schemes for distributing wealth to the people. In the foreign policy sphere he bypassed the Foreign Ministry by dispatching his own emissary to Washington in July 1991, and in August failed adequately to liaise with the Ministry of Defence over the attempted Soviet *coup*. However, Wałęsa clearly respected Bielecki and despite the former's propensity to act autonomously, relations were quite good. Wałęsa strongly supported the government's plea for special powers. It affirmed his growing hostility to the *Sejm*, which was becoming increasingly fragmented and wracked with internal acrimony.

THE ROUND TABLE *SEJM*

The Polish Round Table parliament was a bicameral legislature divided into *Sejm* and Senate. Politically, power remained concentrated in the *Sejm*. The Constitution described the *Sejm* as 'the supreme organ of state authority' and 'the incarnation of the will of the Nation' (Art. 20). The Senate did often delay and complicate the legislative procedure, for a two-thirds majority of the *Sejm* was necessary to overrule its amendments to legislation. With one hundred members the Senate was far smaller than the 460-member *Sejm*. Between 1989 and 1991 it was also more homogeneous, being composed (with one exception) of Solidarity members (as a result of the freely competitive election of the Senate in 1989). However, given its lesser political significance, this factor was not a crucial one in 1989–90. In 1991 it tended to support the president, but the *Sejm* was able to assert its dominance.

The most important function of the new *Sejm* was that of legislation. It also had significant investigative powers to control the executive. As it had done under the communist regime, it organized its work in specialist commissions. Despite criticisms to the contrary, the commissions and the *Sejm* itself worked at an intense rate. In the course of its 28 months the *Sejm* passed 247 new laws. Over that period, however, it mutated from an organ of social consensus with massive public support into one bitterly divided and lacking public confidence. The dissolution of the PZPR spawned new groups within parliament. Before the presidential election animosity increased among Solidarity deputies. The Democratic Union and Labour Solidarity left the OKP, while internal factions such as that of the Christian National Union (ZChN) and Christian Democrats undermined its cohesion. Solidarity peasant groupings battled with one another and with their common rival the PSL. After the presidential election the *Sejm* became positively unruly.

Up to December 1992 (when the Little Constitution came into force) government ministers were collectively and individually responsible to the *Sejm*. The *Sejm* could dismiss the government or individual ministers on its own initiative, but the Round Table *Sejm* (June 1989 to October 1991) played no part in the dismissal of government. Prime Ministers Mazowiecki and Bielecki resigned as a result of elections, Mazowiecki having been defeated in the presidential election and Bielecki following the 1991 parliamentary election.

Mazowiecki and the *Sejm*

Tadeusz Mazowiecki led a Grand Coalition of Solidarity with the political forces of the old regime, the communists and their ancillary parties. The communists held the ministries of Defence and Internal Affairs. Solidarity controlled the economy, with the key Finance Ministry entrusted to Leszek Balcerowicz, vigorously committed to the free market and rapid privatization. Despite the varied political complexion of the government, and a majority in the *Sejm* of the old ruling parties, the system benefited from consensual attitudes and co-operation, from both president and parliament, between September 1989 and December 1990. For example, when parliamentary commissions rejected certain prospective ministers, the *Sejm* agreed to vote the government's composition *en bloc*. Popular support for the Mazowiecki government was very high (about 95 per cent according to opinion polls) in the early months, but it declined rapidly – a direct consequence of the inflation and recession which resulted from the government's economic policies and of the 'war at the top' which began in the spring of 1990.

That summer Mazowiecki responded to his critics by removing ministers associated with the old regime, notably General Kiszczak

(Minister of the Interior) and General Siwicki (Minister of Defence). This left Solidarity (or a wing of Solidarity) in control. However, the change did not alter the government's relationship with the *Sejm*. The now former communists continued to support Mazowiecki, although Geremek's negotiating skills were often called upon. Even the withdrawal of the Peasant Party in protest against the government's agricultural policies presented only a temporary difficulty (the *Sejm* refused to endorse the nomination of Artur Balazs as Minister of Agriculture), since the peasants, although a strong element in the *Sejm*, were far from constituting a majority. Nor did the intensifying divisions within the Solidarity parliamentary club (the OKP) find reflection in obstruction of government policies.

Bielecki and the *Sejm*

After the presidential election, the rules of the game changed. The SDRP (successor to the Communist Party), the Peasant Party (PSL) and Mazowiecki's Democratic Union could no longer be relied upon to support the government. The rhetoric of the election campaign had sorely alienated the Democratic Union from the president's wing of Solidarity. Economic decline required hard choices on public spending. Increasing pressure for 'reckoning with the communists' was bound to be resisted by former communists and their allies, who retained considerable strength in the *Sejm*.

Although much legislation had been initiated by the previous government, Bielecki was anxious to press ahead with more controversial matters, especially privatization of large state enterprises. Critics attacked the government for a rigid monetarist stance, the absence of an industrial strategy, and (resulting from these) a breakdown of public services. Neither did Bielecki have the social quiescence characteristic of Mazowiecki's first months in office. Strikes and protests intensified. A series of public corruption scandals erupted. All these factors contributed to open political conflicts with the *Sejm*.

Bielecki complained that parliamentary obstruction was thwarting his economic initiatives. Indeed, by mid-June the *Sejm* had passed none of the 27 bills initiated by the government, although it promised Bielecki a 'fast track' for urgent legislation. Frustrated with the backlog of parliamentary work, the president and prime minister made common cause in the summer of 1991, urging that special powers be granted to the government to legislate by decree in the crucial sphere of the economy. Such powers required a constitutional amendment, and thus a two-thirds parliamentary majority, which the government had little hope of mustering. The *Sejm* took exception to Bielecki's continuing comments on the 'legislative blockage', which it in turn attributed to sloppy government drafting of legislation.[16]

Wałęsa and Bielecki also supported the idea of a Little Constitution. In September Bielecki proposed constitutional changes entailing a shift in the relative power of parliament and government to the advantage of the latter. This Little Constitution found no favour with the *Sejm*. It took the general view that parliament should not bind a future parliament on such significant constitutional matters.

The President and the Round Table *Sejm*

The most blatant manifestation of Wałęsa's conflict with the *Sejm* developed over the electoral law in the first months of 1991. Fully competitive parliamentary elections depended on the passage of a new law: the existing one had been tailored to the Round Table agreement. The *Sejm*'s internal divisions made the drafting process a protracted one, but it finally achieved a compromise; at that very point the president stepped in with a new proposal. By March 1991 there were two draft electoral laws before the *Sejm*, one emanating from its Constitutional Commission and one from the presidential Chancellery. There were substantial differences between the two, although they agreed on the size of the *Sejm*, to remain at 460 deputies, and both advocated a mixed system inspired largely by German electoral law. Each voter would have two votes, one in a single-member constituency and one in a multi-member constituency. In May the *Sejm* approved a compromise, seeking to meet some presidential objections. However, the president vetoed the new law.

To overturn a presidential veto required a two-thirds majority, which the *Sejm* failed to achieve. It moved quickly to accommodate

16 Marshal of the *Sejm* Kozakiewicz notes with some bitterness that the *Sejm* was preoccupied for two months dealing with 65 pages of corrections issued by the government to its budget proposals; Kozakiewicz, op. cit., p.43.

some of Wałęsa's concerns, but it retained the most controversial provision, which required voting for an individual rather than a party list. It then rejected the Senate's attempt at further compromise. Wałęsa was clearly very angry. Within the *Sejm* his support was limited, although Centrum deputies lobbied vigorously on his behalf. It was at this time that Wałęsa launched his series of factory gatherings 'to assess public support', but the response was too mixed to use to political advantage. He threatened to dissolve parliament; this in turn evoked the spectre of constitutional crisis, for the dubious grounds for dissolution was Article 32, namely, that the *Sejm* was preventing the president from carrying out his duties. Wałęsa drew back from confrontation and repeated his veto. This time the *Sejm* easily overturned it; the issue had become an open battle between the two. A reluctant Wałęsa signed the electoral law and parliamentary elections were scheduled for 27 October.

No one approved of the final electoral law (though many defended it as the best compromise in the circumstances). Both president and *Sejm* had urged a mixed system; but in the final version the first-past-the-post element disappeared altogether. The new law was based on proportional representation, with multi-member constituencies supplemented by additional deputies drawn from national party lists. Wałęsa emerged weakened and with no hope of constructing a parliamentary majority of his own to buttress the government's feeble position. Both he and parliament lost popularity and prestige. The *Sejm*'s 90 per cent approval rating registered by opinion polls in November 1989 had become a 60 per cent disapproval rating by July 1991.[17]

These political tensions certainly led the *Sejm* to unite as an institution against incursions by the president or the government. The *Sejm* became a rallying point when unpopular measures were on the agenda. When the Minister of Labour proposed a fundamental shift in the basis of allocating family allowances, the public outcry led him immediately to reverse his decision. However, the government usually managed to get its way, if only after lengthy, often acrimonious battles. The issue of pensions was one which caused a political storm towards the end of Bielecki's tenure, but the *Sejm* ultimately yielded to arguments on financial grounds, although the echoes were to create

17   The poll is from CBOS; see *Życie Warszawy* 253, 28 October 1991.

huge problems for Olszewski's government.

By the time the Round Table *Sejm* convened for the last time in October 1991 it was rent by internal conflicts. Speaker Kozakiewicz in his final address referred to '... the incursion of the manners and style of the street market ...'.[18] The *Sejm* was also in a state of almost open warfare with the president. Wałęsa, who had addressed the Senate the previous day, was ostentatiously absent from the *Sejm*'s closing session. Many divisions resulted from ideological differences and personal animosities. Some resulted from a lack of clarity in the legal framework. Others were a consequence of the political inexperience of new political elites. Some represented attempts to mobilize public support for the forthcoming parliamentary election.

The new constitutional agenda was fairly clear. The main issue for the new parliament was that of the respective powers of the executive and the *Sejm*. The next problem was how to define the relationship between president and prime minister. Ironically, the nature of the new parliament made it unlikely that these questions would be speedily resolved. Its acute political fragmentation was a recipe for the intensification of internal conflicts and thus for the continuation of solutions seen originally as short-term interim ones.

INSTITUTIONAL RELATIONSHIPS AFTER THE 1991 ELECTIONS

The Problem of Government Formation

Wałęsa's problems did not diminish after the elections, for the indecisive result gave institutional ambiguities greater salience. The first pressing problem was that of government formation in a situation with no strong party or obvious coalition. Wałęsa caused a stir in proposing (as one of several variants) to take the office of prime minister himself (as, for example, Boris Yeltsin had done in Russia). This met with strong negative responses from the political parties. Most constitutional lawyers also opposed it. Wałęsa then asked Bronisław Geremek to try to form a government based on the largest party,

---

18 Polish television transmission of the proceedings.

the Democratic Union, but he failed: there was too much hostility to the UD from the other parties. Some argued that Wałęsa expected Geremek to fail and would use this as a springboard for accumulating more power for himself. Indeed, it became customary to see a hidden agenda for increased presidential power in Wałęsa's actions. His typical verbal ambiguities, references to secret plans and a notebook listing possible combinations lent themselves to conspiracy theories, which would intensify throughout the coming months. However, Geremek believed Wałęsa's intentions to be serious. Wałęsa's relations with the Democratic Union's leaders, including Mazowiecki and Geremek, improved as his relations with the Centrum declined.

After the 1991 election the president became alienated from his close colleagues in the Centrum. Hostility between Kaczyński and Wałęsa became increasingly public during negotiations over the composition of a new government. Wałęsa was reluctant to accept the candidacy of Jan Olszewski, who had withdrawn almost exactly one year earlier from a similar position because of programmatic and personnel differences with the president. Kaczyński, however, was pressing hard on the grounds that Olszewski would prove a unifying figure for the complex coalition needed. Wałęsa favoured Bielecki; but Bielecki was never a likely candidate given the hostility of other coalition contenders to his economic policies. In the event, the Liberals withdrew, the president yielded and Olszewski's minority government received parliamentary approval, well within the three-month constitutional limit. The *Sejm's* endorsement owed much to anxiety over Wałęsa's possible responses to continuing uncertainty.

In June 1992 the Olszewski government lost the formal confidence first of the president and then of the *Sejm*. Wałęsa had already been taking soundings on a successor. His nomination of Pawlak proved successful, and Pawlak endorsed the president's view that the Interior Minister and the Secretary of the Council of Ministers be immediately replaced. Wałęsa seemed to have regained the initiative. Yet not only did Pawlak fail to form a government, but he experienced great difficulty in directing a caretaker government composed of hostile ministers from Olszewski's coalition. Pawlak's failure then gave new impetus to the search for a stable majority and more workable institutional solutions. The president was initially reluctant to accept Suchocka, despite the fact that inter-party negotiations had led to agreement on the entire shape of the government. Although the new prime minister stressed her commitment to a cooperative relationship with the presidency, Wałęsa continued for some time to posit the recasting of the government, preferably with a central role for Pawlak.

Suchocka was the last prime minister nominated under these procedures, for the chronic problems experienced in government-formation demonstrated the need for constitutional clarification of the respective roles of the president and *Sejm*. The next prime minister would fall within the terms of the Little Constitution,[19] which addressed the issue in some detail. The basic thrust of the Little Constitution was the notion of a balance of powers, to replace the strong parliament-centred nature of the old system. Thus the process of government-formation would now shift from president to *Sejm* to president and back again, with weakened conditions following successive failures. The process begins with presidential nomination of a prime minister and, on the latter's motion, government ministers. This government must win a vote of confidence in the *Sejm* by absolute majority; otherwise the *Sejm* has to muster an absolute majority for its own candidate. If it cannot, the president's candidate need achieve only a plurality of votes in the *Sejm*. Failure shifts responsibility back to the *Sejm*, which now also requires only plurality. In the event of continued deadlock, the president may either dissolve parliament or appoint a government for six months; if neither it nor an alternative proposed by the *Sejm* can achieve support, automatic dissolution follows.

The Little Constitution also enhances the government's tenure and control of its personnel. Only the *Sejm* can now move the government's dismissal. If the *Sejm* defeats the government on a vote of no confidence but fails to propose an alternative prime minister (the 'constructive vote of no confidence' used in Germany), the initiative shifts to the president. When this happened in May 1993, the president chose to reject Suchocka's resignation; he ordered the immediate dissolution of parliament and the election date was appointed for 19 September.

---

19 An unofficial version of the Little Constitution was published in *Rzeczpospolita* 185, 7 August 1992.

Formal provisions can assist the political process, but political will remains an important ingredient of success. However, in conjunction with other measures, for example a rather different electoral system, and a likely reduction in the number of political parties after the next election, the Little Constitution offers hope, but no certainty, of easing the process of government-formation.

The *Sejm* and the Government, 1991–92

The tempo of parliamentary work continued to be intense in the new parliament, which determined to continue work on some legislation from the previous session. In 1992 deputies initiated twice as many legislative proposals as the government, while the president tended to restrict his initiatives to fundamental matters such as constitutional issues or broad questions of civil liberties. Olszewski took office with no clear strategy and deputies hurried into the breach. The practice was to continue, often with duplication of effort. By the autumn there was a queue of 102 draft laws, of which 26 had come from government. Four dealt with combating alcoholism, four with de-communization or lustration, and ten with retirement pensions. Some proposals that reached the *Sejm* were dismissed outright as irresponsible, but they still took up parliamentary time. For example, the tiny Union of Political Realism (UPR) introduced a bill providing monetary compensation for the owners of property seized by the state from lands once (but now no longer) part of the territory of the Polish state. However, there were also serious initiatives coming from the political parties. During Olszewski's tenure the 'small coalition' of Liberals, Democratic Union and the Polish Economic Programme (PPG) presented a number of bills, including one on reprivatization. The Democratic Union was responsible for a draft electoral law and for the draft of the Little Constitution.

Debates were of uneven quality and, as previously, were marred by extensive raising of points of order and failure to address the matter at hand. The new *Sejm* regulations retained many points subject to legal dispute[20] and procedural wrangles often seemed interminable. Depu-

---

20 See J. Pilczyński, 'Reguły parlamentarnej gry', *Rzeczpospolita* 205, 1 September 1992. The new regulations are *Regulamin Sejmu Rzeczpospolitej Polskiej*, Warsaw, 1992.

ties were accused of various machinations with their voting buttons. Lack of party discipline often undermined decisions of the Convent of Seniors. The lustration resolution, passed in June without a debate, would have made good high farce had the consequences not been so serious. In February 1992 the Olszewski government, frustrated like its predecessor with the cumbersome nature of the legislative process, similarly presented a package of proposals for special powers. Government decrees with the force of law would speed the process of law-making and would provide the ability to close loopholes and eliminate inconsistencies between laws on a pragmatic, *ad hoc* basis as they arose. Many gaps and legal contradictions existed, not least because numerous laws from the communist period remained in force with elements incompatible with new ones. Certain areas, such as elections, individual liberties and presidential prerogatives, were excluded. Parliament would retain all its own legislative power, so it could override or suspend the government's delegated ones. These proposals made good sense in the abstract, but the government was distrusted and its political base was too slender to hope for their adoption.

The Little Constitution included several measures to facilitate government legislative initiatives. Within circumscribed limits, and with the approval of an absolute majority of the *Sejm* (previously two-thirds), the government can rule by decrees having the force of law in a defined sphere for a specified period of time. The government's right to initiatives in these areas is exclusive, so the question of multiple bills on the same subject should not arise. The Little Constitution also provides that the government may require the *Sejm* to give priority to 'urgent' legislative proposals.

Special powers are no panacea, however. The parliamentary backlog is not simply a matter of overloaded commissions dealing with a mass of legislation. Many laws have returned to parliament for subsequent amendment, because of poor drafting, ill-considered consequences, or a change of government direction. Many new laws have lain dormant for long periods because successive ministries have failed to provide the necessary implementing regulations.[21] The Senate has

---

21 See, for example, J. Pilczyński, 'Nie tylko ustawy', *Rzeczpospolita* 47, 25 February 1992.

delayed laws because of the need for its amendments to be overturned by a two-thirds majority of the *Sejm* or accepted by a simple majority. The Little Constitution should reduce this blockage by its provision that Senate amendments are automatically accepted unless overturned by an absolute majority of the *Sejm*. Nor have the *Sejm*'s achievements been inconsiderable. In 1992 it passed 62 laws, including the seminally important Little Constitution, vital taxation and banking measures, controversial laws on radio and television and abortion; and 106 resolutions, requiring action by government ministries. The Little Constitution aims to improve parliament's efficiency by reducing the number of parliamentary clubs (caucus status is now granted to clubs of fifteen members, rather than three), imposing fines for unexcused absences, preventing last minute changes to the agenda, and expanding the Speaker's disciplinary powers. These changes helped to make the Suchocka government hesitant to request a wide sphere of special powers. Certainly for their effectiveness there needs to be a clearly defined government strategy, close inter-ministerial cooperation, and a willingness to take the risk of sole political responsibility.

The Presidency

We have already noted the deterioration in the relationship between Wałęsa and the government of Jan Olszewski. Disputes over control of foreign and security policy and over defence ministry organization and personnel were further exacerbated by the government's overt hostility to the president's closest advisers. Lack of policy coordination was manifest when Wałęsa, in Moscow in May 1992 to sign a treaty with Boris Yeltsin, was embarrassed by the arrival of a coded telegram detailing government reservations to a clause dealing with Soviet troop withdrawals. Lustration provided the proverbial last straw for Wałęsa, who rose to the occasion as a defender of civil liberties but came to be regarded as an object of almost pathological hatred by the grouping around Olszewski's Movement for the Republic and Kaczyński's Centrum. The idea that Wałęsa was the Soviet collaborator identified by the code name 'Bolek' seemed too ludicrous to contemplate; but such charges continued to dog him.

Wałęsa's feud with the Olszewski government eased his relationship with the *Sejm* somewhat, especially with the parties of the small coalition, but also with the successor parties. On the issues of defence policy and lustration, the *Sejm* was firmly behind the president. Olszewski's defeat facilitated cooperation between parliament and president and although Wałęsa was highly critical of the Little Constitution's provisions regarding the presidency, he did not veto the measure. Certainly views were mixed as to the clarity and likely effectiveness of the new arrangements, particularly over this vexed question of presidential power.[22]

The president retains most powers enumerated previously, but his responsibilities in foreign and defence policy are now explicit. The prime minister must seek the president's views on appointments to the ministries of Foreign Affairs, Defence and Internal Affairs, while the president names the chief of the General Staff of the armed forces 'in agreement with', rather than 'on the nomination of' the Defence Minister. Innovatory is the requirement of government counter-signatures for his decisions, save in enumerated areas (including the legislative veto, calling a referendum or elections, convening or dissolving parliament, and granting pardons). The president's staff unsuccessfully urged a longer list of exemptions.

The Little Constitution did not remove institutional friction. Wałęsa's decision to veto legislation restricting retirement pensions for the uniformed services caused an outcry. The president's veto accorded with the Ombudsman's view that the law implied an unacceptable notion of collective responsibility, but as with Wałęsa's other acts of reconciliation, it raised the hackles of vocal anti-communists, including one coalition partner, the ZChN. The Christian nationalists were also unsympathetic to the president's proposals for a Charter of Rights and Freedoms, and Wałęsa aggravated them further when, after protests from representatives of the creative intelligentsia, he refused to sign the nomination of one of their number as Minister of Culture; this immediately raised problems of how to interpret the new constitutional relationship between president and prime minister.

The Little Constitution, then, provides greater foundation for political compromise in a new presidential–parliamentary hybrid, but it cannot eliminate institutional rivalry or political conflict. There are

22 P. Miodowski, 'Mała konstytucja: rewelacja, kompromitująca czy kompromis', *Rzeczpospolita* 190, 13 August 1992; J. Pilczyński, 'Powrót do trójpodziału', *Rzeczpospolita* 177, 29 July 1992; Vinton, op. cit., pp.25–6.

still problems of a technical nature, arising from imprecise drafting.[23] There remain important issues for constitutional regulation, including the sphere of human rights (the president's Charter went to the *Sejm* commission in January 1993) and judicial institutions. The latter, too, have proved controversial and politicians have not scrupled to judge them by political criteria.

CONSTITUTIONAL SAFEGUARDS

Three major institutions serving to safeguard the legal order date from the reforms of the communist regime: the Constitutional Tribunal (*Trybunał Konstytucyjny*), the Tribunal of State (*Trybunał Stanu*) and the Civil Rights Ombudsman (*Rzecznik Praw Obywatelskich*). Their role has facilitated, though not ensured, the establishment of the rule of law.

The Constitutional Tribunal

The Constitutional Tribunal has been limited as a fully independent constitutional court by the legislative-centred nature of the political system, for the *Sejm* has retained the capacity to reject its verdicts by a two-thirds majority. In practice, however, the Tribunal benefited first from the consensus, then from the fragmentation of the *Sejm*, which made achieving a two-thirds majority unlikely. Still, anxiety remains that the Tribunal may be swayed in its decisions by political considerations. The *Sejm* also controls the composition of the tribunal, electing half of its twelve members every four years for a single eight-year term. Members must have appropriate qualifications and an incompatibility rule prevents them from holding other offices of state.

The Constitutional Tribunal assesses the compatibility of laws and regulations with the Constitution, but only for laws coming into force after 1982. It cannot therefore rule on the constitutionality of martial law and this provision is much criticized, not least for that reason. It has been very active, and the politically controversial nature of its

---

23 Piotr Winczorek, 'Zagadki konstytucyjne', *Rzeczpospolita* 294, 15 December 1992; J. Pilczyński, 'Cena kompromisu', *Rzeczpospolita* 39, 16 February 1993.

verdicts has led to calls for changes to its composition and even for its abolition.[24] Although as a legal instrument it is necessarily conservative, the Tribunal has consciously attempted to function as a mechanism of system transformation, largely by using Article 1 of the Constitution, with its general affirmation of democracy and social justice:[25] the social justice provision was the key argument in overturning much of the 1991 pensions law, for example. The Tribunal also annulled part of the legislation confiscating PZPR property because the deadline established for protests by the party's heirs was too short for justice to be done. It has not, however, consistently sought to expand its jurisdiction. It did this in its rejection of the lustration resolution, when the Tribunal interpreted its jurisdiction widely, in opposition to those who claimed that resolutions, unlike laws, were not subject to its ruling. It failed to do so in ruling on the incompatibility of the Code of Ethics of the ('self-governing') Chamber of Physicians, prohibiting abortion, with the then current abortion legislation permitting it; in that case the Tribunal ruled itself incompetent to decide on conflicting ethical norms.

The Church has not hesitated to speak out on rulings of the Constitutional Tribunal. It expressed gratification at the decision to uphold the provisions on religious education in schools. The Ombudsman had referred this issue on the grounds that its introduction required legislation, not merely a ministerial decision, for religious education breached the 1961 law specifying a secular education programme; the Tribunal argued that the measure was acceptable, given that religious instruction was voluntary. The Church was aggrieved, however, at the Tribunal's failure to endorse its claims to recover buildings confiscated from it by the tsarist authorities during the nineteenth century.[26]

The Tribunal is potentially a fundamental safeguard of the rule of law. Its decisions have drawn attention to the requirements of procedural propriety as well as substance. However, its independence needs to be firmly established to safeguard it from political controversy and its jurisdiction needs to be extended to the ability to judge the compat-

24 See, for example, S. Podemski, 'Ludzie, Historia, Przyszłość', *Polityka* 44, 31 October 1992.
25 Janina Zakrzewska, 'Trybunał Konstytucyjny – Konstytucja – państwo prawa', *Państwo i Prawo*, vol.XLVII, no.1, 1992, pp.3–12.
26 S. Podemski, 'Rachunek za historię', *Polityka* 38, 19 September 1992.

ibility of domestic law with Poland's international obligations. Along with the Ombudsman it has begun to prove a valuable instrument of the legal order.

The Civil Rights Ombudsman

The office of Ombudsman dates from 1987. Its task, similar to that of the Ombudsman elsewhere,[27] is to protect citizens' rights and freedoms by investigating whether the actions or omissions of state bodies are in accordance with 'law, the principles of community life and social justice' (Statute, Article 2). Elected by the *Sejm* with the consent of the Senate for a maximum of two four-year terms, the Ombudsman has the right to take the initiative and to respond to requests by groups or individuals. The office has wide-ranging investigative powers, with the right to demand redress of grievances resulting from maladministration and to refer legislation to the Constitutional Tribunal for judgement.

The first Ombudsman, Ewa Łętowska (1988–92), aimed to make the best of a decorative post: '... in the early period', she said, 'even lame dogs didn't take me seriously.'[28] Rapidly, however, she became one of the most respected figures in Polish political life. This prestige undoubtedly increased the compliance of state bodies with her findings (she had few powers to compel adherence), although she felt that her position was not taken seriously: indeed, she saw it as remaining fundamentally unchanged by the Round Table of 1989: 'I was and remained an unwanted child.'[29] Yet there can be little doubt that the new order permitted this institution greater autonomy and a wider field of action. Citizen access is easy, and the use made of the Ombudsman has been enormous. Although about 80 per cent of letters received concern matters outside the Ombudsman's jurisdiction, Łętowska ensured that each one, even the most abusive, received a sensitive, personal reply.[30] To one beginning 'Hello, Whore' came the

---

27 For some useful comparisons with Britain see Howard Elcock, 'Working for Socialist Legality: The Polish Commissioner for Citizens' Rights', *Public Policy and Administration*, vol.5, no.3, 1990, pp.37–47.
28 Ewa Łętowska, *Baba na Świeczniku*, Warsaw, 1992, p.46.
29 Ibid., p.27.
30 Examples may be found in ibid., pp.38, 200–212; see also the selection of letters in each issue of the *Biuletyn Rzecznika Praw Obywatelskich*.

Bureau's answer that 'we regard as a compliment the assumption that at her age Professor Łętowska could earn a living by providing love for payment.'[31] Łętowska also saw her task as an educative one, performed through newspaper articles and regular television appearances. Tadeusz Zieliński, the second Ombudsman, continued the meticulous commitment to the impersonal application of the law. Both office-holders proved courageous defenders of the individual against the bureaucracy, whose officials often responded with uncomprehending anger at the view that redress of grievances should be provided for incompetence or maladministration; at the same time Łętowska's last annual report attacked the 'excessive legalism' of the bureaucracy, that is, its tendency to take decisions without reference to particular circumstances.[32] Many protests have been concerned with maintaining procedural propriety, as in the case of religious instruction, which Łętowska referred to the Constitutional Tribunal. She questioned the disqualification of Party X in the 1991 elections on numerous procedural grounds, including secrecy, the use of out-dated information and failure to justify the decision. The Ombudsman also raised the new Code of Medical Ethics for its incompatibility with laws regulating abortion, confidentiality and medical experiments. She questioned alterations to military insignia made before the law had been formally changed.

Major issues of substance also emerged. There was a continual backlog of work due to shortage of staff,[33] but the Ombudsman has tackled issues involving prisoners' and conscripts' rights, discrimination on grounds of gender or political attitudes, property rights and socio-economic rights.[34] Many decisions attracted major criticism of Łętowska and the institution itself, which continued into the term of her successor, Tadeusz Zieliński. 'My party considers the Ombudsman unnecessary,' stated Henryk Goryszewski of the ZChN, soon to become a government minister 'because it does not honour Papal

31 Łętowska, op. cit., p.201.
32 'Sprawozdanie Rzecznika Praw Obywatelskich za okres 1 XII 1990 r. – 19 XI 1991 r.', *Państwo i Prawo*, vol.XLVII, no.2, February 1992, pp.3–16.
33 For further detail see Howard Elcock, 'Making Bricks Without Straw?: The Polish Ombudsman and the Transition to Democracy', *International Journal of the Sociology of Law*, vol.20, no.2, 1992, pp.175–6.
34 The best source here is the journal issued by the Ombudsman's Bureau, *Biuletyn Rzecznika Praw Obywatelskich*.

social teachings.'[35] Zieliński experienced a major collision with members of the Church hierarchy, the ZChN, and the Catholic press in September 1992. They expressed outrage and demanded his replacement over his formal protest against a Ministry of Education directive introducing ethics into the curriculum and requiring formal assessment of religious education on school reports; for the Ombudsman it violated the principle of separation of Church and state.[36]

Like the Constitutional Tribunal, the Ombudsman is a major safeguard of liberal democratic principles. Critics of the institution regard procedural concerns as empty formalism and the protection of minorities as violating the rights of the majority. The nature of the criticisms alone is an indication of why the Ombudsman is vital in a fragile aspiring democracy.

The Tribunal of State

No one faced the Tribunal of State between 1989 and the dissolution of parliament in May 1993: it thus remained untested, but the list of prospective accused grew rapidly. The Tribunal, elected by the *Sejm* from among its own members and presided over by the President of the Supreme Court, may rule unconstitutional or illegal actions of senior state officials undertaken in the course of their duties. This provides a mechanism of individual accountability, although unlike impeachment, for instance, the Tribunal may hear cases after individuals have left office. In 1992 the Tribunal's scope was extended to include the president, who may be called to account jointly by the two houses of parliament.

The first decision to refer a case to the Tribunal was taken by the Round Table *Sejm* in its final days. Mieczysław Rakowski, contrary to the view of the *Sejm*'s Commission on Constitutional Responsibility, was required to account for his decision to close the Lenin Shipyard in Gdańsk in September 1988. The commission found insufficient evidence to judge Rakowski's decision to have been politically (rather

35 Quoted in *Wprost* 7, 14 February 1992.
36 See, for example, 'Czy rzecznik praw obywatelskich pragnie dobra młodzieży?', *Słowo Powszechne* 150, 8 September 1992; *Życie Warszawy* 219, 14 September 1992; see also H. Kuligowski, 'Wojna Religijna', *Polityka* 42, 17 October 1992.

than economically) motivated;[37] the minority took its dissenting view to the *Sejm*. After a protracted and hostile debate the *Sejm* voted by a single vote to refer the former prime minister to the State Tribunal. During the next vote, on the co-responsibility of the Ministers of Industry and Finance and the deputy prime minister at that time, the absence of a quorum was discovered, manufactured when Left Alliance deputies failed to press the buttons signalling their presence. This meant that Rakowski would stand alone before the Tribunal. The vote on Rakowski took place along party lines: the OKP, Democratic Union and Labour Solidarity voted in favour; the Democratic Left and PSL voted against.

The use of the Tribunal of State as an instrument of ministerial responsibility reappeared after the 1991 parliamentary elections. A group of fifty deputies (later increased) may refer an individual to the *Sejm*'s commission on responsibility, for recommendation to refer the case to the Tribunal. By autumn 1992 it was investigating a number of former communist officials over the introduction of martial law; another group of ministers under Rakowski and Mazowiecki over the anti-alcohol affair; Jaruzelski and Kiszczak for the destruction of Politburo protocols dating from 1982–89 (deemed part of the national archive); and Pawlak for his dismissal of Ministers Macierewicz and Siwek. Subsequent proposals to add Bielecki, Lewandowski, Balcerowicz, Olszewski and Macierewicz to this list increased fears that the Tribunal of State would become a political plaything, rather than a serious mechanism of accountability. However, it appears wise to withhold judgement until the Tribunal begins to deal with cases presented to it.

THE CHARACTER OF INSTITUTIONAL CHANGE

The relationships between different elements of the government structure have been complex and often confused in the three years following the Round Table settlement. Hopes that a consensual vision

---

37 The Commission's report is reproduced in Mieczysław Rakowski, *Zanim stanę przed Trybunałem*, Warsaw, c.1992, pp.25–31; Rakowski rehearses his defence here, pp.7–25.

of the desired political structures would quickly result in a new constitutional settlement proved unfounded. The immaturity of political parties, legal ambiguities and friction between strong personalities prevented negotiation of a comprehensive new order. The political transformation was often painful, and it seemed to be occurring on a different plane from the daily concerns of the population, which was bemused and often angered by the heated nature of the conflicts and their apparent lack of relevance.

None the less, the first stage of constitutional change, the amendment of the 1952 Constitution, provided the basis for further evolution of the polity by eliminating the essential features of the communist political system. In the ensuing political struggles the new holders of power maintained their commitment to the principle of the rule of law. President Wałęsa, often judged to harbour authoritarian tendencies and undoubtedly motivated to concentrate power in his own hands, cannot be accused of illegal or unconstitutional actions. Rather, he has sought to expand his power through the legal order. It is also worth emphasizing that successive governments, including the controversial Olszewski government, have yielded power peacefully. New behavioural norms have begun to take root and the guardians of the legal order have proved vigilant.

The Little Constitution, operative from December 1992, has not removed all areas of uncertainty and ambiguity. There will surely be a process of continuing trial and error to refine the formula for the presidential–parliamentary variant of liberal democracy. Conflicts over the nature of the state are by no means settled. Yet the groundwork has been laid, experience has been accumulated, and a measure of institutional stability has been achieved.

7. Privatization, De-communization and Civil Liberties

The determination of new elites to base the post-communist system on democratic values has been one of our recurring themes. Democratic government is limited government; hence, the rule of law and individual rights are simultaneously prerequisites and conditions of democracy. The acknowledgement and protection of individual civil liberties constitute a fundamental dimension of system transformation, and most of the key issues which have emerged in the first years of the transition period have implications for civil liberties, although none can be simply reduced to questions of civil rights. This chapter will illustrate the problems of transformation in three broad areas, each involving attempts to redefine rights and entailing significant conflicts of rights: the area of property rights, focusing on the issue of privatization; secondly, that of de-communization, not only in regard to lustration but also in the wider sense of the rejection of communist values; and third, the broad area of socio-economic rights, concentrating on the examples of health service and pension rights.

Civil liberties were carefully enumerated in the Polish Constitution of 1952. The concept of civil liberties was wide, incorporating both the so-called 'negative' freedoms, providing scope for individuals to act without hindrance, and 'positive' freedoms, requiring positive actions by the state. The first category includes the freedoms of expression, association, assembly and conscience; it embraces the concept of the right to a fair trial and due process of law, plus the inviolability of the person and the right to property. These are the rights associated with liberalism, embracing the view that a clear line should be drawn between the public sphere, defined by the activities of the state, and a private sphere, where the state should not intrude. In communist practice, the rights of the collective took precedence over the rights of the individual, while collective rights were interpreted and confined by the PZPR. The permitted scope of individual rights fluctuated greatly over time, and this was aided by the vague and elastic nature of many legal provisions.

The second category of 'positive' rights, which embraces socio-economic rights such as the right to work, health, education, and welfare. In Western Europe the state increasingly made provision for its citizens to enjoy such collective goods, but they rarely achieved the status of 'rights'. The communist system attached greater value to socio-economic rights, which were portrayed as a major ingredient of the superiority of the socialist system. Full employment, comprehensive education and health-care systems, and social security benefits were highly developed, if never fully adequate.

The main consequence of the experience of the first years of post-communist government has been a strengthening of certain 'liberal' rights and a weakening of socio-economic rights. The erosion of socio-economic rights has been partly deliberate and partly an unintended consequence of policy in other areas, particularly in the economy. The extensive system of state social provision has been whittled away by the economic measures of successive governments. Although the old system was inefficient, inadequate and distorted by *nomenklatura* privileges, its dismantling has been met with dismay.

PRIVATIZATION

Throughout Eastern Europe the transformation of bureaucratized central planning into free market capitalism became the desired end of post-communist development. Proponents of a 'third way' between capitalism and 'really existing socialism' found themselves shunted aside in the wholesale rejection of communist or socialist ideology and the wholehearted embrace of the market's invisible hand. Given the dominant role of state ownership in the economy on the one hand and the urgency of economic transition on the other, privatization became the unquestioned instrument of economic change and a mantra of hope for the future.

Poland was viewed as fertile ground for privatization and, more generally, the acceptance of new legal regulations governing property rights. Poland had considerable experience of private enterprise, with most peasants owning their own land and a traditional handicraft and artisan sector, plus some small shopkeepers and manufacturers. The communist governments of the 1980s had acquiesced in a rapid expansion of the private sector.[1] Leasing arrangements became common in the retail sphere. The government also facilitated the establishment of enterprises by Poles abroad (Polonia firms). Beginning in 1987 state enterprises could transform themselves into joint-stock companies. Often they became a vehicle of *nomenklatura* capitalism, the transformation of the old *nomenklatura* into a new bourgeoisie. Most commonly, state firms would sell off lucrative elements of the business to favoured insiders.[2] Advocates of a wider privatization process emerged in academic and entrepreneurial circles.[3]

When Solidarity assumed control, transformation of the economic system became an explicit objective. Powerful (if oversimplified) arguments were adduced in favour of extending capitalism by lifting restrictions on private enterprise and by privatizing state enterprises. First, the prosperous countries of the capitalist West are based largely on private ownership. Many, such as Britain, had been reducing the role of their nationalized industries. Margaret Thatcher was extremely popular in Poland not only because of her vigorous anti-communist stance but because of her perceived economic achievements. Clearly, capitalism provided a successful model of economic development. Secondly, it was argued that private enterprise is inherently more efficient, more innovative, and more responsive to its consumers than are publicly owned producers because of the discipline of competition and the effectiveness of the profit motive. Thirdly, the long experience of reform in Soviet-type systems had failed; this proved that they were in essence unreformable. Fourthly, private ownership would undermine the basis of the old regime's political power by firmly entrenching the right to own property. Indeed, the 'people', who had constituted the nominal owners of state enterprises, would have the

1   Jacek Rostowski, 'The Decay of Socialism and the Growth of Private Enterprise in Poland', *Soviet Studies*, vol.XLI, no.2, 1989, pp.194–214.
2   Jadwiga Staniszkis, '"Political Capitalism" in Poland', *East European Politics and Societies*, vol.5, no.1, 1991, pp.127–41.
3   See, for example, the work by the future minister Lewandowski and his colleague: Janusz Lewandowski and Jan Szomburg, 'Uwłaszczenie jako fundament reformy społeczno-gospodarczej: Zarys programu' in L. Siemon (ed.), *Propozycje przekształceń polskiej gospodarki*, Warsaw, 1989.

opportunity to become genuine participants in the capitalist process, while those whose property had been seized by the communist regime would have redress for the wrongs done to them. Polish sociologists reported increasing public sympathy for capitalist ownership. Contempt for private shopkeepers and market gardeners gave way to 'the myth of the market' and its beneficent consequences.[4]

Broadly speaking, then, privatization was seen as the key instrument for creating capitalism. Privatization may take many forms, and much debate has centred on the appropriate mechanisms to be adopted for the industrial giants which dominate Polish industry. Small-scale privatization, however, proceeded apace. In many instances ownership title lay clearly with local government or individual ministries. Sales by auction and management and worker buy-outs transformed retailing and services from state to private owners. By September 1991, 75 per cent of retail trade was in private hands. New owners were endowed with new property rights.

The privatization of large firms was another matter. Balcerowicz had prepared the way with his stabilization programme: state subsidies were being phased out and tariffs lowered in an effort to force enterprises to adapt to the demands of the market or perish. In August 1990 the *Sejm* passed general enabling legislation (Law on the Privatization of State-Owned Enterprises) which authorized a variety of forms of privatization and created the Ministry of Ownership Transformation to oversee the process. These laws also provided for the creation of a stock market, which began to operate in April 1991. Tax concessions were offered as an incentive to privatization, notably from the infamous *popiwek* and the strange tax on capital assets (the *dywidenda*). The Monopoly Commission was also established in 1990.

Numerous obstacles to privatization were certainly acknowledged, but they were underrated, with the result that both the Mazowiecki and Bielecki governments were wildly over-optimistic in their expectations of what could be achieved. The absence of economic infrastructure – banking, communications, capital markets – was one important area. Lack of clarification of ownership relations and the absence of laws governing commercial contracts, liability, and bank-

4   Lena Kolarska-Bobińska, 'Poczucie krzywdy społecznej a oczekiwanie opiekuńczej roli państwa' in Władysław Adamski *et al.*, *Polacy '90. Konflikty i zmiana*, Warsaw, 1991, pp.37–44.

ruptcy was another. There was insufficient expertise in management, accountancy, actuarial assessments and asset valuation, and marketing. Enterprise culture was steeped in the expectation of state assistance. Despite the recognition of these problems, the first two post-Solidarity governments relied largely on the spontaneous regenerative capacity of the 'market', coupled with Western assistance. They failed to recognize 'that even under capitalism nonmarket institutions are critical for the construction of viable economic relationships'.[5]

The first step in the privatization process for medium and large enterprises was their 'commercialization'. This removed any doubts concerning formal ownership title, for commercialized enterprises became joint stock companies (*spółki akcyjne*), with the Treasury holding all shares. The ministries would relinquish their management functions to independent boards of directors, who would in turn develop plans for restructuring and prepare estimates of their firm's value for privatization. Management could not proceed without the endorsement of the workers' council, and employees were given the right to buy up to 20 per cent of shares at half price.

The Mazowiecki government's preference for public sale on British lines, that is, case-by-case preparation and sale, proved complex, costly and clumsy. 157 large-scale enterprises were selected for the first round of privatization, but by November 1990 only twenty of these had been commercialized; only five were offered for sale in the first round. Valuation of assets was particularly difficult and controversial. Lack of domestic capital was another obstacle, as the savings overhang had been quickly absorbed by inflation. Only Exbud, a construction firm, was over-subscribed by the original closing date. State banks were 'persuaded' to buy shares in three companies.[6] The cost of foreign advisers, administration, prospectuses and advertising was high; the five firms generated only some 230 billion (230,000 million) zloties for the state's coffers.[7]

This type of privatization transfers the ownership of firms to those

5   Janusz Dabrowski, Michal Federowicz and Anthony Levitas, 'Polish State Enterprises and the Properties of Performance: Stabilization, Marketization, Privatization', *Politics and Society*, vol.19, no.4, 1991, p.405.
6   George Blazyca, *Poland's Next Five Years*, London, 1991, p.42.
7   Ben Slay, 'Poland: An Overview', *RFE/RL Research Report*, vol.1, no.17, 1992a, p.17.

individuals who can afford to buy shares. Solidarity's long-standing emphasis on workers' self-management found no echo in government proposals, although the government had to ensure the consent of the workers' councils because of the 'self-governing' nature of enterprises under the existing law of 1981. The government rejected workers' ownership for three basic reasons.[8] Workers could be put in double jeopardy, risking both their jobs in the enterprise and the savings invested in it. Workers could prove more inclined to allocate funds to wages than to investment, so workers' ownership would be inefficient. Finally, the process would be inequitable, for workers in more modern industries could expect high yields from their shares, while those operating obsolete plant would earn little (those in hopeless enterprises would of course gain nothing). Opportunities for workers to take over their own enterprises were not entirely precluded, and some success stories could be identified.[9] However, the issue remained contentious and numerous subsequent schemes tried to extend the notion of 'popular capitalism', while the trade unions became increasingly hostile to privatization.

Krzysztof Bielecki's minister responsible for 'Ownership Transformation', Janusz Lewandowski (January–December 1991), set a new tone for discussions of privatization, while issues of restitution and reprivatization – the restoration of property to previous owners – moved up the agenda. The government accepted restitution in principle, as the restoration of rights illegitimately denied by the communist regime. However, it took the view that physical restoration of property which had been expropriated should be limited; the major form of restitution would be financial compensation through the issue of capital bonds. This view was opposed by President Wałęsa. However, the government argued a pragmatic case with two main arguments. The first was the high cost to the state budget, whether from financial compensation to former owners or from the opportunity costs of returning property which could otherwise be sold. The second was that the sheer complexity of trying to resolve conflicting claims to ownership would prolong the privatization process, perhaps by more

8   Adam and Zbigniew Fallenbuchl, 'Privatization and Marketization in Poland', *Studies in Comparative Communism*, vol.XXIII, nos 3–4, 1990, p.352.
9   J. Poprzeczko, 'Sto milionów dla każdego', *Polityka. Prywatyzacja,* January 1993.

than a decade.[10] One dimension of the problem was establishing what to do with property which had been transformed over the 45 years of communist rule.

Neither the Bielecki government nor its successors succeeded in getting a law on reprivatization through the *Sejm*[11] although some restitution was made by the courts where expropriation was declared to have violated the law of the time; 352 such decisions were issued by the end of 1991.[12] The major exception related to the Church: in autumn 1991 the *Sejm* made special provision for restitution of property formerly owned by the Catholic Church.

Lewandowski worked quickly to shape his new 'privatization offensive', and he was willing to countenance a variety of methods. Six more firms were sold by public offer in 1991. Numerous firms, especially small ones, were privatized by means of 'liquidation' or 'asset' privatization, which was a means of both forcing firms into bankruptcy and preparing relatively healthy firms for purchase or leasing; this was to prove the most popular route. The government also began to woo foreign investors to purchase strategic stakes in major firms. Foreign capital had been discouraged by lack of stability in the legal arrangements (for example, taxes and tariffs), as well as by political uncertainties. The Johnson & Johnson heiress Barbara Piasecka-Johnson finally withdrew her offer to buy the Gdańsk shipyard after controversies over asset valuation, complicated by the sale of parts of the enterprise to private firms which continued to operate on the yard's premises. However, Phillips, Unilever, Coca-Cola, Thomson, Gerber and a few other multinationals took advantage of favourable terms to acquire majority stakes in eighteen firms. By September 1991 sixteen Western financial institutions had been awarded contracts to oversee planned 'sectoral privatizations', including paper and packaging (Hambros), ball bearings (Kleinwort Benson) and power engineering (Samuel Montague).

In June 1991 Lewandowski announced the details of the 'leap into

10 Slay, op. cit., p.19.
11 The Bielecki government's Bill was published in *Rzeczpospolita* 154, 4 July 1991; its successor, presented by the small coalition of the UD, KLD and PPG, is in *Rzeczpospolita* 199, 25 August 1992.
12 These decisions mainly affected mills, hotels and bakeries: see *Rzeczpospolita* 28, 28 January 1992.

capitalism', the PPP or Mass Privatization Programme (*Program Powszechnej Prywatyzacji*). He had been a long-standing advocate of mass privatization through the direct distribution of vouchers as a means of extending property rights to those without capital. However, his final version opted for a system based on intermediary institutions.[13] Four hundred large firms would be commercialized and a number of investment funds would be created, with their shares distributed to the public. The funds in turn would receive 60 per cent of the stock of the 400 firms; they would be the majority shareholders, and they were expected to be largely foreign; their task would be to maximize the value of the enterprises in their portfolios. The state would retain 30 per cent of shares, and ten per cent would be given to the firms' employees. The public would own the investment funds, whose own shares would be traded at a later stage, bringing them close to United States mutual funds or British unit trusts.[14]

The viability of the programme was called into question by deepening recession and rising unemployment, with fears that inflationary pressures would be generated by creating new paper assets which could be sold for cash. Furthermore, the state budget deficit not only made it difficult to give away profitable assets but to find the funds necessary to finance privatization. There were also fears that the investment funds would be controlled and manipulated by foreign firms, while the role of the public would remain entirely passive.[15]

Aside from the economic viability of Lewandowski's plan, there were also political obstacles. The government, of course, did not have a majority in the *Sejm*, and this was a highly controversial issue (the enabling legislation of 1990 had gone through seventeen successive drafts). Opposition on the ground was increasingly important, and it grew stronger as it became clearer that the benefits of capitalism could not be achieved painlessly. Managers, trade unions and workers' councils formed a 'Bermuda triangle' of opposition to privatization,

13 For a general discussion of the economic case for financial intermediaries see Eduardo Borensztein and Manmohan S. Kumar, 'Proposals for Privatization in Eastern Europe', *IMF Staff Papers*, vol.38, no.2, 1991, pp.309–13.
14 Jan Szomburg, 'Prywatyzacja powszechna', *Rzeczpospolita* 167, 22 July 1991.
15 See, for example, H. Bochniarz, J. Krawczyk and A. Wiśniewski, 'Prywatyzacja masowa i dobrze przemyślana', *Rzeczpospolita* 163, 15 July 1991 and *Rzeczpospolita* 164, 16 July 1992; Slay, op. cit., p.18; Barbara Błaszczyk and Marek Dąbrowski, 'Krok w nieznane', *Polityka* 28, 13 July 1992.

which could not take place without their consent. At the same time they engaged in self-destructive tactics such as systematic sale of assets, which served for purposes of short-term survival, while undermining any future prospect of privatization.[16] By mid-1991 the government had shifted somewhat from its hands-off approach to industry. Henryka Bochniarz, the Minister of Industry and Trade, developed a strategy of prioritization of industries, entailing the ranking of firms. At the top would be potential 'winners', to be assisted by government to restructure before privatization; at the bottom hopeless 'losers', to be rapidly liquidated. By October 1991 Lewandowski was also developing plans to counter managerial collusion in the 'deterioration of enterprises to enable them to be bought cheaply at the time of their privatization'.[17] Bureaucratic muddle and cross-cutting jurisdiction, the absence of clear criteria, and outright corruption added to the practical problems and reinforced public anxieties that privatization was a denial of their rights.[18]

The Olszewski government called a virtual halt to privatization, expressing the view that a period of stocktaking had become imperative; in order to go faster, it was argued, one had first to go more slowly. Only six firms were privatized in the first half of 1992, with foreign companies acquiring large holdings. Certainly there was a case for rethinking the early experience. Numerous sources of confusion had emerged. Public confidence had been eroded. The condition of the state enterprises had deteriorated as a result of lack of domestic demand, the collapse of the Soviet market, recession in capitalist countries, and the anxieties of foreign capital regarding the uncertain political situation. Little progress had been made with restructuring the state sector. Indeed, the hard budget constraints, intended to discipline enterprises by making them adapt or perish, proved illusory. Instead, enterprises accumulated an enormous burden of debt through mutual credit and non-payment (these *zatory płatnicze* or cumulative

---

16 Wojciech Bienkowski, 'Poland's Bermuda Triangle', *RFE/RL Research Report*, vol.1, no.17, 1992, pp.22–4.
17 Janusz Lewandowski, quoted in *Gazeta Wyborcza* 232, 4 October 1991.
18 See Joanna Solska, 'Sami Sobie', *Polityka* 35, 31 August 1991; see also Tadeusz Gruszecki's comments in *Rzeczpospolita* 41, 17 February 1992; Andrzej Mozołowski, 'Wnuki nie doczekają', *Polityka* 4, 25 January 1992.

arrears were not a wholly new phenomenon[19]), non-payment of taxes and social security contributions, and borrowing. By the end of May 1992 about 45 per cent of state firms were in debt. In the first half of 1992 570 state firms owed the state budget over 14 billion zloties.[20] Bankruptcy was almost unknown.

However, the Olszewski government never developed an industrial policy to enable the practical implementation of its notion of a unified, coherent policy linking privatization to industrial policy. Gradually the Industry Ministry abandoned the attempt at prioritization, partly because deteriorating conditions made it difficult to assess firms' current financial position and future potential. Most observers condemned the wasted months of Olszewski's period in office. Wałęsa's own privatization programme, envisaging credit of up to 100 million zloties per citizen for the purchase of shares,[21] was also poorly received, not least because of its hyper-inflationary consequences.[22]

Although mass privatization made no progress during the year from mid-1991 to mid-1992, by March 1992 173 of the 400 firms had been commercialized. Increasingly, however, public attitudes to privatization grew less favourable. The oldest research institute for investigating public opinion found that between August 1991 and June 1992 there had been a steady fall in the numbers regarding privatization as beneficial to the Polish economy; 58 per cent of those surveyed thought that large enterprises should remain entirely in state hands.[23] A study of 500 enterprises carried out by the Polish Academy of Sciences, also in June, found a strong sense of injustice among the workers. While in 1991 individual liberties were most highly valued, now they came close to the bottom of the list; equality and social security replaced them.[24]

Lewandowski returned to office with the Suchocka government determined to get the 'privatization express' moving again, with the original 400 firms intended for public privatization increased to 600.

19 See Adam Lipowski, *Mechanizm rynkowy w gospodarce polskiej*, Warsaw, 1988.
20 J. Macieja, 'Nie chcą płacić czy nie mogą?', *Rzeczpospolita* 261, 5 November 1992.
21 'Belwederski wariant masowej prywatyzacji', *Rzeczpospolita* 74, 27 March 1992.
22 See for example Barbara Błaszczyk and Marek Dąbrowski, 'Trzecia próba', *Polityka* 14, 4 April 1992.
23 CBOS *Serwis Informacyjny* 6/1992, pp.44–9.
24 J. Mojkowski, 'Dylemat więźnia', *Polityka. Prywatyzacja*, February 1993.

Now, however, there would be a reconsideration of workers' participation in the process. Lewandowski took seriously the erosion of public confidence. He aimed to coordinate with Kuroń (once again Minister of Labour) negotiations with trade unions for the new social contract. He also hoped that the emergence of a majority government would allay foreign investors' anxieties. Much, however, would depend on the speed of the legislative process: new laws were needed on mass privatization, reprivatization and commercialization, while the existing law on privatization needed amendment.[25] The outbreak of industrial unrest was not calculated to strengthen Poland's appeal to foreign capital, which had amounted only to some 800 million US dollars by mid-1992.[26]

Indeed, the strikes of July and August (see Chapter 4) signalled a growth of serious opposition to privatization, with added suggestions of a xenophobic antipathy to foreign capital. Trade unionists who had hitherto reserved their most bitter invective for one another (for example, Marian Jurczyk of Solidarity '80 and Ewa Spychalska of the OPZZ) now joined forces. Demands for an immediate cessation of privatization were echoed by a number of opposition political parties – not only the KPN, which registered its own new trade union, Kontra, and the SDRP, still allied to the OPZZ, but also the new groupings of Parys and Olszewski. Privatization was attacked as constituting a process of theft of national assets and a denial to workers of their basic rights. In September 1992 Janusz Lewandowski narrowly survived a vote of no confidence in his stewardship of privatization.

The new social contract represented by the Pact for Industry (see Chapter 4) reflected the Suchocka government's desire to accelerate the privatization process and give labour a stake through increased ownership rights. The pact gave some cause for hope of industrial peace, although continuing 'populist demagogy' was perceived as a threat to its gaining social acceptance.[27] However, widespread expectations of a debt forgiveness programme did not encourage enterprises to take action to reduce their debts, and indebtedness to the state budget from non-payment of taxes and social security contributions con-

---

25 Interview with Janusz Lewandowski, *Rzeczpospolita* 170, 21 July 1992; the Bill to amend the 1990 law is in *Rzeczpospolita* 225, 24 September 1992.
26 See Andrzej Mozołowski, 'Zniechęcenie', *Polityka* 31, 1 August 1992.
27 See, for example, *Życie Warszawy* 214, 8 September 1992.

tinued to rise (one demand of striking miners in December was for a cancellation of all enterprise debts), making restructuring programmes more difficult.

The new corporatist approach envisaged a tripartite system of national wage bargaining. In exchange workers would help determine their enterprise's privatization strategy (worker or managerial buyout, public offer, or sale to a single buyer). They would receive ten per cent of their firm's stock and their trade union representatives were to be guaranteed seats on the new boards of directors of the privatized companies. The mass privatization programme (PPP) squeaked through the *Sejm*, but much of the Pact fell with the dissolution of parliament in May.

Thus the mood had soured as the realities of the capitalist system had begun to make themselves felt. Privatization processes had rejected the concept of workers' ownership stressed for so long by Solidarity. However, the growth of resistance must also be linked to the general mood of economic pessimism. Fears that private firms would provide greater labour discipline and fewer jobs played their part, especially when several large and apparently thriving private firms collapsed towards the end of 1992. However, unemployment was bound to result from the restructuring of industry and the bankruptcy of inefficient firms, regardless of ownership. Antipathy to privatization should be seen as a substitute for more diffuse concerns. The loss of the right to work was keenly felt, and the acquisition of new ownership rights was inadequate compensation. Civil liberties in the new Poland did not merely enhance rights, but undermined and revoked them too.

DE-COMMUNIZATION AND CIVIL LIBERTIES

When Mazowiecki became prime minister, he faced a number of major dilemmas of a philosophical nature. One was the question of how the rule of law is to operate in a system where the norms and values embodied in much existing law are alien to democracy and even to the rule of law itself; furthermore, how is respect for and obedience to law to be fostered when so much law is bad law. Secondly, how are the principles of justice, requiring a settling of accounts and restitution of past wrongs, to be combined with the principle of the rule of law and respect for the rights of the individuals who perpetrated these wrongs? Mazowiecki took the position that existing law should be regarded as binding until abrogated by new legislation. Changes in the Constitution, and its recognition as the supreme source of law, would guide judicial interpretation in accordance with the new democratic ethos. There were a number of practical difficulties, however. The process of legislation was lengthy and cumbersome. Defective drafting[28] often meant that legislation had to be resubmitted for amendment and the whole tortuous process repeated. The sheer volume of new laws and regulations led to a state of 'legal chaos' in which it was difficult to determine what legal norms actually applied in given circumstances.[29]

Apart from the practical problems of a piecemeal, evolutionary approach, there were political consequences too. On the one hand, it was apparent that many former communists were happily taking advantage of 'old' law to feather their own nests. Wałęsa made this the rationale for his call for de-communization and 'acceleration' in the spring of 1990 (the 'war at the top'). Although this criticism unfairly suggested a lack of determination to push ahead with new legislation, public outrage was perfectly understandable: most people were getting poorer, but the new red capitalists were visibly getting richer. Similarly, the trade union wing of Solidarity was incensed that the unions were expected to obey communist laws regulating industrial relations. Laws providing considerable security of tenure for those working in the state administration also caused controversy. Some political parties, such as the KPN, argued openly that there was no moral imperative to obey communist law. It was difficult to inculcate a respect for law in such circumstances.

Thus, although the passions aroused by de-communization reached their height with the lustration resolution of June 1992, the issue itself was more far-reaching. The view taken by the Mazowiecki government reflected not merely the continuing presence of communists and

---

28 Wojciech Sokolewicz, 'The Legal–Constitutional Bases of Democratisation in Poland: Systemic and Constitutional Change' in George Sanford (ed.), *Democratization in Poland, 1988–90*, London, 1992, p.71.

29 Anna Sabbat-Swidlicka, 'Poland: Toward the Rule of Law', *RFE/RL Research Report*, vol.1, no.27, 1992, p.30.

ex-communists in the administration, but a generally cautious, evolutionary, approach. Democratization would constitute the main method of de-communization. His government would assume full responsibility for developments during its tenure of office but not for the previous system; a thick line would be drawn between the two. Nor could a principle of collective guilt apply to the Communist Party, its members or successors. Collective guilt violated all basic precepts of individual rights and its boundaries could not be clearly established. Indeed, the whole of society was complicit, either directly or indirectly. As Jacek Kuroń put it at an election rally, the logic of total de-communization would require that 'we all be given a rope with which to hang ourselves'.[30] Mazowiecki's approach, also followed by Bielecki's government, meant that individuals would be judged case by case. National and provincial 'verification commissions' were set up to examine officials of the Interior Ministry to ensure that they possessed appropriate qualifications and experience for their jobs. Those who had violated the laws of the day would be called to account through the judicial process. Many resigned, including most senior and middle-ranking functionaries. About 14,500 presented themselves for verification; of these some 9,800 were finally accepted as suitable for further service,[31] often amid allegations that the commissions were excessively lenient.

Mazowiecki's opponents transformed his expression the 'thick line' (*gruba linia*) into a 'thick full stop' (*gruba kreska*) and his denial of responsibility for communist malpractice into forgiveness or even condoning of the same. They cited slow progress in disbanding the communist media empire, problems over the character and control of television and radio, and the retention of many former communist officials in government ministries. The absence of trials for criminal acts committed for political reasons (that of Płatek and Ciastoń, suspected of masterminding the Popiełuszko murder, did not begin until June 1992) appeared further evidence of attempts to forestall the necessary reckoning with the communist past and to protect 'communist friends'.

---

30 Election rally at the Central School of Planning and Statistics, Warsaw, 15 October 1991.
31 Jan Widacki, *Czego nie powiedział Generał Kiszczak*, Warsaw, 1992, pp.26–8.

During the parliamentary election campaign of October 1991 the Centrum, the ZChN and the KPN prominently carried the banner of de-communization. It then became a major factor holding together the parties of the Olszewski coalition government. Those who endorsed the thick line were almost by definition communist sympathizers. Olszewski and his colleagues were in turn labelled 'Olszewiks' or 'White Bolsheviks' and were accused of willingness to condone departures from the presumption of innocence and the requirement that evidence be provided of individual guilt. President Wałęsa's willingness to acknowledge the loyalty and patriotism of ex-communist military officers was taken as *prima facie* evidence of Wałęsa's sympathy for the old order itself. The issue came to a head in June 1992.

The Lustration Resolution

The lustration issue of how to deal with collaborators of the former regime did indeed constitute a major aspect of de-communization with significant implications for civil liberties. Lustration was defended on a number of grounds. It was necessary in order to demonstrate that collaboration was not just distasteful but also morally repugnant; society required a cleansing or purifying process. It was necessary that people holding high office should have demonstrated their probity. Furthermore, there was a risk that former collaborators could be susceptible to blackmail if their past were not openly revealed; the issue was thus bound up with the vital security interests of the state.

None the less, even many proponents of lustration criticized the *Sejm* for precipitous and cavalier action in adopting the surprise resolution without a substantive debate.[32] The resolution of 28 May 1992 was deeply flawed as regards its civil liberties implications. It will be recalled that it required the Minister of the Interior, Antoni Macierewicz, to provide full information about current public functionaries who had cooperated with the security service in the years 1945–90. It did not specify the criteria to be applied in drawing up the list of 'collaborators'. It provided punishment, namely a ban on holding public office, for actions not prohibited by law. In addition, the method

32   See the verbatim report in *Gazeta Wyborcza* 150, 27–28 June 1992.

chosen by Minister Macierewicz provided no opportunity or mechanism for the accused to clear their names. Both the Chairman of the Supreme Court, Adam Strzembosz, and the Civil Rights Ombudsman, Tadeusz Zieliński, expressed the view that the mere existence of a signature confirming willingness to cooperate with the security services could not constitute sufficient evidence, for in many instances signatures were exacted by coercion and blackmail, with no subsequent substantive acts of 'collaboration'.[33] Others such as Professor Andrzej Ajnenkiel, who had served on the so-called Michnik commission established in 1990 to investigate documents of the Interior Ministry, pointed to the ease with which the word 'informer' could be added to lists of persons in whom the security police took 'an interest' and also the problem of mistaken identity.[34] Mazowiecki's Interior Minister Henryk Mażewski adduced similar arguments to support his refusal to release the names of alleged collaborators; he also stressed that many persons registered as sources of information did not realize that they were conversing with functionaries of the security service.[35]

The opposing view was that Macierewicz had acted properly by providing names in confidence to parliament, while it was the *Sejm*'s responsibility to establish procedures to safeguard individual rights.[36] The head of the controversial Research Department of the Interior Ministry, responsible for identifying former collaborators, vigorously defended the thoroughness of its investigations and the authenticity of its findings,[37] as did Macierewicz himself, despite acknowledging one case of mistaken identity, that of Solidarity Senator Janusz Mazurek.[38]

The Constitutional Tribunal accepted the former view, declaring the lustration resolution to be incompatible with the Constitution's commitment to democratic principles and human rights, as well as in violation of laws governing state secrecy and the protection of an

---

33 'Państwo prawne i lustracja' (Interview with Adam Strzembosz), *Gazeta Wyborcza* 191, 14–16 August 1992; Zieliński, quoted in *Rzeczpospolita* 178, 30 July 1992.
34 Quoted in *Rzeczpospolita* 116, 18 May 1992.
35 Mażewski's speech to the *Sejm* is quoted in Widacki, op. cit., pp.126–8.
36 J. Karpiński, 'Agenci i lustracja – politycy i przeszłość', *Rzeczpospolita* 165, 15 July 1992; Jan Olszewski, *Olszewski. Przerwana Premiera*, Warsaw, 1992, p.16.
37 Interviews with Piotr Woyciechowski in *Życie Warszawy* 151, 27–28 June 1992; and *Tygodnik Solidarność* 27, 3 July 1992.
38 Interview with A. Macierewicz in Jacek Snopkiewicz *et al.*, *Teczkii, czyli widma bezpiek*, Warsaw, 1992, pp.96–7.

individual's reputation. In addition, only legislation, not a resolution, could authorize the Minister of the Interior to encroach on the sphere of individual civil liberties. The *Sejm* had violated its own procedures. The *Sejm*'s own investigative commission accused Macierewicz and Olszewski of personal responsibility for acts of 'political provocation ... aimed at compromising and paralysing the highest organs of state ...'.[39] They were later cleared, however, of attempting to organize or precipitate a *coup d'état*.[40]

Some of those on Macierewicz's list acknowledged the allegations against them; some issued statements of clarification,[41] and others refused all comment. Inevitably other names on the list leaked out, and rumours continued to spread about secret agents in high places. Wałęsa received a humiliating reception from the Fourth Solidarity Congress, and it appeared that there were many who were ready to believe that a communist agent had helped defeat the communists. The serious issue underlying lustration, the legitimate task of the state to protect itself, was buried in a mire of gossip and innuendo.

De-communization after June 1992

After the fall of the Olszewski government de-communization did not weaken as a political issue. Animated rumours circulated regarding secret agents Bolek (allegedly Wałęsa) and Zapalniczka. It was difficult for individuals to defend themselves. Wałęsa was reduced to pleading for all files connected with himself to be made public, while Zdzisław Najder published an affidavit and an open letter to the Minister of the Interior in connection with the Zapalniczka affair, with which his name was widely associated.[42] Although a number of draft lustration bills were still being examined in parliamentary commissions in May 1993, there was some anxiety that the atmosphere of

---

39 Reports of the commission's findings may be found in *Rzeczpospolita* 156, 4–5 July 1992; *Życie Warszawy* 157, 4–5 July 1992; *Gazeta Wyborcza* 156, 4–5 July 1992.
40 These allegations were published widely, with alleged documentation, in the third week of June 1992; see for example 'Pucz czerwcowy?', *Nie* 25, 18 June 1992. For the findings of the *Sejm* commission see *Rzeczpospolita* 270, 12 November 1992.
41 For example Włodzimierz Cimoszewicz issued a formal statement, published in several newspapers of 6–7 July 1992; Ewa Spychalska referred to the fact that she found herself 'in good company' on the list; see *Glob* 24, 11 June 1992.
42 Both appear in *Rzeczpospolita* 235, 6 October 1992.

hysteria and the difficulties of protecting individual rights would be difficult to overcome.[43] The attitude of the Olszewski–Kaczyński axis to President Lech Wałęsa kept the issue of the president's own status in the public eye. In the autumn of 1992 Jarosław Kaczyński also began a campaign to reward the true patriots of the past. In particular he pleaded for a pardon for Colonel Ryszard Kukliński, who had defected to the United States in November 1981 with high-level defence secrets of Poland and the Warsaw Pact. Kukliński had been sentenced to death in absentia in 1984. Kaczyński (and others, including Professor Zbigniew Brzezinski) argued that betraying state secrets to the United States was not treason, but heroism.[44]

No progress was made with draft legislation, whether dealing narrowly with lustration or with wider questions of de-communization. Poland's accession to the European Convention on Human Rights (but not all its protocols) provided a touchstone against which to assess draft bills and find them wanting. New issues emerged under the rubric of de-communization, blurring into areas only tenuously linked to the communist past. Olszewski had put the question 'Whose Poland?', and it became a key slogan of the anti-communist right. Was Poland to remain in the hands of ex-communists, collaborators, communist sympathizers and atheists; or were the forces of patriotism and Christianity to prevail? The answer, of course, was expected to be in the affirmative. Increasingly the concept of de-communization became far more widely defined than when it emerged in spring 1990 as a major element in the 'war at the top'.

DE-COMMUNIZATION, CIVIL LIBERTIES AND THE CHURCH

The widening of the concept of de-communization took it into realms far afield from lustration. Kaczyński, Olszewski and Macierewicz (who founded a new political group called Catholic Action after his

---

43 See Mariusz Janicki, 'Lustracja w impasie', *Polityka* 46, 14 November 1992.
44 On the Kukliński affair see, for example, 'Idealny agent', *Prawo i Życie* 33, 15 August 1992; 'Nie wyjaśnione tajemnice', *Prawo i Życie* 34, 22 August 1992; 'Nie ma mowy, żebym za życie wrócił', *Rzeczpospolita* 290, 10 December 1992.

expulsion from the ZChN) joined forces with the ZChN to embrace the sphere of ethics. In this context de-communization was very broadly conceived to embrace the substitution of Christian moral values for the secular, atheist values promoted by the communist system. Concepts of Christian doctrine and Catholic values had formed an essential element of the political programmes of various Christian democratic parties, and of the ZChN and a number of peasant parties. Law should be Christian in essence, having no truck with the tolerance and moral relativism preached by liberalism.[45]

Conflicts of religious and secular values had surfaced in the summer of 1990 with the introduction of voluntary Catholic education into the schools. Taking place as it did under the Mazowiecki government, the issue was of little use as ammunition for the de-communizers. Indeed, the proponents of Christian values won every political battle in the first three years of post-communist Poland, although not always as speedily as they would have liked and not with the unanimous support of the political institutions. Both Ombudsmen, for example, challenged decisions on religious education, in response to which the Catholic Church issued sharply critical statements,[46] and leading ZChN figures called for the recall of the Ombudsman. Zieliński's challenge was stronger, however, for it rested on the constitutional separation of Church and state. This is the area where de-communization overlaps with the secular–clerical conflict.

The tensions evoked by the issue of religious instruction were not isolated. They were reinforced by heated conflicts over abortion, seen by the Church and its allies as a symbol of the evil of the communist system, permitting and encouraging the murder of the unborn child. Surprisingly, abortion was not a persisting dominant theme of Church–state relations under the communist regime, although of course individual priests spoke against it in their sermons. It did not surface in a major way until 1988,[47] after which it remained on the political agenda until the passage of an anti-abortion law late in 1992.

45 See S. Niesiołowski in *Ład* 42, 20 October 1991.
46 See, for example, *Słowo Powszechne* 150, 8 September 1992.
47 See Jacqueline Hernier, 'Polish Democracy is a Masculine Democracy', *Women's Studies International Forum*, vol.15, no.1, 1992, p.129; on the history of abortion see also Małgorzata Fuszara, 'Legal Regulation of Abortion in Poland', *Signs*, vol.17, no.1, 1991, pp.117–28.

In truth there was a wide gulf between the secular liberal approaches to the law and that of the Christian right. In the eyes of the Church, the notion of a state neutral in its attitudes to religion was merely a mask for anti-religious and anti-clerical sentiments fundamentally at odds with the 'will of the nation', which was in its vast majority Catholic. Its opponents, argued the Church, protested against the Church's role in purveying ethical and moral teachings, while tolerating the blasphemy, falsehood and pornography which had engulfed the mass media.[48] The proponents of a sharp separation between Church and state argued that only neutrality in religious matters could protect freedom of conscience for adherents of different faiths or none. At the same time, violation of this principle would not only give the Catholic Church a privileged position compared with those professing different beliefs but risked the replacement of the old system of secular, atheist propaganda by an equally intolerant Catholic propaganda professing its own absolute truths.

The advocates of fundamental de-communization were joined by the ZChN on issues of the relationship between Church and state. In August 1992 they failed by one vote to include in the new law on radio and television the requirement that these media should respect Christian values, a decision regretted by the Church.[49] In December 1992 the *Sejm* approved the Bill, after the Senate had restored the clause requiring broadcasters 'to respect the religious feelings of their audience and especially to respect the Christian value system'. Immediately, there were strong positive and negative reactions, with some advocates of Christian values endorsing the idea of a Catholic censor[50] and others, including representatives of the Church, deploring the possibility of any return to censorship.[51] The Democratic Left Alliance referred the controversial clause to the Constitutional Tri-

---

48 See the Pastoral Letter for 15 September 1991 in *Gazeta Wyborcza* 214, 13 September 1991.
49 On the major provisions of the new law, retained in the final version, see Louisa Vinton, 'Sejm Approves New Law on Radio and Television', *RFE/RL Research Report*, vol.1, no.43, 1992c, pp.32–4. The text of the Law is in *Rzeczpospolita* 17, 21 January 1993, and *Rzeczpospolita* 18, 22 January 1993.
50 See for example *Niedziela* 3, 17 January 1993.
51 Father Adam Boniecki, 'O Katolickiej cenzurze i wartościach chrześcijańskich', *Tygodnik Powszechny* 4, 24 January 1993; see also M. Pęczak, 'Swoboda i dyktat', *Polityka* 7, 13 February 1993.

bunal on the grounds that it violated the constitutional principles of freedom of expression and equality before the law.

The battle-lines were drawn over the constitutional question of the relationship between Church and state; but the divisions did not wholly coincide with those between the advocates and opponents of wide-reaching de-communization measures. When the president introduced his Charter of Rights and Freedoms to the *Sejm* in January 1993, the ZChN, the Centrum and the Movement for the Republic opposed it on the grounds that it 'legalized the Stalinist principle of separating the Church from the state', which would lead to the removal of the Church and religion from public life.[52] However, Aleksander Hall's new parliamentary club, the Polish Convention (KP), also opposed the Charter on similar grounds. The future of the Charter looked uncertain because to these opponents were added those declaring against it (or parts of it) on other grounds, including excessive protection for minorities, the incompatibility of the popular referendum with parliamentary democracy, its irrelevance in the absence of threats to individual citizens' rights from the state, and the absence of a socio-economic dimension of civil rights (the latter was taken up in a separate charter by the Democratic Left Alliance: see below).

Given the unresolved constitutional questions and important remaining issues on the agenda of the Christian right, conflicts between secular and religious approaches are bound to remain salient. The role of the Church hierarchy in relation to civil liberties will play a fundamental role in the ability of Polish democracy to take root and acquire stability. The Roman Catholic Church is very powerful. It speaks out on major political issues and has so far achieved two of its fundamental aims, anti-abortion legislation (although it intends to push further for a total prohibition) and religious education in the schools. It approved the decision regarding the broadcasting media and important figures within the Church have endorsed the idea of a new moral censorship system. However, the Church has seen its popularity decline, and there is growing feeling that it has become too overtly political. If it fails to temper its instinctive anti-liberalism there could be major consequences for the still fragile democratic system.

52 Marek Jurek of the ZChN, quoted in *Rzeczpospolita* 18, 22 January 1993.

ISSUES OF WELFARE RIGHTS

The erosion of certain socio-economic rights (*qua* rights) is a necessary concomitant of the acceptance of a capitalist economic system. The European welfare states periodically experience huge strains, especially in times of economic recession; and they take different forms;[53] but they show that capitalism is compatible with a variety of measures by which the state acts to support capitalism or to limit its negative social effects. If the right to work is incompatible with capitalism, state action to promote employment is clearly not. If the right to housing conflicts with the property rights of private owners, none the less measures can be adopted to protect tenants. State provision of education and health care brings both economic and social benefits. From an historical perspective, the state versus market dichotomy is a highly misleading one.

Still, the question of the extent to which state social provision can be maintained in the transition to capitalist democracy in Eastern Europe remains open.[54] The communist system of bureaucratic provision was highly developed, but to a great extent it depended on functioning within a particular configuration of central planning. As the bureaucratic planning system has been dismantled, so too has social provision been reduced. Removing sources of inefficiency has benefits and also costs: the removal of subsidies for foodstuffs and basic consumer goods and services, for example, may structure supply and demand in accordance with scarcity relations, but it has led to a growth in poverty and deprivation for significant sections of society. Similarly, permitting unemployment aids the restructuring of the economy but it has costs to society in unused potential and to individuals in human dignity as well as material security. State enterprises have closed their crèches, vocational schools and health facilities as part of their cost-cutting programmes. The scope of social policy was considerably reduced by the economic decisions of post-communist governments, while those policies have given rise to new social problems, such as unemployment, homelessness and rising levels of crime.

53   Ramesh Mishra, *The Welfare State in Capitalist Society*, Hemel Hempstead, 1990.
54   Bob Deacon *et al.*, *The New Eastern Europe*, London, 1992; also Adam Przeworski, *Democracy and the Market*, Cambridge, 1991.

Although much of this shrinkage has been spontaneous, uncontrolled, and a product of economic policy rather than conscious social policy choices, there are also ideological justifications for a reduced state role in the sphere of social policy. The common liberal perspective stresses the negative consequences of an 'excessively protective state' as leading to welfare dependency and stunted individual development. The whole category of socio-economic rights is thus deemed problematic. There are social consequences too, namely the opportunity costs of excessive consumption, for services provided free of charge or heavily subsidized are consumed unnecessarily. This argument has been particularly pervasive in discussions about the health service. It also surfaced in debates over unemployment benefit, with the argument that generous benefits discourage job-seeking. On the other hand, there remains great public commitment to extensive state social provision and generally to a welfare state ethos.[55] Health, housing, education and welfare benefits, especially pensions, have remained salient political issues. There is widespread support for continuing a state-provided health-care system and anger at the continuing deterioration of the health service. Yet there is no organized consumer health lobby to challenge the medical professionals, anxious for greater scope for the private sector, or bureaucrats, striving to reduce state health expenditure. Similarly, protests over pensions have been largely led by trade unions keen to protect the pension privileges of certain groups such as miners. Technical arguments concerning pension calculations and entitlement are complex and the decision-making process remains opaque.

Health Care

Instead of defending the citizens' constitutional right to free health care at the point of delivery,[56] the Ministry of Health has seen its abrogation as one of its main aims. It does not espouse the total dismantling of the state system, but it has consistently argued that the state lacks the resources to provide comprehensive health-care provision for all citizens. Therefore a 'realistic' perspective is needed, to

---

55 Kolarska-Bobińska, op. cit., pp.37–44.
56 This was Article 70 of the amended Constitution of 1952.

identify a guaranteed 'basket' of patient services, provided by both public and private sectors, with options for additional care or higher standards paid for by patients. The Constitution was perceived as a major obstacle to such a system. In addition, the Ministry favoured the introduction of an insurance-based system of funding.

Bureaucratic incompetence and political weakness have long characterized the Polish health sector. Reform of the health service appeared on the political agenda in the late 1970s. The old regime was cognisant of its inefficiencies and deficiencies and the poor quality of much provision. At the same time the deterioration in the health of the population was reflected in a reduction of life expectancy, high infant mortality rates, and worrying levels of premature adult mortality and disability. Efforts to strengthen primary care and health promotion and prevention remained largely confined to the sphere of rhetoric, and no coherent health-care strategy emerged. For much of 1989–91 the system remained more or less in limbo, but it was also being shaped by spontaneous processes. In 1990 the Ministry relinquished social care to Jacek Kuroń at the Ministry of Labour without a political battle. In 1991 a new law on drug charges came into effect. A law on health service establishments came into force in January 1992, but the Ministry was dilatory in providing the necessary implementing regulations. It was not until late 1992 that certain formal proposals began to take shape within the administration regarding the 'basket' and a separate health insurance scheme. By this time patients were already increasing their own direct financial contribution very considerably.

The economic changes inaugurated by the Balcerowicz programme, coupled with inadequate public finance, led the health-care sector into massive debt and *ad hoc* reduction of provision. The increased costs of foodstuffs, rent, energy, drugs and pharmaceutical supplies exceeded official estimates and by the end of 1991 the total health service debt was approximately 4,500 million zloties, while the provisional budget for the first quarter of 1992 was 10,000 million zloties, 80 per cent of which was required for labour costs.[57] Temporary closures of hospital wards and health clinics became permanent. In 1991 health service employment was reduced by 18,000; 200 industrial health

57   *Rzeczpospolita* 15, 18 January 1992.

clinics closed along with some 2,500 hospital beds.[58] The introduction of direct charges was also widespread, either under the guise of an 'administrative charge' or with patient access conditional upon a 'voluntary' donation. The law on health establishments envisaged further direct charges for those 'misusing the ambulance service' and for those whose condition resulted from a state of inebriation.

The law of November 1991 on prescription charges introduced a subsidy of drugs to replace the subsidy of persons which had meant, in effect, that most patients received their prescriptions free of charge. The new system provided a token payment for drugs listed as 'basic', a 30 per cent payment for 'supplementary' drugs, with the remainder being charged at full cost. Demand dropped considerably in the first months following the introduction of the new system, but it remained unclear whether this was because patients were no longer hoarding supplies, because they had stocked up with reserves prior to the new regulations, or because of financial hardship. Separate provision for those on low incomes and for the chronically ill was promised but proved very slow in coming.

Opinion surveys revealed strong public commitment to a free health service and ambivalent attitudes to the private sector. Even when support for privatization was relatively high, a considerable proportion was wholly opposed to the privatization of hospitals: 47.6 per cent in one 1990 survey; by mid-1992 it had risen to 60 per cent.[59] A study of attitudes to payment found that three-quarters of respondents opposed the introduction of obligatory charges for health care. There was considerable anxiety (80 per cent) that ability to pay could become a condition of access, while only 24 per cent thought that direct charges might improve the quality of provision.[60]

Despite public anxieties, there are no real mechanisms for the articulation of their health interests in the decision-making processes. The parliamentary health commission has been extremely critical of

58 See the *Sejm* health commission debates, *Biuro Informacyjny Sejmu*,166/I kad., 12 February 1992 and 191/I kad., 19 February 1992; also *Rzeczpospolita* 44, 21 February 1992.

59 Władysław Adamski, 'W obliczu prywatyzacji: poparcie i przeciw' in Adamski *et al.*, op. cit., p.83; CBOS, *Serwis Informacyjny* 6/1992, p.49.

60 J. Halik *et al.*, 'Społeczeństwo polskie wobec opłat za niektóre świadczenia służby zdrowia', Warsaw, 1992 (unpublished).

the Ministry of Health, but generally deputies, and the political parties, are ill informed on technical issues of health organization and
financing. The medical professions favour 'reform' but they are
divided over its meaning and the manner of implementation. Demonstrations and protests within the health service have been frequent and
widespread, but they have largely centred on issues of remuneration.
A main aim of the physicians has been to achieve a situation where
they obtain reimbursement (from the state or private insurance firms)
for private consultations. In the meantime, state provision has further
deteriorated, and in some spheres (most notably dentistry) the choice
is now one of private care or none.

The abortion issue has also provided a source of controversy for the
Ministry of Health. This is an issue where the conflict of rights is particularly stark, namely that between those who claim rights for the
unborn child and those for whom the woman's right to control her
own body is paramount. In May 1992 a new provision of the Medical
Ethics Code, passed controversially by the profession's regulating
body, the Self-Governing Chamber of Physicians, introduced a prohibition against termination of pregnancy. Although the permissive
1986 law remained in force, the number of abortions dropped dramatically. Doctors feared that they would be struck from the medical
register if they failed to comply with the new code. The Ombudsman
raised the matter with the Constitutional Tribunal, which declined to
adjudicate (see Chapter 6), while the Ministry of Health merely pre-
tended that the problem did not exist. Nor did the Ministry make
preparations for the introduction of the new anti-abortion legislation
which took effect in March 1993.[61]

Pension Rights

Pensions policy is another area which has proved contentious and
more politically fraught than health care, despite general agreement
that the old system was too complex and too bureaucratized. Retirement and invalidity pensions are dealt with by the State Social Insur-

---

61   As a result of the new legislation, many Polish women began to seek abortions in the
     Russian enclave of Kaliningrad, bordering on north-east Poland.

ance System (ZUS), along with sickness and maternity benefit and other welfare payments, financed by employer contributions based on the size of the wage fund. Inflation, however, was the immediate problem for post-communist governments. Jacek Kuroń, during his first term as Minister of Labour and Welfare, introduced quarterly index-linking of pensions to the average wage and in November 1990 secured the revaluation of pensions for those aged over eighty. Kuroń also introduced measures linking the pensions of the newly retired to the current average wage to eliminate the problem of the 'old wallet' immediately for this group.[62] The provisions were very generous, resulting in pensions at or above 90 per cent of the average wage. This fact, coupled with the encouragement of early retirement to assist industrial restructuring, led to a flood of new pensioners.[63] This in turn increased pressure on the state insurance system, which required an injection of funds from the state budget, just when a substantial deficit was emerging.

Kuroń's successor, Michał Boni, caused a political furore by suspending index-linking; it intensified with his new Bill, which attempted to reduce some of the disproportions between the pensions of the newly retired and those who had retired earlier. The *Sejm* first rejected, then reluctantly acceded to it. The new law[64] included a new employee contribution and an explicit linking of the pension to the employment record, along with a lengthier employment requirement. It also changed the method of calculating the amount of pension, introduced a maximum pension along with mechanisms for reducing pensions for those continuing in some form of employment, and eliminated the privileges of certain groups, including miners, teachers and railway personnel. About 2.5 million persons were expected to suffer reduced pensions as a result. This, along with the removal of privileges and the earnings ceiling, provoked angry protests and demonstrations by pensioners' organizations and trade unions and became a significant election issue.

The Olszewski government inherited a major political problem. The state coffers were empty and the IMF was exerting pressure against

---

62 Jacek Kuroń, *Moja zupa*, Warsaw, 1991, p.91.
63 Ewa Nowakowska, 'Jacek wśród seniorów', *Polityka* 31, 3 August 1991, p.4.
64 It may be found in *Rzeczpospolita* 265, 14 November 1991.

running an 'excessive' deficit. Yet in February 1992 the Constitutional Tribunal ruled a large part of the new law unconstitutional, chiefly because it was retroactive and breached the Constitution's commitment to 'social justice'. It, and later the *Sejm*, agreed with the Ombudsman's view that economic factors could not override legal and procedural requirements. Following this defeat the Ministry of Labour began work on a complete revision of the system of state insurance. Kuroń, resuming his previous post under Suchocka, endorsed new proposals for employee and employer contributions to separate funds for pensions, sickness and maternity benefit, and occupational disease and industrial accident. In some cases company shares would be offered as part of a retirement package. Kuroń's commitment to improved consultation with trade unions and pressure groups provided some grounds for optimism that a consensus could be agreed. However, budget pressures ensured that the issue would retain a high public profile.

That pensions aroused such a high level of political controversy seemed to take successive governments by surprise. However, this is another area where generalized ideas of social justice are very important. Public sympathy for impoverished pensioners faced with high inflation has gone hand in hand with fury at excessively high pensions for some.[65] At the same time the trade unions have sought to enhance their credibility by fervently defending their members' interests, especially where there are special privileges at stake.

Socio-Economic Rights and the Constitution

The president's proposed Charter of Rights and Freedoms, having constitutional status, did not embrace a developed concept of socio-economic rights, contenting itself with a notion of 'basic' social rights. The president maintained that the Constitution could not provide what society could no longer afford. Many parties placing high stress on health and welfare issues, such as the ZChN and the KPN, preferred such matters to be regulated by individual statute rather than by constitutional commitment, although the KPN's deputy chairman, Krzysztof Król, thought it 'unacceptable' that free education should

65 See *Rzeczpospolita* 137, 11 June 1992.

be limited to primary schooling.[66] The SLD's complementary Charter of Social and Economic Rights, inspired by the social charter of the European Community, did not find favour with parliament. The broad area of social and economic rights will, however, constitute a sphere of continuing political strife, for the public has begun to feel acutely the loss of these rights and it is particularly sensitive to populist appeals. The evolution of the Polish welfare state will depend not on abstract philosophical concepts but on *ad hoc* resolutions arising from the changing constellation of political forces.

66   Quoted in *Rzeczpospolita* 18, 22 January 1993.

8. Poland's External Relations

APPROACHES TO FOREIGN POLICY

The state has been a major focus of approaches to the study of international relations in this century, and political nationalism, broadly conceived as an ethnic drive for independent statehood, has remained a persistent force. Although ethnic homogeneity is a far from universal characteristic of states, it has become customary to refer to the key international actors as 'nation-states'. At the same time there has been an increasing awareness of the importance of other international actors such as multi-national enterprises and international organizations; great emphasis is now focused on the globalization of the economy and of world politics and thus of increasing interdependence and interconnection.[1] These insights can inform our understanding of Poland's changed role in the international arena and of its foreign policy responses.

In Polish political culture the concept of the nation-state is vital, and since 1945 it has been roughly accurate. The minority ethnicities should not be forgotten – indeed, they can complicate relations with neighbouring states; but in the absence of external revisionism, they are too small to constitute a threat to the integrity of the state. Nor are all Poles gathered within the nation-state. There are significant Polish minorities in Lithuania, Belorussia, and the Ukraine, who under Soviet rule were broadly isolated from contacts with Poland itself, and large Polish communities abroad, especially in the United States, elements of which have retained strong emotional ties with the homeland.

One reason why the Poles are so sensitive to issues of statehood is the historical experience of its deprivation, for in the eighteenth cen-

---

1 See Anthony G. McGrew, 'Conceptualizing Global Politics', in Anthony G. McGrew, Paul G. Lewis *et al.*, *Global Politics. Globalization and the Nation-State*, Oxford, 1992, pp.1–30; and M. Smith, 'Modernization, Globalization and the Nation-State', ibid., pp.253–69.

tury the once-powerful Polish state was extinguished by its successive division amongst the imperial neighbouring powers. A sense of national oppression was a powerful stimulus to the spread of Polish nationalism in the nineteenth century. Yet the regaining of independent statehood following the First World War did not fully restore national self-confidence. Ethnic and class conflicts, conflicts over the very nature of the state, economic travails, and the insecurity of a geopolitical position wedged between two powerful revisionist states, Germany and the Soviet Union, made for political turbulence; in the international sphere this culminated in what came to be known as the Fourth Partition of Poland, the Nazi–Soviet Pact of 1939. The territories lost in the east to the USSR contained most of Poland's non-Polish citizens (but also the Polish cities of Lwów [Lviv, Lvov] and Wilno [Vilnius] with important historical and cultural significance). Their loss was confirmed as part of the post-war settlement, with compensation in the 'recovered territories' from Germany in the west. Then, for almost fifty years, the eastern relationship with the USSR was central to and conditioned Poland's external relations.

'Poland', observed Andrzej Walicki, 'is a country where everything has a historical dimension. We are living, as it were, with the entire burden of our history ...'.[2] Given the Polish experience with the predatory tendencies of its neighbours, emphasis on the national interest and the struggle for survival is unsurprising; these concepts were fundamental to the 'realist' critique offered by the Polish nationalist thinker Roman Dmowski of the strong Polish tradition of romantic nationalism.[3] They also coincide substantially with 'realist' perceptions of international relations. The realist school, 'the dominant normative view in international relations for most of the twentieth century', conceives of international relations as a struggle between sovereign states for power and security.[4] In the post-war period of Soviet dominance the lament for lost sovereignty was a frequent, if often implicit, dimension of social protest. Since 1989 there has been

---

2   Andrzej Walicki, 'The Three Traditions in Polish Patriotism', in Stanisław Gomułka and Antony Polonsky (eds), *Polish Paradoxes*, London, 1990, p.21.
3   Ibid., p.34.
4   John Baylis and N.J. Rengger, 'Introduction: Theories, Methods, and Dilemmas in World Politics' in John Baylis and N.J. Rengger (eds), *Dilemmas of World Politics*, Oxford, 1992, p.9; see pp.9–12 on the origins and development of the realist school.

a tension between those who share the 'realist' emphasis on national sovereignty and the primacy of security needs and those who seek security through the process of European integration, which in turn adds to the resources of the nation-state by pooling resources to deal with common problems.

Soviet acceptance of a broad coalition government dominated by Solidarity in August 1989 altered the Soviet–Polish relationship dramatically and profoundly. The disintegration of the USSR and its final demise in December 1991 changed the entire basis of post-war international and inter-European relations. For its part, Poland could at last perceive itself as a genuinely sovereign state. The terms 'sovereignty' and 'independence' appeared in virtually every political tract and party programme. In autumn 1992 two events symbolized this new sense of national independence: the final withdrawal of Russian combat troops and the handing over by Boris Yeltsin of documents proving Stalin's authorization of the Katyń massacre. The conflict between those who saw Poland's national sovereignty, security and integrity as violated by the Soviet alliance and those who saw the alliance as a vital guarantor of that sovereignty had resolved itself. The geopolitical dilemma was now altered by the creation of new independent successor states lying between Poland and Russia; the small enclave of Kaliningrad on the Baltic now constituted the only border between Poland and the Russian Federation.

Realist perceptions of international politics (whether they are formally articulated by methodologically self-conscious scholars or represent the instinctive responses of politicians) themselves influence the reality they are perceiving: seeing states as assertively pursuing self-interest leads them to emphasize security and thus to the classic 'security dilemma', whereby one side's defensive preparations are seen as a threat to the other and thus must be countered, causing an escalation of tension and further reciprocal response. Poland, like the other states of the Soviet bloc, was caught in the Soviet Union's security dilemma *vis-à-vis* the United States. It is still possible that security concerns could create their own dilemmas for Poland in the aftermath of the Soviet Union's disintegration, not only because of traditional fears of Russia but also because of possible instability in the new states, especially the potentially powerful Ukraine.

However, since 1989 other factors have been pulling in a different direction, that of cooperation rather than confrontation, and of recognition that the sovereignty of the modern state can never be absolute. This approach accords with interdependence theories of international politics, which are widely endorsed by Polish academics and by the new practitioners of the Polish government. It embraces a belief in the demonstrable superiority of Western European institutions, with the promise of increased prosperity for those who adopt them; the view that European integration remains vital to preventing a resurgent Germany; ethical convictions about the civilizing values of Western democracy; and acceptance of the value of collective security arrangements. These attitudes strengthened as the Soviet Union declined.

THE EVOLUTION OF POLISH FOREIGN POLICY

One can already, to 1993, distinguish three stages in post-communist Polish foreign policy. In the first, lasting just a few months from the assumption of the premiership by Mazowiecki in autumn 1989 to the early part of 1990, Poland affirmed its alliance with the Soviet Union, despite questioning of the Soviet military presence by groups such as Moczulski's Confederation for Independent Poland (KPN). Indeed, Poland continued to envisage the USSR as a guarantor of its western border, a topic reopened by Chancellor Kohl's ambiguous statements about the Oder–Neisse line in the context of impending German unification. The second period, not much longer, lasted from the spring of 1990, when the demise of communism in Central and Eastern Europe already seemed secure, to the disintegration of the USSR in December 1991. In this period the eastern relationship was based on the so-called 'two-track' policy: on the one hand policy was oriented toward the central Soviet government; on the other, it was directed towards the governments of the constituent republics of the USSR, which had been variously declaring independence (beginning with Lithuania in March 1990) or asserting 'sovereignty'; after the failed coup of August 1991 all the republics declared their independence. At the same time, from autumn 1989 the Poles were vigorously seeking to integrate themselves into Western European institutions, to confirm their detachment from the Soviet sphere of influence and, not least, to gain support for their programme of economic transformation. After December 1991 the Soviet–Russian relationship ceased to be the paramount element of Polish foreign policy, whose nature became at once more multi-faceted, but also more explicitly oriented to Western Europe.

Despite government instability, with five prime ministers since 1989, there has been considerable continuity in Polish foreign policy, not least because of a continuity of personnel. Foreign Minister Krzysztof Skubiszewski retained his post throughout the period from 1989 to 1993. Minister of Finance Leszek Balcerowicz held his post for two years, until Olszewski took office; even Olszewski could not find a finance minister prepared to depart from the basic principles of Balcerowicz in dealing with Poland's foreign debtors and international financial institutions. When the Suchocka government acceded in July 1992 previously experienced ministers returned to government. They included former Prime Minister Krzysztof Bielecki, Minister without Portfolio for relations with the European Community, and Minister of Defence Janusz Onyszkiewicz, who had served as deputy minister in the Mazowiecki and Bielecki governments.

The broad foreign policy line was developed and orchestrated for the Mazowiecki government by Foreign Minister Skubiszewski, while Balcerowicz dealt with foreign economic relations, especially negotiations with international economic organizations and with Poland's foreign creditors. Skubiszewski's policy goals consisted of developing and maintaining cooperative relations with all Poland's neighbours; the gradual integration of Poland into the structures and networks of mutual European interdependence, such as the Council of Europe and the Conference on European Security and Cooperation and including accession to the European Community; developing mechanisms of regional cooperation such as the Baltic Council and the Visegrad Triangle with Hungary and Czechoslovakia; and gaining support for the economy through international organizations such as the IMF and the World Bank. In all these areas tensions have surfaced, largely reflecting different conceptions of the national interest; but a remarkable measure of consensus has remained, not least because of the growing sense of physical security derived from the perceived absence of any external threat. The Foreign Ministry and Skubiszewski himself survived the lustration dispute which brought down the Olszewski government, despite attempts to tar the minister with the brush of communist collaboration. The tensions over national security between President Wałęsa and Olszewski's Minister of Defence Jan Parys from January to April 1992 provided a brief period of discontinuity between foreign and security policy, although in practice there was more noise than substance in the differences. Broadly, this is an area where the government, politicians and public have been in rough accord. The vast majority feel secure within the boundaries of their state; they no longer fear their neighbours (although they do not love them); and they retain confidence in their armed forces, which (as for much of the communist period) for most of 1991 and 1992 enjoyed higher public esteem than parliament, government or president.[5]

POLAND AND THE SOVIET UNION

One astonishing dimension of the Gorbachev reform programme in the USSR was its fundamental redefinition of Soviet interests in Eastern Europe. It was astonishing not because there was no objective basis for a changed relationship; indeed there were valid economic and military reasons for a reassessment: it was possible to argue that the East European buffer zone had been rendered obsolete by new weapons technology, while the economic relationship was no longer clearly advantageous to the USSR. The dysfunctions of the communist system were becoming increasingly apparent.

However, perceptions usually lag behind objective possibilities; Great Powers are slow to recognize their own decline, and the perceptions were deeply rooted on both sides of the already threadbare 'Iron Curtain'. For decades scholars and politicians had argued with rare unanimity that the maintenance of a level of control over Eastern Europe was a 'core Soviet interest' and thus by definition not negotiable: the Soviet Union had not only vital strategic interests in this

5 Opinion poll findings coincided substantially on the question of external danger: see CBOS, *Serwis Informacyjny 6/92*, Warsaw, June 1992, pp.82–90, 109–10; also the report of Sopot polls in *Rzeczpospolita* 162, 11–12 July 1992. In January 1993 the armed forces were regarded as the institution 'best serving society' by 72 per cent, a reduction of 4 per cent since November 1992: CBOS poll reported in *Polityka* 8, 20 February 1993.

area, but also economic, political and ideological interests.[6] The global order was based on the mutual acknowledgement of two super-power blocs which had solidified in the aftermath of the Second World War and seemed set in the hardest concrete. Widespread schol-arly disagreements occurred over the nature of intra-bloc relation-ships: the fraternal East European allies were variously portrayed as extensions of Soviet domestic politics, as dependent satellites of the Soviet imperial state, or as relatively autonomous elements of an asymmetrical alliance system. Still, it was universally accepted that the sovereignty of the East European states was limited. The Soviet Union had proved its capacity to intervene directly in suppressing riots in East Germany in 1953, and then to mobilize full-blown military intervention in Hungary in 1956 and in Czechoslovakia in 1968; and it had threatened Poland with force on a number of occasions. A *de facto* Brezhnev Doctrine existed well before his enunciation of the principle that foreign intervention in the interests of saving socialism should be seen not as a violation of sovereignty but as a guarantee of the collective security interests of all members of the socialist com-monwealth.[7] However, bloc dynamics had evolved considerably even before the accession of Gorbachev as General Secretary of the CPSU. He inherited an open debate within the Warsaw Pact on the relation-ship between national interests and bloc interests, stimulated by Brezhnev's acceptance of the principle of national Eastern European initiatives on the road to *détente*.[8]

Yet Gorbachev did not at once depart from the perspective of his predecessors. The early years of his tenure were ones of evident conti-nuity in Soviet policy towards Eastern Europe, albeit in a rather sub-dued atmosphere.[9] The Soviet–American relationship was paramount and change in Eastern Europe was gradual. Gorbachev encouraged

---

6   See Karen Dawisha, *Eastern Europe, Gorbachev, and Reform*, Cambridge, 1988, pp.7–29.

7   The speech enunciating the so-called Brezhnev Doctrine is published in Gale Stokes (ed.), *From Stalinism to Pluralism: A Documentary History of Eastern Europe since 1945*, Oxford, 1991, pp.132–4.

8   Robin Remington, 'Changes in Soviet Security Policy toward Eastern Europe and the Warsaw Pact' in George Hudson (ed.), *Soviet National Security Policy under Pere-stroika*, Boston, 1990, p.240.

9   Margot Light, 'Foreign Policy' in Martin McCauley (ed.), *Gorbachev and Perestroika*, London, 1990, p.186.

perestroika in the more conservative East European countries, and the reform wings of the communist parties could now claim the legitimacy of following the Soviet model down the path of change. Gorbachev's 'new thinking',[10] with its emphasis on cooperation and interdependence in international affairs, gradually altered the confrontational mind-set of Soviet foreign policy makers. The boundaries of the permissible were shifting outwards, but few doubted their continuing existence. One illustration of the depth of the shift was the endorsement by *Pravda* and *Izvestiya* of proposals for Polish Round Table negotiations with Solidarity.[11] Still, Neal Ascherson was probably correct in assuming that Gorbachev's point of reference in 1988 was still change *within* the socialist system, not change *of* the socialist system: 'he [Gorbachev] has not yet faced directly the idea that – sooner rather than later – one of these states is going to attempt the non-violent removal of a ruling Communist Party from power.'[12]

Even when Gorbachev did face the problem by endorsing the result of the Polish elections of June 1989, it is not clear that the full implications were apparent. The official line was that the USSR would work with any democratically elected neighbouring government, but the PZPR's position in Poland was not yet defined as hopeless and the collapse of the other East European dominoes had not yet begun. When the collapse came, the rapidity of change in successive East European states throughout the autumn of 1989 meant that there was no clear point at which intervention could have stemmed the tide, even if that option had been politically acceptable to Gorbachev or economically feasible.[13] Soviet acquiescence in German unification served to demonstrate just how radical a change had taken place in Soviet thinking, although it entailed a good measure of bowing to the inevitable.

10 Neil Malcolm offers a historical perspective in his 'De-Stalinization and Soviet Foreign Policy: The Roots of "New Thinking"' in Tsuyoshi Hasegawa and Alex Pravda (eds), *Perestroika: Soviet Domestic and Foreign Policies*, London, 1990, pp.178–205.

11 For example in *Izvestiya* 15 September 1988 and in *Pravda* 19 October 1988 and 23 February 1989.

12 Neal Ascherson, 'Rumblings in the East' in Jon Bloomfield (ed.), *The Soviet Revolution: Perestroika and the Remaking of Socialism*, London, 1989, pp.241–2.

13 He had publicly renounced the use of force in his speech to the Council of Europe in July 1989: 'The philosophy of the concept of a "common European home" rules out the ... very possibility of using force or the threat of force.': see Stokes, op. cit., p.267 (the speech is reproduced on pp.266–8).

The advent of non-communist governments in Eastern Europe as a result of the 1989 revolutions obviously constituted a change of mammoth proportions for global international relations, as well as providing another sharp stimulus to continuing change within the USSR itself. For the latter, response pulled in two directions. On the one hand, the demise of communist monopartism provided a fillip to separatist nationalism in the Soviet republics; on the other it mobilized those conservative forces which regarded the 'loss' of Eastern Europe not only as a grave error of foreign policy but as an act of betrayal. They were not appeased by the conclusion in Paris of the Conventional Armed Forces in Europe Treaty (CFE) which effectively ended the Cold War in November 1990. Throughout 1990 Gorbachev was also preoccupied with the manoeuvrings of his own internal balancing act. The formal abandonment of the legal basis for the CPSU's 'leading role' signalled a shift in the locus of policy-making to the state institutions, particularly the new executive presidency. In a slow trickle Gorbachev's reformist colleagues left the party, leaving him no longer at the centre of the see-saw but dangerously exposed on one end. Determined to keep the union together, however, he acquiesced in a concerted attempt to resist the growing wave of Baltic separatism.

Developments in Poland's relations with Lithuania inaugurated Skubiszewski's two-track policy towards the USSR. The Polish parliament, press and political parties welcomed enthusiastically and almost unanimously the March 1990 Lithuanian declaration of independence, and visits to Warsaw by the Lithuanian Foreign Minister in May and the Prime Minister in June assumed a symbolic importance when Lithuania faced Moscow's military and economic pressure with little support from the international community.

The settlement of Poland's borders with Germany with a new border treaty in November 1990 freed the Polish government to pursue a more determined line with Moscow, and simultaneously to develop good relations with the westernmost Soviet republics. In October 1990 Skubiszewski visited the Soviet Union, where he not only conducted talks with central government officials but also signed declarations of friendship and cooperation with Russia and the Ukraine. Belorussia, however, demurred, accusing the Poles of mistreating their Belorussian minority. All the republics which bordered Poland had Polish minorities, and Poland itself had Belorussians and Ukrainians (although fewer Lithuanians) in its eastern provinces. The questions of safeguards for minority rights and recognition of existing borders temporarily soured relations with Belorussia.

Rumours of an imminent Soviet *coup* surfaced at the end of 1990 and East European anxieties were fuelled by Moscow's use of force in Lithuania in January 1991, continued by Gorbachev's apparent concessions to conservative forces throughout the spring. A group of Polish parliamentarians travelled to Vilnius in January to offer moral support and Polish government condemnation was forceful and unambiguous. The massive relief effort which followed was 'perhaps the greatest ever undertaken in Poland'.[14] The Polish government stopped short of recognizing Lithuania; despite public pressure it remained cautious with regard to Moscow, which had reacted angrily to Iceland's recognition.[15] This situation was resolved by the failed *putsch*, which finally took place in August 1991 in an attempt to prevent the signing of the new treaty of union negotiated by Gorbachev with the majority of Soviet republics. The *coup* attempt acted as a catalyst for the acceleration of the disintegration of the Soviet Union, which gasped its last breath at Christmas 1991.

Throughout this period the main task had been one of disentangling Poland from the networks of ties binding the Soviet bloc, especially but not only the Warsaw Pact and the CMEA (Comecon), without alienating Moscow. By and large the process was not confrontational, although public invective on both sides became bitter at times. Hungary and Czechoslovakia had already begun negotiations on Soviet troop withdrawals in the first months of 1990. Poland's failure to follow suit led to severe criticism of the government (Wałęsa, still then leader of Solidarity with no political office, made news headlines with a peremptory demand to the Soviet ambassador in January that all Soviet troops should withdraw that year), which gave priority to maintaining Soviet support on the issue of the border with Germany. However, in September 1990 the Polish government formally requested the Soviet Union to negotiate the withdrawal of Soviet mili-

---

14 Stephen R. Burant, 'Polish–Lithuanian Relations: Past, Present, and Future', *Problems of Communism*, vol.XL, May–June 1991, p.77.

15 Ibid., pp.77–8 on the official reasons offered for non-recognition.

tary units. The process was difficult and protracted,[16] partly because of the complexity of the negotiations, which had to be coordinated with plans for the transit through Poland of Soviet troops leaving Germany. In January 1992 Russia assumed responsibility for the now defunct USSR's Polish commitments and in May agreement was concluded after a lengthy direct meeting between Presidents Yeltsin and Wałęsa.

Although negotiations on Soviet troop withdrawals were important for the East European governments, they assumed for a time that the Warsaw Pact would continue in some form, albeit as a political alliance with a circumscribed mission to deal with issues of European security and disarmament.[17] Withdrawal from the Pact's Joint Command structure was obviously essential to gaining military autonomy, and with it some eastward redeployment of forces, which had been exclusively mobilized against borders with Western countries. The Pact was altered by the loss of the defunct German Democratic Republic and it was already 'gradually withering away'.[18] However, the process of dissolution was speeded up more than originally foreseen. At a meeting of Pact Foreign and Defence Ministers in February 1991 the Pact's demise was agreed: all military activities would cease on 1 April. Similarly, there was a recognition of the need to maintain economic links. It was at the insistence of the East European states and 'with an eagerness bordering on naiveté'[19] that agreement was reached to trade in convertible currency from January 1991 and to disband Comecon, which was dissolved at its final session in June 1991. This decision was to prove more profoundly disruptive of econ-omic relationships, especially with the USSR, than its signatories realized.

16 See Jan de Weydenthal, 'Polish–Russian Relations Disturbed by Troop Dispute', *RFE/RL Research Report*, vol.1, no.11, 1992c, pp.32–4; Jan de Weydenthal, 'Poland Free of Combat Troops', *RFE/RL Research Report*, vol.1, no.45, 1992d, pp.32–5.

17 Curt Gasteyger, 'The Remaking of Eastern Europe's Security', *Survival*, vol.XXXIII, no.2, 1992, pp.118–19.

18 K. Skubiszewski, lecture to the Royal Institute of International Affairs, London, January 1991, published as 'New Problems of Security in Central and Eastern Europe', *East European Reporter*, vol.4, no.4, 1991, pp.61–4.

19 Ronald H. Linden, 'The New International Political Economy of East Europe', *Studies in Comparative Communism*, vol.XXV, no.1, 1992, p.14.

POLAND AND THE SUCCESSOR STATES

The main focus of eastern policy has, naturally enough, centred on Russia and the neighbouring states of Lithuania, Belorussia and Ukraine. After the abortive *coup* there was a peculiar interim period as Gorbachev fought to save some sort of political union (but now clearly excluding, at the least, the Baltic states and Georgia), while the republics had announced their independence but were moving at different rates to establish their identities as independent states. In addition to settling Polish–Russian disputes over troop withdrawals in May 1992, Presidents Yeltsin and Wałęsa also signed a treaty of friendship and cooperation, pledging mutual acknowledgement of sovereignty and agreeing to expand bilateral economic and cultural contacts. The meeting was a difficult one because of conflicts between the Polish president and Olszewski's government over elements of the draft treaty, resulting in coded demands being sent to Wałęsa in Moscow to amend the section concerning the establishment of Polish–Russian joint enterprises in some vacated Russian garrisons. The dispute was resolved by Yeltsin's willingness to delete the offending paragraph, but the dispute continued to rumble on in Polish domestic politics. The conflict may be seen as a surrogate in the conflict over jurisdiction in foreign policy matters, and as an indication of continuing anti-Russian suspicions within the Polish political establishment.[20] The Suchocka government's more flexible attitudes, the passage of the Little Constitution, and the good will demonstrated by Yeltsin in the documentary revelations over Katyń were factors helping to cement the new relationship with Russia by the end of the year. The movement of Polish troops eastwards, partly because of the concentration of Russian forces at Kaliningrad, remained a sensitive issue,[21] but developments in 1992 appeared to augur favourably for overcoming the long-standing Polish fear and distrust of its great neighbour. The imponderable factors concerned internal political developments in Russia. In February 1993 President Wałęsa warned of the possibility of a new communist revolution in Russia and urged a policy of greater preparedness for such an eventuality.

20 This view is shared by Jan de Weydenthal, 'Poland and Russia Open a New Chapter in Their Relations', *RFE/RL Research Report*, vol.1, no.25, 1992b, pp.46–8.
21 *The Guardian*, 21 November 1992.

Similarly harmonious relations developed rapidly with Ukraine and Belorussia, whose independence Poland recognized on 2 December and 27 December 1991 respectively. Belorussia in particular was seen as a point of access to members of the new Commonwealth of Independent States, with whom it enjoyed good relations, as well as a significant Polish trading partner in its own right. Issues affecting the respective minorities were settled amicably, the inviolability of existing borders was recognized in a new state treaty of June 1992, and economic and cultural agreements have been cemented by numerous reciprocal visits by political leaders.[22]

The achievement of cordial relations with Ukraine has been a greater success because of the historical legacy of deep mutual enmity, Ukrainian fears of Polish territorial claims, and Polish fears of the emergence of a new, possibly unstable major nuclear power on its longest eastern frontier. In addition, there was some anxiety lest Ukrainian tensions with Russia should spill over into Polish–Russian relations.[23] Ukraine for its part aimed to reorient its own policies westwards, thus reducing its dependence on the Commonwealth of Independent States. Establishing good relations with Hungary and Poland would provide a window on the West, and Ukraine expressed interest in closer cooperation, or even membership of the Visegrad Triangle.[24] In May 1992 the Ukrainian President Leonid Kravchuk visited Warsaw for the signing of a friendship treaty.

Relations with Lithuania, however, deteriorated in the aftermath of independence. The main sources of estrangement were the large Lithuanian Polish minority, viewed by Lithuanians with suspicion because of its history of reluctance to endorse their independence, and Lithuanian fears of Polish claims to territory lost to Stalin. A mutual Declaration of friendly relations in January 1992 did not improve matters. In his annual report to the *Sejm* in May, Skubiszewski noted that '... Lithuania has to this day failed to meet its obligations to the Polish community', with successive postponement of regional elec-

---

22　Stephen R. Burant, 'Polish–Belarusian Relations', *RFE/RL Research Report*, vol.1, no.37, 1992, pp.41–5; P. Kosiński and R. Malik, 'Dobrzy sąsiedzi', *Rzeczpospolita* 270, 17 November 1992.
23　See the views of Leon Bojko in *Gazeta Wyborcza* 14, 21 January 1992.
24　Bohdan Nahaylo, 'Ukraine and the Visegrad Triangle', *RFE/RL Research Report*, vol.1, no.23, 1992, pp.28–9.

tions and continuing discrimination against Poles in matters of privatization and re-privatization.[25] Historic grievances surfaced over the
circumstances leading to the incorporation of Vilnius into Poland in
1922, for which the Lithuanians demanded an official apology,
arousing a predictably angry response in the Polish press.

Foreigners in Poland

The main anxiety for Poland's policy makers in dealing with the
Soviet successor states has been that political instability will generate
a massive outflow of refugees across Europe, with Poland as the
major route of transit. President Wałęsa has issued a number of
warnings of possible consequences, not only for Poland but for Western Europe as a whole. However, the whole issue of the place of
foreigners in Poland began to acquire increasing political salience in
1992, not least because of German proposals to tighten their regulations governing asylum-seekers, with the risk that large numbers
would be expelled from Germany to Poland as their port of entry.
With regard to this general issue of foreign influx, however, a number
of separate elements must be distinguished: those engaging in normal
cross-border traffic for trading purposes; illegal entry and transit for
work in the second economy or for purposes of organized criminal
activity; and refugees seeking a safe haven from persecution. To the
question of foreigners must be added anxieties about the potential for
Poles resident in the former USSR to seek to repatriate themselves as
ethnic tensions increase in the successor states.

The issue of increasing cross-border population flows became a
matter of concern for all the neighbouring successor states and served
to stimulate the development of cross-border diplomacy in Eastern
Europe.[26] The initial expansion of unlicensed trading encouraged
attempts to regularize and control the large spontaneous increase in
border traffic, which led to waiting times of up to several days for
motor vehicles on Poland's eastern borders. Limited financial
resources have prevented the rapid opening of the new border cross-

25 K. Skubiszewski, 'Polityka zagraniczna RP w 1992', speech delivered in the *Sejm* on 8
May 1992, *Przegląd Rządowy*, no. 6, June 1992, p.27.
26 Jan de Weydenthal, 'Cross-Border Diplomacy in East Central Europe', *RFE/RL
Research Report*, vol.1, no.42, 1992f, pp.19–23.

ings agreed with all neighbouring states save Lithuania. In many towns and cities, however, local authorities have made provision for bazaars and street markets for the temporary visitors. They are not always welcome, and there is an irony in recalling popular Polish incomprehension of the negative attitudes their own propensity for trading aroused in Western Europe during the communist period.

Similar comment applies to workers in the second economy. In the view of many such immigrants compete with the local labour force, export currency and do not pay taxes.[27] Coupled with this attitude is a genuine fear of both petty and organized crime, with major international smuggling operations proving difficult for border guards and customs officials to control; and prostitution, with attendant fears of the spread of AIDS. Although official figures showed 8.5 million visitors from the former USSR in 1992,[28] there is no way of knowing how many were engaged in some form of illegal activity. Pressure to tighten border controls and to introduce visas (also for Romanians and Bulgarians) was beginning to make itself felt, with political parties (notably the ZChN) appearing particularly responsive to negative public attitudes to immigrants and refugees.

POLAND'S NEIGHBOURS IN CENTRAL AND EASTERN EUROPE

The Visegrad Quartet

The Visegrad Triangle was inaugurated in February 1991 as a mechanism of regional cooperation between Poland, Hungary, and Czechoslovakia, arising out of their common aim of integration with Western European economic and political institutions. After 1 January 1993, when Czechoslovakia split into two states, the Triangle became the Quartet, despite tensions between Slovakia and Hungary over the Hungarian minority in Slovakia and over the Slovak Gabčikova dam's effect on the Danube and with it the Slovak–Hungarian border.

27 CBOS poll of October 1992, cited in Marek Henzler, 'Rzeczpospolita przechodnia', *Polityka* 7, 13 February 1993.
28 Ibid.

Broadly, regional cooperation was intended as a stabilizing factor, and also a means of increasing members' credibility as prospective partners by demonstrating their ability to work together constructively. Additional benefit derived from the factor of strength through numbers, especially regarding joint negotiations with the European Community. 'If we join our voices,' said Czechoslovak President Havel, 'our demands will be heard more strongly than if we act individually.'[29] The three countries concluded negotiations for associate membership with the EC, as well as gaining observer status in the North Atlantic Assembly. They also agreed (with independent Slovakia) to initiate a free trade area, with all customs duties to be eliminated progressively between 1993 and 2001. This was a very tangible response to the trade dislocations caused by the dissolution of Comecon and the subsequent mutual imposition of tariffs intended to prevent their different subsidy arrangements from distorting trading patterns. Although the Quartet provided the framework for frequent official contacts, there appeared no desire to establish an institutional machinery to support it. Its informal nature seemed easily able to accommodate expansion, but proposals that Ukraine should become a member were rejected as weakening the group's cohesion.

Indeed, informality appeared best to accommodate the national sensibilities of many Polish politicians, who expressed themselves in February 1993 during a heated parliamentary debate on proposals to formalize mechanisms of regional cooperation in a 'Carpathian Euroregion' involving border provinces of Poland, Slovakia, Hungary and Ukraine. Deputies from opposition parties joined forces with deputies of the Christian National Union (ZChN), part of the government coalition. Jan Łopuszański of the ZChN accused the Foreign Minister of preparing the way for a new partition of Poland and asked Skubiszewski why he was prepared to collaborate with the 'dark forces planning to dismantle our frontiers'.[30]

29 *The Financial Times*, 7 May 1992.
30 Quoted in *Rzeczpospolita* 44, 22 February 1993.

Polish–German Relations

Although lacking a direct frontier with West Germany, Poland's attention in autumn 1989 was focused firmly on Bonn, which was optimistically viewed as the main source of the foreign capital needed for the transformation of the economy. Poles had the greatest direct experience of West Germany, which was the easiest Western European country for them to visit, and the FRG became the model for their consumer aspirations. The existence of the separate East German state also made it possible for people to develop differential attitudes to the two Germanies. West Germany was favourably regarded, while traditional anti-German sentiments tended to be focused on the East.

Of course, this period was short-lived. The appearance of German unification on the political agenda aroused atavistic Polish anxieties about a resurgent Germany which were given credence by Chancellor Kohl's refusal to pledge the eternal immutability of the border on the Oder–Neisse line. It also rapidly became clear that the East German economy would become the foremost absorber of German capital. None the less, the resulting tensions were softened by the resolution of the border issue, by German aid and by the firm voicing of continued German support for Poland within the European Community.

However, it is not the case that Polish fears of Germany have been altogether alleviated. When in July 1991 the Prime Minister of Brandenburg, Manfred Stolpe, proposed a comprehensive programme of bilateral cooperation for the Polish–German border zone, elements of the Polish press portrayed it as a new weapon of German imperialism. In Silesia demands of the German minority for autonomy have also stirred fears of a potential fifth column (Skubiszewski dismissed German minority aspirations as a 'political fantasy'[31]). A spiral of mutual misunderstanding accompanied the proliferation of anti-immigrant attacks by German neo-fascists, which in turn stimulated Polish nationalism in German areas, while elements of the German community in Poland proved themselves highly insensitive to Polish historical sensibilities by erecting statues to honour German wartime dead. The problem of German asylum regulations increased fears in Poland of a mass influx of refugees expelled from Germany.

31 Skubiszewski, interview, op. cit.

Yet official relations have remained good. The Polish–German Treaty of June 1991 institutionalized the Polish–German Commission as a mechanism for dealing with border issues, including the continuation of negotiations on the Stolpe Plan.[32] Germany has replaced the Soviet Union as Poland's major trading partner. It has provided more support, more aid and more capital to Poland than any other European country.

POLAND AND WESTERN EUROPE

Poland and the EC

It would be something of an understatement to suggest that the European Community, individually and collectively, was pleased about the demise of communism in 1989–90, or that the level of rhetoric has not quite been matched by the level of assistance. The broad aim of the EC has been to support the transition to capitalism and democracy by laying down conditions which would make the process of change irreversible. However, neither the individual states nor the international institutions of which they are members have managed fully to sacrifice their short-term interests to their long-term perspectives, the latter arguing the benefits to the international community of a stable, democratic and prosperous Eastern Europe. The European Community proved 'a reluctant imperialist. ... Yet the fear of instability in its neighbours is pulling [it] ... towards its destiny in Eastern and Central Europe.'[33]

In July 1989 the EC set up the PHARE programme (Polish and Hungarian Assistance for the Reconstruction of Europe) and moved quickly to conclude trade agreements with Poland, Hungary and Czechoslovakia, but its general line cannot be regarded as generous. Negotiations of EC agreements of association with these three states proved arduous and often bad-tempered, with the Poles threatening to terminate negotiations on several occasions. The final agreement was

32 Jan de Weydenthal, 'German Plans for Border Region Stirs Interest in Poland', *RFE/RL Research Report*, vol.1, no.7, 1992a, p.41; see also *Financial Times*, 24 August 1992.
33 A. Robinson and M. Wolf in *Financial Times*, 2 December 1991.

signed in December 1991, designed to facilitate economic cooperation and trade with the EC and providing assurances that the Community would assist it (and Hungary and Czechoslovakia, which signed identical agreements) to achieve the conditions necessary for full membership.[34] Previously, association agreements had not been linked to membership of the Community. The agreement was, according to one Polish observer, 'not perfect, not the most beneficial of all possible, but the sum of many compromises'.[35] Indeed, the EC proved highly reluctant to commit itself to greater access for Polish goods, especially the 'sensitive products' of steel, textiles and agricultural products, because of its own existing surpluses. The head of the European Bank for Reconstruction and Development took the East European side in September 1992, urging the EC to renegotiate the agreements and in so doing to abandon its own protectionist tendencies.[36] In London in November 1992 Prime Minister Suchocka achieved observer status at ministerial meetings of the twelve member states, but failed to secure a firm commitment to Poland's admission as a full member of the Community. As one observer commented, 'for the Community a decision on starting negotiations on full membership will be a clash between the political rationale (in favour) and the economic rationale (against)'; the annual costs of regional assistance to the Visegrad Quartet under current EC regulations would be $US8,000 million.[37] Foreign Minister Skubiszewski is an ardent proponent of European integration and an enthusiast of the Maastricht Treaty, including its doctrine of subsidiarity; but as it stands at present, it looks extremely unlikely that Poland could be in a position to meet the Maastricht conditions within ten years (of course, in 1993 this looked dubious for the twelve existing members as well).

It has often been argued that the requirements and conditions laid down for admission to European institutions will assist the process of democratization in Eastern Europe because the East Europeans will have to bring their legislation and practices into line with those of Western Europe. Certainly, both the EC and the Council of Europe

34 *Financial Times*, 5 December 1991.
35 Interview with Jacek Saryusz-Wolski, Government Spokesman on European integration, *Polityka* 39, 26 September 1992.
36 *Financial Times*, 8 September 1992.
37 M. Ostrowski, 'Wspólnota na dystans', *Polityka* 45, 7 November 1992, p.11.

have theoretical membership prerequisites of democratic principles and the safeguarding of human rights. The increasing institutionalization of the Conference on Security and Cooperation in Europe (CSCE), whose charter now includes a commitment to respect the rule of law, to uphold the rights of ethnic minorities, to respect fundamental human rights, and to hold free and fair elections,[38] is a further attempt to promote democratic practices. However, the conditions are not entirely clear: when Skubiszewski signed the European Convention on Human Rights on Poland's behalf in November 1991, he omitted the ten protocols elaborating and providing human rights safeguards, including that of individual access to the European Court;[39] but this did not prevent Poland's becoming the twenty-sixth member of the Council of Europe. It took domestic pressure and stern remonstrations from the Polish Helsinki Committee, strengthened by President Wałęsa's assumption of a human rights brief, to bring a change of government heart in 1993.

Poland's Security and the Atlantic Alliance

Poland's desire to join NATO has been tempered by the recognition that NATO has rejected the notion of additional members, at least until it fully clarifies its own objectives in the aftermath of the disintegration of the Warsaw Pact.[40] NATO's Secretary-General, Manfred Wörner, has suggested rather disingenuously that the countries of Central and Eastern Europe 'benefit already from the security and stability that NATO provides. They know that they are full partners in a structure of consultation for developing assistance and advice on regional security.'[41] President Wałęsa's concept of a second, parallel NATO ('NATO–bis') continued to be endorsed by the chief of his National Security Bureau[42] as a means of uniting the successor states

---

38 Richard Weitz, 'The CSCE's New Look', *RFE/RL Research Report*, vol.1, no.6, 1992, p.28.
39 See Marek Nowicki, 'Polska nie podpisała całej Konwencji Europejskiej', *Rzeczpospolita* 170, 21 July 1992.
40 On the adaption of NATO's objectives see Fergus Carr, 'NATO and the New Europe', *Talking Politics*, vol.5, no.2, 1992, pp.90–93.
41 Manfred Wörner, 'A Vigorous Alliance – A Motor for Peaceful Change in Europe', *NATO Review*, vol.40, no.6, 1992, p.6.
42 Interview with Jerzy Milewski in *Rzeczpospolita* 211, 8 September 1992.

of the western USSR (without Russia) and the Warsaw Pact into a new defensive mutual security system to quell localized conflicts; it would ultimately be superseded by admission to NATO itself. However, successive Polish governments have shown no enthusiasm for the concept of a second NATO, preferring instead to strengthen their links with the United States bilaterally, including US provision of support for military training, and through the North Atlantic Co-operation Council. The Council, which includes former Warsaw Pact members and Soviet successor states (with the exception of Georgia) held its inaugural meeting in December 1991 and meetings of its foreign ministers took place in March and June 1992. NATO's Secretary-General is also chairman of the North Atlantic Council.

Without doubt the Polish preference is for the development of an international security system involving Europe, the United States and Canada. Its own security doctrine currently envisages no threat and sees no country as a potential foe. Its aim is 'sufficiency', maintaining sufficient capability to respond to an external threat, and it has taken expert advice, including that of NATO, on force sizes (reducing to 200,000 in peacetime) and structures,[43] including a rapid deployment force for any trouble spots.

INTERNATIONAL ECONOMIC INSTITUTIONS

The accelerating globalization of the economy along with the demise of the Soviet superpower and the loss of US economic hegemony has not only drawn attention to shifting loci of economic power, notably in the Pacific: it has also altered and increased the role of international economic organizations such as the International Monetary Fund and the World Bank. Fred Bergsten has argued that with the end of the Cold War, 'the salience of security issues will decline sharply; economics will move much closer to the top of the global agenda.'[44] The IMF and World Bank, and new bodies such as the European Bank for Reconstruction and Development (EBRD), founded explicitly to aid

43 Interview with Minister of Defence Janusz Onyszkiewicz in *Rzeczpospolita* 176, 28 July 1992; also *Rzeczpospolita* 250, 23 October 1992.
44 C. F. Bergsten, 'The World Economy after the Cold War', *Foreign Affairs*, vol.69, no.3, 1990, p.96.

the former communist states, have been accorded a key role in facilitating the transition to a market economy in Eastern Europe. This role has been welcomed and applauded by some;[45] it has been seen as offering the best substitute for national governments, given their reluctance to provide massive aid to the former communist countries.[46] Others have questioned it as imposing a particular, inappropriate ideological framework of economic liberalism insufficiently cognizant of the social consequences of its policies.[47] Indeed, one recent review concluded that the impact of IMF programmes on inflation is uncertain, and found no strong correlation between IMF programmes and economic growth.[48]

The Balcerowicz strategy clearly owed much to the conventional wisdom of the dominant Anglo–American economic strategies of the 1980s. 'Although Eastern Europe is brimming with visiting "suitcase economists"', noted William Keegan, 'it is an open question whether their theories and experience have equipped them for problems of this scale.'[49] The confidence and certainty of the visitors at first seemed unbounded: the IMF, the World Bank, the OECD all gave the seal of approval to Balcerowicz's shock treatment. Only gradually did enthusiasm give way to the realization that the bitter pill was not having the expected effects: it had effectively wiped out people's savings,[50] it had reduced living standards[51] and output and increased unemployment; but there was little evidence of any fundamental restructuring.[52]

45 A.D. Crockett, 'The International Monetary Fund in the 1990s', *Government and Opposition*, vol.23, no.3, 1992, pp.267–82.
46 Michael Hughes, 'Can the West Agree on Aid to Eastern Europe?', *RFE/RL Report on Eastern Europe*, vol.1, no.11, 1992, pp.35–42.
47 See Bob Deacon, 'The Impact of Supranational and Global Agencies on Central European National Social Policy', Workshop on Social Responses to Political and Economic Transformation, Prague, May 1992 (unpublished paper).
48 *Financial Times*, 26 February 1992.
49 William Keegan, *The Spectre of Capitalism*, London, 1992, p.98.
50 As, indeed, it was intended to do: this is the concept of the monetary overhang which must be removed as part of any stabilization programme; 'you can confiscate it, you can inflate it away, or, if you had thought about it at the beginning, you might have arranged something like swapping part of frozen financial assets for real assets. ..': A. Gelb, quoted in 'Panelists Discuss Hyperinflation in Former Centrally Planned Economies', *IMF Survey*, 3 August 1992, p.249.
51 This is not universally accepted; see, for example, Andrew Berg and Jeffrey Sachs, 'Structural Adjustment and International Trade in Eastern Europe: The Case of Poland', *Economic Policy* 14, April 1992, pp.138ff.
52 Two Polish economists associated with the IMF and World Bank respectively have

The emphasis was on an idealized version of the American model of capitalism, rather than attempting to utilize studies of market socialism or assessing the Japanese and Western European experiences. Poland's high levels of foreign debt ($US40,700 million in January 1990) made it especially susceptible to IMF influence, since an IMF programme was considered a condition for further negotiations with Western creditors. The IMF for its part was caught in a web of assumptions about how economies would behave, without recognizing that the East European economies differed from their previous clients in their lack of infrastructure, the highly concentrated nature of their industry, different management structures, absence of financial accounting and inexperience with competition.[53]

Yet it would be misleading to see Polish economic strategy as dictated and imposed by international institutions and visiting advisers from abroad under schemes such as the British Know-How Fund. Polish economists had already been seduced by the propaganda of the Thatcherite 'economic miracle' in Britain and by their extensive contacts with liberal economists in the United States. They took the initiative with proposals which found approval with the IMF and World Bank and led to the provision of an internationally-financed stabilization fund at the end of 1989.[54] Poland agreed a stand-by arrangement with the IMF in February 1990. This also opened the way to significant World Bank funding, and it facilitated agreements on debt reduction with the Paris Club, which in March 1991 accepted 50 per cent debt forgiveness contingent upon the agreement of a three-year economic programme with the IMF.

However, the relationship with the IMF has not proved easy, especially since the departure of Leszek Balcerowicz following the parlia-

---

argued that while the shock therapy approach was correct, it was wrongly implemented; G. Kolodko and M. Rutkowski, 'The Problem of Transition from a Socialist to a Free Market Economy: the Case of Poland', *Journal of Social, Political and Economic Studies*, vol.16, no.2, 1991, pp.159–79.

53 Pawel Bozyk, 'The Transformation of East Central European Economies: A Critical Assessment', *Studies in Comparative Communism*, vol.XXXV, no.3, 1992, pp.266–8; Linden, op. cit., p.6, rightly characterizes the planned economies as 'not just "shortage economies" ... but internationally dependent shortage economies because they depended on one key supplier for their inputs ...'.

54 For Balcerowicz's view of negotiations with international organizations and Poland's creditors see Leszek Balcerowicz, *800 dni*, Warsaw, 1992, especially pp.129–45.

mentary elections of October 1991. It was widely believed that despite efforts from President Wałęsa, the IMF kept Balcerowicz in office. Paweł Bożyk argued that the 'defeat of Balcerowicz and Poland's rejection of the IMF program would mean a defeat suffered by the creditors and a shattering of their hopes for the fast recovery of their debt.'[55] In September 1991 the IMF suspended disbursements on its original extended loan facility because the budget deficit was deemed excessive and the rate of inflation too high. The advent of the Olszewski government gave rise to a confused picture, arising out of the different views expressed by the coalition parties, some of which were more interventionist than others. Finance Minister Olechowski's visit to Washington in March 1992 was regarded as the first step on the road back to fulfilling the conditions established by the IMF, but Olechowski resigned after his policies failed to find requisite support from his government colleagues. The Suchocka government was again dominated by liberals who accepted the need to establish macro-economic stability through cuts in public expenditure and control of the money supply, quite in accordance with IMF orthodoxy. The IMF has not been totally inflexible, however; it has several times accepted a greater budget deficit than it would have liked. By the autumn the IMF delegation in Warsaw was praising the government for its 'impressive' package of economic stabilization measures to lay the ground for sustained growth and restore financial equilibrium[56] and its determined efforts to come to terms with the trade unions through the 'Pact for Industry'. A new standby agreement concluded in November covered the period from the beginning of 1993 to the first quarter of 1994, providing access to credit of some $US700 million but imposing strict conditions regarding the budget deficit, inflation, progress with the privatization programme, and the growth of production.

The EBRD for its part took a more flexible approach to lending, although confined by its charter's requirement that 60 per cent of its funds was to be earmarked for large-scale private sector projects and 40 per cent for restructuring state firms. It was viewed suspiciously by sponsoring governments because of President Jacques Attali's socialist

55 Bozyk, op. cit., p.270.
56 *Financial Times*, 9 September 1992; *Gazeta Wyborcza* 212, 9 September 1992.

background and his choice of senior officials, deemed too statist in their orientation. The Bank's failure to respect the conditions of the 60:40 split in its first year aroused further criticism, rejecting Attali's argument that the private sector was insufficiently developed to absorb the aid.[57] Attali's view stressed infrastructural investment and restructuring of military and defence establishments (including nuclear power plants). He argued that it was 'ill-advised to free market forces in the short term without first having put in place the necessary institutions.'[58]

Foreign Investment

At the outset of its economic transformation programme Poland seemed to have a number of advantages which its leaders assumed would lead to large-scale foreign investment. First there was its experience in encouraging investment by Poles abroad, the Polonia community. Joint venture legislation had been liberalized several times in the 1980s. Secondly, it was a large market of almost 40 million aspiring consumers and it possessed extensive raw materials. Yet the promise has not been fulfilled. The scale of investment channelled through joint ventures was low: in 1990 their share in sales was 2.5 per cent and in hard currency exports 3.4 per cent.[59] Western investment was discouraged by poor infrastructure, limited opportunities for profit repatriation, a constantly changing tax system, high rates of inflation, and political instability. By the end of 1991, according to official figures, there were 5,000 joint ventures and foreign-owned projects with a declared investment value of $US690 million; this was only a third of the level in Hungary, with a far smaller population.[60] This figure increased to 7,648 enterprises by June 1992, but it was still regarded as disappointing.[61] Most investments have been small or medium, although a number of well-known international corporations have joined the list of investors: Fiat, Unilever, Coca-cola, Pepsi

57 Karoly Okolicsanyi, 'The EBRD's First Year', *RFE/RL Research Report*, vol.1, no.23, 1992, pp.45–6.
58 Quoted in Keegan, op. cit., p.124.
59 George Blazyca, *Poland's Next Five Years*, London, 1991, p.45.
60 *Financial Times*, 28 April 1992.
61 Życie Warszawy 216, 10 September 1992.

Cola, Levi Strauss, Philips, Siemens, the German detergent producer Benckiser and the Swedish–Swiss Engineering Group ABB. Poland led all its former Eastern European allies in attracting US investment during the last quarter of 1991 and the first quarter of 1992, a sizeable amount of which is believed to have come from Polish Americans.[62] However, Poland has not been very successful in selling its large enterprises to foreign strategic investors offering new technology and management and marketing experience.[63] Overall there is no disguising Polish disappointment at the relative lack of response from the Western private sector.

FOREIGN POLICY AND THE DOMESTIC POLITICAL PROCESS

Those who enthusiastically embrace the direction of foreign policy speak of Poland's 'return to Europe'. In particular, they see accession to the EC as a means of enhancing Poland's status, security and economic position. The Democratic Union and the Liberals are the main supporters of this line, viewed not as a sacrifice of sovereignty but a recognition of Poland's links with the values of Western European civilization and of the changes to the concept of sovereignty wrought by the process of increasing globalization; they see no conflict in simultaneously asserting a 'Polish' and a 'European' identity. Skubiszewski himself argued that European integration 'is no threat to national identity but rather enhances its fuller development'.[64] The most fervent opponents of this 'return to Europe' argue that joining the EC will once again limit Poland's sovereignty and its ability to defend its national interests. For certain groups this is coupled with anxiety about perceived IMF 'diktats' and about the penetration of foreign capital and foreign ownership of Polish land. The Christian National Union (the ZChN), a member of both the Olszewski and

---

62 *Financial Times*, 28 April 1992.
63 Marko Simoneti, 'A Comparative Review of Privatisation Strategies in Four Former Socialist Countries', *Europe–Asia Studies*, vol.45, no.1, 1993, p.87.
64 'Dodawanie ułamków', Interview with Krzysztof Skubiszewski, *Polityka* 42, 17 October 1992.

Suchocka coalitions, shares these tendencies, as do the groupings in Olszewski's Movement for the Republic. This makes the Liberals and Democratic Union suspect because of their 'cosmopolitanism' and disregard for Polish sovereignty, expressed for example in the Liberals' acknowledged passion for a 'Europe of regions' rather than a loose alliance of states. Such attitudes were the source of some tension within the Suchocka government (from July 1992), with its uneasy alliance of ZChN, Democratic Union and Liberals; the peasant partners also displayed some ambivalence about Europe, given the vocal demands of their constituency for continuing subsidies and protection against imports and the challenge of Leppers's Self-Defence, with its propensity for direct action.

However, the Suchocka coalition held firm and won an easy victory in the *Sejm* for the EC association agreement, despite reservations of a nationalist nature. In part this success represents an acknowledgement, sometimes grudging and reluctant, of the benefits of EC aid and the gains in security from linkage with Western Europe. The issue of national security also feeds into and depends on attitudes to the former Soviet Union.

Although the departure of Russian troops removed a major bone of contention, some still see Russia and the other Soviet successor states as a potential source of threat to Poland's security. This reinforces the desire to join NATO; they argue that the government has been far too passive in accepting NATO's reluctance to expand its membership instead of pressing for it as a fundamental strategic objective designed to free Poland definitively from the Russian sphere of influence. Olszewski's and Parys's supporters take this line,[65] which formed a crucial aspect of the jurisdictional dispute between Parys and Wałęsa. It provided an ingredient of the lustration issue, which strengthened links between Olszewski, Parys and Macierewicz, expelled from the ZChN over his role, and certain elements of the Centrum (see Chapter 4). They share the view that lustration is essential to national security, for Poland cannot be secure so long as former communists, Soviet agents, and collaborators are still able to occupy positions of importance within the state apparatus, particularly the military. Their oppo-

---

65 See, for example, J. Kwieciński, 'O bezpieczeństwo – dziś i w roku 2010', *Rzecz-pospolita* 211, 8 September 1992.

nents argue that a literal interpretation of their demands would be a suicidal blow against the armed forces, which had already been 'cleansed' by the departure of over 18,000 officers but which would lose some 12,000–15,000 more to lustration.[66]

It is to be expected, however, that foreign policy issues would be left largely to the foreign policy establishment. Public concerns focus mainly on social and economic issues, although these may have a foreign policy resonance. Numerous peasant protests have claimed the need for protection against unfair EC agricultural imports. In September 1992 Fiat displayed uncertainty about continuing its Polish investment programme when its allegedly exploitative role became an issue in the strike at the FSM car plant in Tychy after the workers protested their inferior wages in comparison with those in the Italian Fiat plants. There is always some risk that dissatisfaction will lead to instability accompanied by an outburst of xenophobia, but the road to Europe will depend on laying down economic paving stones rather than political ones.

RESULTS AND PROSPECTS

The achievements of foreign policy have been considerable in the first period of Poland's post-communist politics. Optimism concerning the beneficence of external support has been tempered by realism, but real gains can be counted in the association agreement with the EC, negotiations with foreign creditors, and the regularizing of relations with the successor states of the USSR. External circumstances have been particularly favourable in the sphere of security, although the potential dangers of instability on Poland's eastern borders cannot be ignored. They have been less favourable with regard to Poland's integration into the global capitalist economy, not least because of the depth of recession in major capitalist states and the unwillingness of the EC states to place long-term political considerations above short-term interests. Poland's external relations are in great measure beyond the control of the country's foreign policy makers, for external con-

---

66 See the interview with Zbigniew Skoczylas, head of the Cadres Department at the Ministry of Defence in *Polityka* 42, 17 October 1992.

straints are great. Yet given Poland's turbulent history, the state's territorial integrity and its autonomy in domestic affairs are more secure now than at any time since the regaining of independence after the First World War.

9. Post-Communist Politics in its First Phase

The parliamentary election of September 1993 brought to an end the first four years of post-communist politics in Poland. This was a period of destruction, decomposition and dislocation as well as one of construction, adaptation and modification. Of course, the second fully competitive election of the post-communist period did not provide a terminal end-point to processes which were continuous and disparate. Turning-points or watersheds are analytical constructs largely dependent on hindsight. However, the September election provided a symbolic terminus. The process of change was by then irreversible: however deep the nostalgia for the old system, there was no going back. The two contending gladiators of the communist period, the PZPR and Solidarity, were dead or transformed beyond recognition. There was no significant conservative force; indeed, all major political actors favoured democracy and the market mechanism, however much important sections of the public longed for capitalism with a human face. The dust had settled from the election of 1991. The second free election indicated a routinization of the electoral process.

The consequences of these four years may plausibly be portrayed in both positive and negative terms. In the most optimistic variant, Poland was well on the road to constructing an enduring capitalist democracy. One could identify the entrenching of competitive political processes, the vibrant development of private sector capitalism and the absence of major social upheavals. In the bleakest, pessimistic variant, one could see in Poland a crippled democracy accompanied by a deformed capitalism and a psychologically maimed society. Both depictions are exaggerated; yet they both contain important elements of truth.

The main motor of economic dynamism appeared to be the private sector. More than half of the economically active population worked in private enterprise by 1993. Economic dependence on large-scale heavy industry was reduced. The deep recession continued, but there were gains in production, while unemployment levelled off over a period of several successive months. Improved economic signals won the applause of the international organizations. The IMF endorsed the Suchocka government's performance and offered a new credit deal. The World Bank's representative paid his own backhanded compliment: Polish goods 'may not always match up to goods produced in the West, but there is a market for mediocre products at low prices.'[1] Although the privatization process continued to be sluggish, and further complicated by the absence of solutions to reprivatization and restitution, the Suchocka government did succeed in legislating the terms of its Mass Privatization Programme (PPP).

On the debit side, the restructuring of the old system's large-scale economic enterprises proceeded very slowly. Although few major giants went bankrupt in the first four years, unemployment was still 15 per cent in mid-1993. Grand plans for regional restructuring, such as that of Wałbrzych, failed to provide the promised gains. Inflation remained worryingly high, if variable according to sector of the economy. The private sector enjoyed numerous tax exemptions and privileges, and corruption scandals appeared endemic. Both public and private firms were adept at avoiding or evading their tax and social security obligations to the state budget. Broadly, successive governments continued to place too much stress on privatization, that is on changes in ownership, as a stimulus to economic efficiency. The major departure, the corporatist approach of the Pact for Industry, was equally unrealistic in its expectations of the trade unions.

In the political sphere, too, significant gains were apparent. These included the holding of competitive elections, gains in freedom of expression, the passage of the Little Constitution, and the reincorporation, if incomplete, of the communists' heirs, the SDRP and the OPZZ, into political life. The relationship between president and prime minister was clarified by the Little Constitution, despite the legal ambiguities that remained. Numerous gains were made in the sphere of individual civil liberties. Institutional safeguards of the rule of law proved controversial, especially the Civil Rights Ombudsman, but they were by and large respected. The implications of political change were not always apparent, even to their authors. For example, when the *Sejm* defeated Suchocka on a vote of confidence in May 1993, few deputies understood that dissolution was a serious constitutional option. Yet the process proceeded smoothly and legally.

1　*The Independent*, 9 March 1993.

Yet these developments, while crucial, affected only the institutional superstructure. They did not democratize the relationship between state and society. Indeed, there emerged important indications of a new legitimation crisis. Parliament proved ineffective as a representative body. Trust in politicians evaporated, as widespread perceptions of their self-aggrandizement took hold. The prestige of all political institutions save the army declined. Grass-roots activity remained very limited – indeed, the most active groups were those of the old regime, especially trade unions and pensioners' associations. New intermediate structures of interest articulation remained undeveloped. Although new trade unions emerged, they were divided among themselves, they competed in demagogic terms, and their capacity for coordinated, coherent political action was limited. Local government remained weak. Hopes of a regenerated, animated civil society proved premature. Political apathy, a sense of inefficacy and demobilization reigned.

Much of this political demobilization can be illuminated by looking at the factors that have contributed to the emergence of a political culture of resentment. Some are general factors, broadly pertaining to the region as a whole. First, because the twin tasks of refashioning both the polity and the economy were pursued simultaneously, people found it difficult to distinguish the two and they were easily conflated. At the same time, throughout Eastern Europe the new elites perpetrated the confusion of economy-building and polity-building: universally they promised rapid prosperity, thus linking their own legitimacy to economic success. Secondly, the changing role of the state served as a source of social disorientation, complicated by the predominance of anti-state rhetoric and the previous experience of the over-centralized, corrupt, mono-party state. Pluralism creates new centres of decision-making which are not instantly transparent (for example, economic and political, central and local, public and private), so people did not necessarily know either where the decisions affecting them were taken (previously, they knew only too well), or how to set about influencing them. There was uncertainty about what precisely the state was able to guarantee and how to claim rights or services from it. Thirdly, social cleavages were unstable, especially those of class, and old reference points disappeared. The new private sector employers proved demanding in terms of labour discipline and unreceptive to trade union activity. Disparities of wealth became highly visible. Unemployment removed the economic security of the old system. Social service provision deteriorated and major socio-economic rights were lost or eroded. Poverty was widespread and debilitating. Almost 40 per cent of households lived below the social minimum by the middle of 1993.[2] The old social networks of mutual assistance were no longer essential in circumstances when money rather than access to goods and services was the prime requisite. The three major polling organizations consistently found the population to be highly pessimistic, in the assessment both of individuals' prospects and of those of the country itself.[3] In general the only groups displaying any degree of optimism were business people, those in managerial positions and students – a small proportion of the total.[4]

The specific features of the Polish communist system also left an enduring legacy. After the brief respite of the Mazowiecki government (September 1989 to December 1990), strikes again came to be seen as the main instrument for articulating workers' demands, despite the Suchocka government's shift to a consultative stance. In May 1993 strikes by public-sector workers, especially in health and education, gave impetus to the events which culminated in the vote of no confidence in Suchocka's government. Solidarity deputies initiated the motion on the instructions of the union, which also threatened a general strike, as a bargaining counter in their battle with the government. They neither expected nor anticipated the outcome, in which they emerged as emphatic losers. They suffered the loss of the Pact for Industry, however flawed it may have been; they achieved nothing for public-sector workers; and the government which they had challenged remained in power. Developments in May and June 1993 marked the second phase of Solidarity's identity crisis, which was as profound as that caused to the communists by the PZPR's dramatic loss of power in June 1989.

Solidarity had taken power as a symbol of national resistance to the communist system. Yet this unity could not survive once the challenge had succeeded. The first stage in the unravelling of Solidarity was the 'war at the top' between the supporters of Wałęsa and Mazowiecki. Wałęsa kept the trade union element intact and still allied with the

---

2   These figures are from the Bureau of State Statistics (GUS), *Polityka* 28, 10 July 1993.
3   See *Rzeczpospolita* 11, 14 January 1993, *Rzeczpospolita* 22, 27 January 1993 and *Rzeczpospolita* 35, 11 February 1993, respectively.
4   *Rzeczpospolita* 193, 18 August 1992; *Rzeczpospolita* 278, 26 November 1992; *Rzeczpospolita* 279, 27 November 1992; also Lena Kolarska-Bobińska, 'Konflikty w nowej Polsce', *Gazeta Wyborcza* 280, 28–9 November 1992.

citizens' committees during the presidential election of November 1990. It was primarily the Solidarity intelligentsia which continued to fragment along various overlapping axes: into supporters and opponents of the Balcerowicz programme; into secular advocates of the separation of Church and state versus clerical sympathizers of a strong role for the Catholic Church and endorsement of traditional religious values; into the advocates and opponents of the 'return to Europe'.

In June 1992, however, lustration intensified the divisions between the de-communizers and their opponents. Jan Olszewski's fall brought major new tensions to the trade union wing of Solidarity. A number of the union's leaders sympathized with Olszewski's demands for de-communization and an end to the manipulations of *nomenklatura* capitalism, and Wałęsa lost his grip on the movement. The Network (*Sieć*) of committees in large enterprises remained largely loyal to the president but the rest of the movement was divided. Further strains were caused by fear of loss of influence to other, more radical unions. The national executive and the regions did not always speak with one voice; the stridency of the Warsaw region under Maciej Jankowski increasingly appeared as a challenge to the leadership of Marian Krzaklewski. Individual Solidarity organizations, notably at the famous agricultural machinery plant at Ursus, also began to take independent action. Divisions between the trade union and its parliamentary representatives and within the latter group were sharply focused in the spring of 1993, as some deputies resisted union instructions to vote against the government. The dissolution of parliament following the vote of no confidence and the prospect of the September election exacerbated these divisions, and those deputies who had voted for the government came under attack. One was Bogdan Borusewicz, who had made his way alone from Gdańsk to attend the inaugural meeting of KOR in 1976. Wałęsa dissociated himself from the movement, as Zbigniew Bujak had done two years earlier. 'This is no longer my Solidarity', said Wałęsa. *Sieć*, however, proved receptive to the president's attempt to mobilize the BBWR, the Non-Party Reform Bloc.

Despite these divisions and a decline in membership to around 1.6 million, Solidarity persisted in regarding itself as capable of representing the national interest, that is of speaking for society as a whole. It wished to confirm its trade union identity whilst remaining reluctant to limit its role to that of a trade union. Yet politically its appeal was reduced by competition from the political parties, especially the SDRP and the KPN. As a trade union it was challenged by its old adversary the OPZZ, former splinter groups of Solidarity itself such as Solidarity '80, and a myriad of new trade union bodies. It also faced the emergence of an explicitly anti-union theme in political discourse, articulated most effectively by members of Aleksander Hall's new Conservative Party.

The legacy of the communist system also made itself felt in the politics of the peasantry, which remained the most consistently disaffected element of society. The impotence of the Solidarity peasant leaders was manifest, despite their involvement in the first four postcommunist coalitions. This was partly due to the objective problems of submitting small family farms to capitalist competition and partly due to the ineptitude of the leadership and their susceptibility to personal squabbling. It served to strengthen the large successor party, the Polish Peasant Party (PSL), which also gained through Pawlak's demeanour during his period as prime minister in June 1992. It gave credence to the direct action and extra-parliamentary activities of Lepper's Self-Defence.

The role of the Roman Catholic Church, which had often played a crucial mediating role between state and society, underwent a major shift in the post-communist period as it abandoned mediation and pressed the concerns of its own agenda. The Church enjoyed acclaim and a special status as the bearer of national values in the communist period, and now it no longer had to fear for its survival. It moved to assert its perceived rightful place in a largely Catholic society, including reclaiming much property previously confiscated by the communists. Its concerns were above all social and moral, reflected in the new salience of issues such as abortion and religious education in schools. It did not necessarily need to exert direct political pressure, since numerous political parties expressed its views and appealed explicitly to Catholic social doctrine. Its support for Christian parties, notably the ZChN, was regarded as a significant factor in the 1991 election. Apart from the introduction of religion into the schools (August 1990) and the anti-abortion legislation (March 1993), the Church also achieved a victory in the clause requiring 'respect for Christian values' in the 1992 broadcasting law. Endorsement of proposed new censorship mechanisms began to appear in the Catholic press. Debate between secular and religious views of the relationship between Church and state took on an acrimonious character. One consequence was a marked decline in the Church's prestige in 1992 and anxiety over its undue political influence.[5] Despite these conflicts, however, it is important to stress the continuing importance of religion as a fundamental element of Polish culture.

In all these respects we can see how the combination of systemic features shared with other post-communist states and the particular characteristics of the Polish experience continued to shape post-communist political development. The respective significance of structural characteristics and constraints, both economic and political, and the particular strategies chosen by the new decision-makers remains problematic,[6] but there can be little doubt that both will remain important. 'Let Poland be Poland' sang the crowds celebrating their solidarity with Solidarity throughout the 1980s. However enduring the communist legacy, and whatever the future pattern of Polish politics, it will be a rich admixture of continuity and change; and it will be indubitably Polish.

---

5 Opinion polls began to show that a clear majority considered the Church's political influence excessive: see *Rzeczpospolita* 18, 22 January 1993.

6 Ben Slay, 'The Dilemmas of Economic Liberalism in Poland', *Europe–Asia Studies*, vol.45, no.2, 1993, pp.237–57; David Stark, 'Path Dependence and Privatization Strategies in East Central Europe', *East European Politics and Societies*, vol.6, no.1, 1992, pp.17–54.

Bibliography

Adamski, Władysław (1991), 'W obliczu prywatyzacji: poparcie i przeciw' in Adamski *et al.*, *Polacy '90*, pp.81–96.
—, Ireneusz Białecki, Krzysztof Jasiewicz *et al.* (1981), *Polacy '80.Wyniki badań ankietowych*, Warsaw: PAN, Instytut Filozofii i Socjologii and Instytut Studiów Politycznych.
— (1986), *Polacy '84. Dynamika społecznego konfliktu i konsensusu* (2 vols), Warsaw: PAN, Instytut Filozofii i Socjologii and Instytut Studiów Politycznych.
—, Krzysztof Jasiewicz, Lena Kolarska-Bobińska *et al.* (1989), *Polacy '88. Dynamika konfliktu i szansa reform*, Warsaw: PAN, Instytut Filozofii i Socjologii and Instytut Studiów Politycznych.
— (1991), *Polacy '90. Konflikty i zmiana*, Warsaw: PAN, Instytut Filozofii i Socjologii and Instytut Studiów Politycznych.
Agh, Attila (1991), 'The Transition to Democracy in Central Europe: A Comparative View', *Journal of Public Policy*, vol.11, no.2, pp.133–51.
Andrzejczak, Jerzy, Premysław Cwikliński and Jacek Ziarno (1991), *Art–B Bluff*, Warsaw: BGW.
Arato, Andrew (1981), 'Civil Society Against the State', *Telos* 47 (Spring), pp.23–47.
— (1982), 'Empire vs. Civil Society: Poland 1981–82', *Telos* 50 (Winter), pp.19–48.
— (1991), 'Revolution, Civil Society, and Democracy' in Z. Rau (ed.), *The Reemergence of Civil Society in Eastern Europe and the Soviet Union*, Boulder, CO, and Oxford: Westview.
Ascherson, Neal (1981), *The Polish August: The Self-Limiting Revolution*, London: Penguin.
— (1989), 'Rumblings in the East' in Bloomfield (ed.), *The Soviet Revolution: Perestroika and the Remaking of Socialism*, pp.234–45.
Ash, Timothy Garton (1983), *The Polish Revolution: Solidarity 1980–82*, London: Cape.
— (1990), *We the People*, Cambridge: Granta Books.
Baczyński, Jerzy (1992), 'Duch Kuronia', *Polityka* 33, 15 August.
— and Władysław Władyka (1989), 'Kampania majowa', *Polityka* 23, 10 June.
— and J. Mojkowski (1993), 'Wokół zera', *Polityka* 6, 6 February.
Balcerowicz, Leszek (1992), *800 dni*, Warsaw: BGW.
Ball, Alan R. and Frances Millard (1986), *Pressure Politics in Industrial Societies*, London: Macmillan.
Barańczak, Stanisław (1989), 'Before the Thaw: The Beginnings of Dissent in Postwar Polish Literature (The Case of Adam Wazyk's "A Poem for Adults")', *Eastern European Politics and Societies*, vol.3, no.1 (Winter), pp.3–21.
Barber, Benjamin R. (1969), 'Conceptual Foundations of Totalitarianism' in Friedrich, Curtis and Barber, *Totalitarianism in Perspective: Three Views*, pp.3–52.
Batt, Judy (1991), 'The End of Communist rule in East–Central Europe: A Four-Country Comparison', *Government and Opposition*, vol.26, no.3, pp.368–90.
Baylis, John and N.J. Rengger (1992), 'Introduction: Theories, Methods, and Dilemmas in World Politics' in John Baylis and N. Rengger (eds), *Dilemmas of World Politicss*, Oxford: Clarendon Press, pp.1–25.

Beksiak, Janusz, Tadeusz Gruszecki *et al.* (1990), *The Polish Transformation: Programme and Progress*, London: Centre for Research into Communist Economies.

'Belwederski wariant masowej prywatyzacji' (1992), *Rzeczpospolita* 74, 27 March.

Bereś, Witold and Jerzy Skoczylas (eds) (1991), *Generał Kiszczak mówi ... prawie wszystko*, Warsaw: BGW.

— and Krzysztof Burnetko (c.1991), *Gliniarz z 'Tygodnika'. Rozmowy z byłym ministrem spraw wewnętrznych Krzysztofem Kozłowskim*, Warsaw: BGW (no date given).

Berg, Andrew and Jeffrey Sachs (1992), 'Structural Adjustment and International Trade in Eastern Europe: The Case of Poland', *Economic Policy* 14 (April), pp.117–74.

Bergsten, C. F. (1990), 'The World Economy after the Cold War', *Foreign Affairs*, vol.69, no.3, pp.96–112.

Bernhard, Michael (1987), 'The Strikes of June 1976 in Poland', *East European Politics and Societies*, vol.1, no.3 (Fall), pp.363–92.

Bielasiak, Jack (1985), 'Solidarity and the State: Strategies of Social Reconstruction' in Misztal (ed.), *Poland after Solidarity*, pp.19–38.

— and Barbara Hicks (1990), 'Solidarity's Self-Organization: The Crisis of Rationality and Legitimacy in Poland, 1980–81', *East European Politics and Societies*, vol.4, no.3, pp.489–512.

— and Maurice D. Simon (eds) (1984), *Polish Politics: Edge of the Abyss*, New York: Praeger.

Bienkowski, Wojciech (1992), 'Poland's Bermuda Triangle', *RFE/RL Research Report*, vol.1, no.17 (24 April), pp.22–4.

Błaszczyk, Barbara and Marek Dąbrowski (1992), 'Trzecia próba', *Polityka* 14, 4 April.

Blazyca, George (1980), 'Industrial Structure and the Economic Problems of Industry in a Centrally Planned Economy: the Polish Case', *The Journal of Industrial Economics*, vol.XXVIII, no.3 (March), pp.313–26.

— (1982), 'The Degeneration of Central Planning in Poland' in Woodall (ed.), *Policy and Politics in Contemporary Poland*, pp.99–128.

— (1991), *Poland's Next Five Years*, London: Economist Intelligence Unit.

— and Ryszard Rapacki (eds) (1991), *Poland into the 1990s: Economy and Society in Transition*, London: Pinter.

Bloomfield, Jon (ed.) (1989), *The Soviet Revolution: Perestroika and the Remaking of Socialism*, London: Lawrence & Wishart.

Bochniarz, H., J. Krawczyk and A. Wiśniewski, 'Prywatyzacja masowa i dobrze przemyślana', *Rzeczpospolita* 163, 15 July 1991

Boniecki, Father Adam (1993), 'O Katolickiej cenzurze i wartościach chrześcijańskich', *Tygodnik Powszechny* 4, 24 January.

Borensztein, Eduardo and Manmohan S. Kumar (1991), 'Proposals for Privatization in Eastern Europe', *IMF Staff Papers*, vol.38, no.2 (June), pp.300–326.

Bozyk, Pawel (1992), 'The Transformation of East Central European Economies: A Critical Assessment', *Studies in Comparative Communism*, vol.XXXV, no.3 (September), pp.257–73.

Brierley, W. (ed.) (1987), *Trade Unions and the Economic Crisis of the 1980s*, Aldershot: Gower.

Brogan, Patrick (1990), *Eastern Europe 1939–1989: The Fifty Years War*, London: Bloomsbury.

Brown, A.H. (1974), *Soviet Politics and Political Science*, London: Macmillan.

Brumberg, Abraham (ed.) (1983), *Poland: Genesis of a Revolution*, New York: Random House.

Brzezinski, Zbigniew (1990), *The Grand Failure: The Birth and Death of Communism in the Twentieth Century*, London: Macdonald.

Bugaj, R. (1991), 'Póki nie jest za późno', *Polityka* 30, 27 July.

Bujak, Zbigniew (1991), *Przepraszam za Solidarność*, Warsaw: BGW.

Burant, Stephen R. (1991), 'Polish–Lithuanian Relations: Past, Present, and Future', *Problems of Communism*, vol.XL, no.3 (May–June), pp.67–84.

— (1992), 'Polish–Belarusian Relations', *RFE/RL Research Report*, vol.1, no.37 (18 September), pp.41–5.

Carr, Fergus (1992), 'NATO and the New Europe', *Talking Politics*, vol.5, no.2, pp.90–93.

Checinski, Michael (1982), *Poland: Communism, Nationalism, Anti-Semitism*, New York: Karz Kohl.

Chrypinski, V. (1989), 'Church and Nationality in Post-War Poland' in Pedro Ramet (ed.), *Religion and Nationalism in Soviet and East European Politics*, Durham, NC, and London: Duke University Press, pp.241–63.

Ciechanowski, Jan Mieczyslaw (1974) *The Warsaw Rising of 1944*, Cambridge: Cambridge University Press.

Clarke, Roger A. (ed.) (1989), *Poland: The Economy in the 1980s*, London: Longman.

Crockett, A.D. (1992), 'The International Monetary Fund in the 1990s', *Government and Opposition*, vol.23, no.3, pp.267–82.

Curry, Jane L. (ed.) (1983), *Dissent in Eastern Europe*, New York: Praeger.

— (1988), 'The Psychological Barriers to Reform in Poland', *East European Politics and Societies*, vol.2, no.3 (Fall), pp.484–509.

Czaczkowska, Ewa (1992), 'Bojownicy', *Rzeczpospolita* 155, 3 July.

Czapiński, J. (1992), 'Partie w (krzywym?) zwierciadle swoich zwolenników', *Rzeczpospolita* 302, 24–27 December.

Czarna księga cenzury PRL (2 vols) (1979), London: Aneks.

'Czy rzecznik praw obywatelskich pragnie dobra młodzieży?' (1992), *Słowo Powszechne* 150, 8 September.

Daab, Włodzimierz, Krzysztof Korzeniowski, Paweł Bożyk *et al.* (1991), *Polski wyborca '90*, vol. 1, Warsaw: Instutut Psychologii PAN.

Dabrowski, Janusz, Michal Federowicz, and nthony. Levitas (1991), 'Polish State Enterprises and the Properties of Performance: Stabilization, Marketization, Privatization', *Politics and Society*, vol.19, no.4 (December), pp.403–37.

Dahrendorf, Ralf (1990), *Reflections on the Revolution in Europe*, London: Chatto.

D'Amico, Robert (1991), 'The Myth of the Totally Administered Society', *Telos* 88 (Summer), pp.80–94.

Davies, Norman (1982), *God's Playground: A History of Poland*, Oxford: Oxford University Press, vol.II.

Dawisha, Karen (1988), *Eastern Europe, Gorbachev, and Reform: The Great Challenge*, Cambridge: Cambridge University Press.

Deacon, Bob (1992), 'The Impact of Supranational and Global Agencies on Central European National Social Policy', Workshop on Social Responses to Political and Economic Transformation, Prague, Central European University (unpublished paper).

—, Nick Manning, Frances Millard *et al.* (1992), *The New Eastern Europe*, London: Sage, 1992.

Długosz, Stanisław (1992), *Służyłem dziewięciu premierom*, Warsaw: BGW.

'Dodawanie ułamków' (1992), Interview with Krzysztof Skubiszewski, *Polityka* 42, 17 October.

Domański, Paweł (ed.) (1991), *Tajne dokumenty Biura Politycznego. Grudzień 1970*, London: Aneks.

Domarańczyk, Zbigniew (1990), *100 dni Mazowieckiego*, Warsaw: Andrzej Bonarski.

Dubiński, Krzysztof (1990), *Magdalenka. Transakcja Epoki*, Warsaw: Sylwa.

Dziadul, J. (1989), 'Opozycja w opozycji', *Polityka* 9, 4 March.

Dziewanowski, M.K. (1959), *The Communist Party of Poland*, Cambridge, MA: Harvard University Press.

Ekiert, Grzegorz (1991), 'Democratization Processes in East Central Europe: A Theoretical Reconsideration', *British Journal of Political Science*, vol.21, no.3 (July), pp.285–313.

Elcock, Howard (1990), 'Working for Socialist Legality: The Polish Commissioner for Citizens' Rights', *Public Policy and Administration*, vol.5, no.3 (Winter), pp.37–47.

— (1992), 'Making Bricks without Straw?: The Polish Ombudsman and the Transition to Democracy', *International Journal of the Sociology of Law*, vol.20, no.2 (June), pp.173–82.

Fallenbuchl, Adam and Zbigniew Fallenbuchl (1990), 'Privatization and Marketization in Poland', *Studies in Comparative Communism*, vol.XXIII, nos 3–4 (Autumn–Winter), pp. 349–54.

Frank, Andre Gunder (1992), 'Economic Ironies in Europe: A World Economic Interpretation of East–West European Politics', *International Social Science Journal* 131 (February), pp.41–56.

Friedrich, Carl J. and Zbigniew K. Brzezinski (1956), *Totalitarian Dictatorship and Autocracy*, Cambridge, MA: Harvard University Press.

Friedrich, Carl J., Michael Curtis and Benjamin R. Barber (1969), *Totalitarianism in Perspective: Three Views*, London: Pall Mall. (ch2, n2)

Fuszara, Małgorzata (1991), 'Legal Regulation of Abortion in Poland', *Signs*, vol.17, no.1 (Autumn), pp.117–28.

Fukuyama, Francis (1992), *The End of History and the Last Man*, London: Hamish Hamilton.

Gasteyger, Curt (1992), 'The Remaking of Eastern Europe's Security', *Survival*, vol.XXXIII, no.2 (March–April), pp.111–24.

Gebert, Konstanty (1989–90), 'The Polish Press Since the Round Table Accord', *East European Reporter*, vol.4, no.1 (Winter), pp.76–7.

— (1991), 'Anti–Semitism in the 1990 Polish Presidential Election', *Social Research*, vol.58, no.4 (Winter), pp.723–55.

Gebethner, Stanisław (1992a), 'Political Reform in the Process of Round Table Negotiations' in Sanford (ed.), *Democratization in Poland 1988–90*, pp.50–67.

— (1992b), 'Wybrane głosy w dyskusji' in Łukasiewicz and Zaborowski (eds), *Szanse i zagrożenia polskich przemian*, pp.92–4.

Geremek, Bronisław (1990), 'Between Hope and Despair', *Daedalus*, vol.119, no.1, pp.91–109.

— (1991), 'I co z Europa Srodkowa?', *Krytyka* 36, pp.90–97.

— and Jacek Żakowski (1990), *Rok 1989. Bronisław Geremek Opowiada. Jacek Żakowski Pyta*, Warsaw: Plejada.

Gerrits, André (1990), *The Failure of Authoritarian Change: Reform, Opposition and Geo-Politics in Poland in the 1980s*, Aldershot: Dartmouth.

Goldfarb, Jeffrey (1989), *Beyond Glasnost: The Post-Totalitarian Mind*, Chicago: University of Chicago Press.

Gomułka, Stanisław and Antony Polonsky (eds) (1990), *Polish Paradoxes*, London: Routledge.

Gotz-Kozierkiewicz, Danuta and Grzegorz Kolodzko (1992), 'Fiscal Adjustment and Stabilization Policies: The Polish Experience', *Oxford Review of Economic Policy*, vol.8, no.1 (Spring), pp.14–27.

Grabowska, Mirosława (1991), 'System partyjny – w budowie', *Krytyka* 37, pp.24–33.

— and Ireneusz Krzemiński (eds) (1991), *Bitwa o Belweder*, Warsaw: Wydawnictwo Literackie Kraków.

Habermas, Jurgen (1990), 'What Does Socialism Mean Today? The Rectifying Revolution and the Need for New Thinking on the Left', *New Left Review* 183 (September–October), pp.3–32.

Hahn, Werner (1987), *Democracy in a Communist Party*, New York: Columbia University Press.

Halik, Janusz, Teresa Borkowska-Kalwas and Maria Pączkowska (1992), 'Społeczeństwo polskie wobec opłat za niektóre świadczenia służby zdrowia', Warsaw: Centrum Organizacji i Ekonomiki Ochrony Zdrowia (July–August) (unpublished).

Halliday, Fred (1992), 'An Encounter with Fukuyama', *New Left Review* 193 (May–June), pp.89–95.

Hankiss, Elemér (1988) 'The "Second Society": Is There an Alternative Social Model Emerging in Contemporary Hungary?', *Social Research*, vol.55, nos 1–2 (Spring–Summer), pp.13–42.

— (1990), 'In Search of a Paradigm', *Daedalus*, vol.119, no.1, pp.183–214.

Hasegawa, Tsuyoshi and Alex Pravda (eds) (1990), *Perestroika: Soviet Domestic and Foreign Policies*, London: Royal Institute of International Affairs.

Henzler, Marek (1986), 'Najlepsi czy loyalni', *Polityka* 23, 7 June.

— (1993), 'Rzeczpospolita przechodnia', *Polityka* 7, 13 February.

Hernier, Jacqueline (1992), 'Polish Democracy is a Masculine Democracy', *Women's Studies International Forum*, vol.15, no.1 (January), pp.129–38.

Heyns, Barbara and Ireneusz Bialecki (1991), 'Solidarnosc: Reluctant Vanguard or Makeshift Coalition', *American Political Science Review*, vol.85, no.2 (June), pp.351–70.

Holmes, Leslie (1986), *Politics in the Communist World*, Oxford: Clarendon Press.

Holzer, Jerzy and Krzysztof Leski (1990), *Solidarność w podziemiu*, Łódź: Wydawnictwo Łódzkie.

Hough, Jerry F. (1981), '"Interest Groups" and "Pluralism" in the Soviet Union', *Soviet Union*, vol.8, no.1, pp.104–9.

Hudson George (ed.) (1990), *Soviet National Security Policy under Perestroika*, Boston, MA: Unwin Hyman.

Hughes, Michael (1992), 'Can the West Agree on Aid to Eastern Europe?', *RFE/RL Report on Eastern Europe*, vol.1, no.11, 13 March, pp.35–42.

'Idealny agent' (1992), *Prawo i Życie* 33, 15 August.

Ionescu, Ghiţa (1967), *The Politics of the European Communist States*, London: Weidenfeld & Nicolson.

Janicki, Mariusz (1992a), 'Władza na wolnym rynku', *Polityka* 7, 15 February.

— (1992b), 'Lustracja w impasie', *Polityka* 46, 14 November.

Janowski, Karol B. (1992), 'From Monopoly to Death-Throes: The PZPR in the Process of Political Transformation' in Sanford (ed.), *Democratization in Poland 1988–90*, pp.162–76.

Jaruzelski, Wojciech (1992), *Stan wojenny DLACZEGO...*, Warsaw: BGW.

Jasiewicz, Krzysztof (1990), 'Election Behavior in Light of Studies from the Series "Poles"', paper presented at the Annual Conference of the Political Studies Association, University of Durham (April).

— (1991), 'Wyborca polski – w dziesięć lat po sierpniu', *Krytyka* 36, pp.23–47.

Kaczyński, Jarosław (1991), *Odwrotna strona medalu*, Warsaw: Oficyna Wydawnicza Most.

— (1992), 'Byłem głównym rozgrywającym', *Polityka* 3, 18 January.

Kaminski, Antoni Z. and Joanna Kurczewska (1991), 'Letter from Poland', *Government and Opposition*, vol.26, no.2, pp.215–28.

Kamiński, Bartłomiej (1991), *The Collapse of State Socialism: The Case of Poland*, Princeton, NJ: Princeton University Press.

Kanet, Roger E. (1984), 'The Polish Crisis and Poland's "Allies": The Soviet and East European Response to Events in Poland' in Bielasiak and Simon (eds), *Polish Politics: Edge of the Abyss*, pp.322–33.

Kania, Stanisław (1991), *Zatrzymać konfrontację*, Warsaw, BGW.

Karpiński, J. (1992), 'Agenci i lustracja – politycy i przeszłość', *Rzeczpospolita* 165, 15 July.

Keane, John (ed.) (1988), *Civil Society and the State*, London: Verso.

Keegan, William (1992), *The Spectre of Capitalism*, London: Radius.

Kemp-Welch, A. (trans.) (1983), *The Birth of Solidarity: The Gdańsk Negotiations, 1980*, London: Macmillan.

Kennedy, Michael D. (1991), *Professionals, Power and Solidarity in Poland*, Cambridge: Cambridge University Press.

— and Ireneusz Bialecki (1989), 'Power and the Logic of Distribution in Poland', *East European Politics and Societies*, vol.3, no.2 (Spring), pp.300–328.

Kiesielewski, Stefan (1980), '"Planning" under Socialism', *Survey*, vol.25 (Winter), pp.19–37.

Kolankiewicz, George (1981), 'Renewal, Reform or Retreat: The Polish Communist Party after the Extraordinary Ninth Congress', *The World Today*, vol.37, no.10, pp.369–75.

— (1988), 'Poland and the Politics of Permissible Pluralism', *East European Politics and Societies*, vol.2, no.1 (Winter), pp.152–83.

Kolarska-Bobińska, Lena (1991a), 'Zmieniający się świat znaczeń i tożsamości politycznych', *Krytyka* 36, pp.52–60.

— (1991b), 'Poczucie krzywdy społecznej a oczekiwanie opiekuńczej roli państwa' in Adamski *et al.*, *Polacy '90. Konflikty i zmiana*, pp.37–44.

— (1992), 'Konflikty w nowej Polsce', *Gazeta Wyborcza* 280, 28–9 November.

—, Piotr Łukasiewicz and Z. Rykowski (1990), *Wyniki badań – wyniki wyborów. 4 czerwca 1989*, Warsaw: Polskie Towarzystwo Socjologiczne.

Kolodko, G. and M. Rutkowski (1991), 'The Problem of Transition from a Socialist to a Free Market Economy: The Case of Poland', *Journal of Social, Political and Economic Studies*, vol.16, no.2, pp.159–79.

Koralewicz, Jadwiga, Ireneusz Białecki and Margaret Watson (eds) (1987), *Crisis and Transition. Polish Society in the 1980s*, Oxford: Berg.

Korbonski, Andrzej (1983), 'Dissent in Poland, 1956-76' in Jane L. Curry (ed.), *Dissent in Eastern Europe*, New York: Praeger, pp.25–47.

Kornai, Janos (1980), *Economics of Shortage* (2 vols), Amsterdam: North Holland.

Korzeniowski, Krzysztof and Krystyna Skarzyńska (1991), 'Wyznacziki popularności trzech głównych pretendentów w wyborach prezydenckich' in Daab *et al.*,*Polski wyborca '90*, vol.1 pp.148–52.

Kosiński, P. and R. Malik (1992), 'Dobrzy sąsiedzi', *Rzeczpospolita* 270, 17 November.

Kozakiewicz, Mikołaj (c. 1991), *Byłem marszałkiem kontraktowego...*, Warsaw: BGW (no date).

Kruszewski, Z.A. (1984), 'The Communist Party during the 1980–81 Democratization of Poland' in Bielasiak and Simon (eds), *Polish Politics: Edge of the Abyss*, pp.241–59.

Krzemiński, Adam (1990), 'Trzeci wariant', *Polityka* 52, 29 December.

Krzemiński, Ireneusz (1992), 'Sami sobie damy radę?', *Rzeczpospolita* 283, 2 December.

'Kubiak Report, The' (1982), *Survey*, vol.26, no.3, pp.87–107.

Kuczyński, Waldemar (c. 1992), *Zwierzenia zausznika*, Warsaw: BGW.

Kuligowski, H. (1992), 'Wojna Religijna', *Polityka* 42, 17 October.

Kumar, Krishan (1992), 'The Revolutions of 1989: Socialism, Capitalism and Democracy', *Theory and Society*, vol.21, no.3 (June), pp.309–56.

Kuroń, Jacek (1991), *Moja zupa*, Warsaw: BGW.

Kurski, Jarosław (1991), *Wódz*, Warsaw: Wydawnictwo PoMost.

— and Piotr Semki (1993), *Lewy czerwcowy*, Warsaw: Editions Spotkania.

Kwiatek, Wojciech (1991), *Gra o wszystko*, Warsaw: Centrum.

Kwieciński, J. (1992), 'O bezpieczeństwo – dziś i w roku 2010', *Rzeczpospolita* 211, 8 September.

Laba, Roman (1991), *Worker Roots of Solidarity: A Political Sociology of Poland's Working Class Democratization*, Princeton, NJ: Princeton University Press.

Lamentowicz, Wojciech (1982), 'Adaptation Through Political Crisis in Post-War Poland', *Journal of Peace Research*, vol.XIX, no.2, pp.117–31.

Leski, Krzysztof (1989), *Coś. Rzecz o Okrągłym Stole*, Warsaw: In Plus.

Łętowska, Ewa (1992), *Baba na Świeczniku*, Warsaw: BGW.

Lewandowski, Janusz and Jan Szomburg (1989), 'Uwłaszczenie jako fundament reformy społeczno-gospodarczej: Zarys programu' in Siemon (ed.), *Propozycje przekształceń polskiej gospodarki*, Warsaw, pp.68–93.

Lewis, Paul G. (1989), *Political Authority and Party Secretaries in Poland, 1975–1986*, Cambridge: Cambridge University Press.

— (1990a), 'Non–competitive Elections and Regime Change: Poland 1989', *Parliamentary Affairs*, vol.43, no.1 (January), pp.90–107.

— (1990b), 'Democratization in Eastern Europe', *Coexistence*, vol. 27, no. 4, pp. 245–67.

— (1990c), 'The Long Good-bye: Party Rule and Political Change in Poland since Martial Law', *The Journal of Communist Studies*, vol.6, no.1 (March), pp.24–48.

Light, Margot (1990), 'Foreign Policy' in McCauley (ed.), *Gorbachev and Perestroika*, pp.169–88.

Linden, Ronald H. (1992), 'The New International Political Economy of East Europe', *Studies in Comparative Communism*, vol.XXV, no.1 (March), pp.3–21.

Lipowski, Adam (1988), *Mechanizm rynkowy w gospodarce polskiej*, Warsaw: PWN.

Lipski, Jan Jozef (1985), *KOR: A History of the Workers' Defense Committee in Poland 1976–1981*, Berkeley, CA: University of California Press.

Lomax, Bill (1992), 'Internal (and External) Impediments to Democratization', Paper presented at the Workshop on Regime Change, Charles University, Prague, September 1992.

Lopinski, Maciej, Marcin Moskit and Mariusz Wilk (1990), *Konspira: Solidarity Underground*, Berkeley, CA: University of California Press.

Lovenduski, Joni and Jean Woodall (1987), *Politics and Society in Eastern Europe*, London: Macmillan.

Łukasiewicz, Piotr and Wojciech Zaborowski (eds) (1992), *Szanse i zagrożenia polskich przemian*, Warsaw: Polska Akademia Nauk (Instytut Filozofii i Socjologii, Instytut Studiów Politycznych).

Łukczak, A. (1992), '33 dni Pawlaka', *Polityka* 38, 19 Septembe.

McCauley, Martin (ed) (1990), *Gorbachev and Perestroika*, London: Macmillan.

246   *The Anatomy of the New Poland*

— and Stephen Carter (eds) (1986), *Leadership and Succession in the Soviet Union, Eastern Europe and China*, London: Macmilan,
MacDonald, Oliver (1983), 'The Polish Vortex: Solidarity and Socialism', *New Left Review* 139 (May–June), pp.5–48.
Macpherson, C.B. (1973), *Democratic Theory: Essays in Retrieval*, Oxford: Clarendon Press.
MacShane, Denis (1981), *Solidarity: Poland's Independent Trade Union*, Nottingham: Spokesman.
McGrew, Anthony G. (1992). 'Conceptualizing Global Politics', in McGrew, Lewis *et al.*, *Global Politics: Globalization and the Nation-State*, pp.1–30.
—, Paul G. Lewis *et al.* (1992), *Global Politics: Globalization and the Nation-State*, Oxford: Oxford University Press.
Macieja, J. (1992), 'Nie chcą płacić czy nie mogą?', *Rzeczpospolita* 261, 5 November.
Malcher, George (1984), *Poland's Politicized Army: Communists in Uniform*, New York: Praeger.
Malcolm, Neil (1990), 'De-Stalinization and Soviet Foreign Policy: The Roots of "New Thinking"' in Hasegawa and Pravda (eds), *Perestroika: Soviet Domestic and Foreign Policies*, pp.178–205.
Markowski, R. (1991),'O psychologicznych "profilach" elektoratów' in.Mirosława Grabowska and Ireneusz Krzemiński (eds), *Bitwa o Belweder*, pp.139–44
Marks, John (1990), *Fried Snowballs: Communism in Theory and Practice*, London: Claridge Press.
Markus, Maria (1982), 'Overt and Covert Modes of Legitimation in East European Societies' in T.H. Rigby and Ferenc Fehér (eds), *Political Legitimation in Communist States*, pp.82–93.
Mason, David S. (1983), 'Solidarity, the Regime and the Public', *Soviet Studies*, vol.XXV, no.4 (October), pp.533–45.
— (1984), 'Solidarity and Socialism' in Bielasiak and Simon (eds), *Polish Politics*, pp.118–37.
— (1985), *Public Opinion and Political Change in Poland, 1980–1982*, Cambridge: Cambridge University Press.
— (1987), 'Poland's New Trade Unions', *Soviet Studies*, vol.XXXIX, no.3, pp.489–508.
Michnik, Adam (1985), *Letters from Prison and Other Essays*, London: University of California Press.
Miliband, Ralph (1992), 'Fukuyama and the Socialist Alternative', *New Left Review* 193, May–June, pp.108–13.
Millard, Frances (1987), 'Trade Unions and Economic Crisis in Poland' in William Brierley (ed.), *Trade Unions and the Economic Crisis of the 1980s*, pp.87–100.
— (1992a), 'Social Policy in Poland' in Deacon *et al.*, *The New Eastern Europe*, London, pp.118–43.
— (1992b), 'The Polish Parliamentary Elections of October 1991', *Soviet Studies*, vol.44, no.5 (September), pp.837–55.
Miodowski, P. (1992), 'Mała konstytucja: rewelacja, kompromitująca czy kompromis', *Rzeczpospolita* 190, 13 August.
Mishra, Ramesh (1990), *The Welfare State in Capitalist Society*, Hemel Hempstead: Harvester–Wheatsheaf.
Misztal, Bronislaw (ed.) (1985), *Poland after Solidarity. Social Movements versus the State*, Oxford: Transaction Books.
Mojkowski, Jacek (1993), 'Dylemat więźnia', *Polityka. Prywatyzacja* (February)..

Mokrzycki, Edmund (1991–2), 'Eastern Europe after Communism', *Telos* 90 (Winter), pp.129–36.

Moltz, James Clay (1993), 'Divergent Learning and the Failed Politics of Soviet Economic Reform', *World Politics*, vol.45 (January), pp.301–25.

Morawska, Ewa (1988), 'On Barriers to Pluralism in Pluralist Poland', *Slavic Review*, vol.47, no.4 (Winter), pp.626–36.

Morawski, W. (1987), 'Self-management and Economic Reform' in Koralewicz, Bialecki and Watson (eds), *Crisis and Transition: Polish Society in the 1980s*, pp.80–110

Mozolowski, A. (1992a), 'Wnuki nie doczekają', *Polityka* 4, 25 January.

— (1992b), 'Zniechęcenie', *Polityka* 31, 1 August.

Myant, Martin (1982), *Poland: A Crisis for Socialism*, London: Lawrence & Wishart.

— (1989), 'Poland – The Permanent Crisis?' in Clarke (ed.), *Poland: The Economy in the 1980s*, pp.1–28.

Nahaylo, Bohdan (1992), 'Ukraine and the Visegrad Triangle', *RFE/RL Research Report*, vol.1, no.23 (5 June), pp.28–9.

Naszkowska, Krystyna (1992), 'Nowy Szela', *Gazeta Wyborcza* 156, 4–5 July.

'Nie ma mowy, żebym za życie wrócił' (1992), *Rzeczpospolita* 290, 10 December.

'Nie wyjaśnione tajemnice' (1992), *Prawo i Życie* 34, 22 August.

Nowakowska, Ewa (1991), 'Jacek wśród seniorów', *Polityka* 31, 3 August.

O'Donnell, Guillermo, Philippe Schmitter and Laurence Whitehead (eds) (1986), *Transitions from Authoritarian Rule*, Baltimore, MD, and London: Johns Hopkins University Press.

Offe, Claus (1991), 'Capitalism by Democratic Design? Democratic Theory Facing the Triple Transition in East Central Europe', *Social Research*, vol.58, no.4 (Winter), pp.865–92.

Okolicsanyi, Karoly (1992), 'The EBRD's First Year', *RFE/RL Research Report*, vol.1, no.23 (5 June), pp.41–6.

Olszewska, Barbara (1992), 'Bez satysfakcji i pieniędzy', *Polityka* 12, 21 March.

Olszewski, Jan (1992), *Olszewski. Przerwana Premiera*, Warsaw: Tygodnik Solidarność.

Osa, Maryjane (1989), 'Resistance, Persistence and Change: The Transformation of the Catholic Church in Poland', *East European Politics and Societies*, vol.3, no.2 (Spring), pp.268–99.

Ost, David (1989), 'Towards a Corporatist Solution in Eastern Europe: The Case of Poland', *East European Politics and Societies*, vol.3, no.1 (Winter), pp.152–74.

— (1990), *Solidarity and the Politics of Anti-Politics*, Philadelphia, PA: Temple University Press.

Ostoja-Ostaszewski, A. *et al.* (1977), *Dissent in Poland 1976-77*, London: Association of Polish Students and Graduates in Exile.

Ostrowski, M. (1992), 'Wspólnota na dystans', *Polityka* 45, 7 November.

Paczkowski, Andrzej (1992), 'Aparat bezpieczeństwa w Polsce: lata 1954-1956', *Puls* 54, no.1 (January–February), pp.62–9.

Pakulski, Jan (1990), 'Poland: Ideology, Legitimacy and Political Domination' in Nicholas Abercrombie, Stephen Hill and Bryan S. Turner (eds), *Dominant Ideologies*, London: Unwin Hyman, pp.38–64.

'Panelists Discuss Hyperinflation in Former Centrally Planned Economies' (1992), *IMF Survey*, 3 August, pp.241 and 249–51.

Pańków, Włodzimierz (1987), 'The Solidarity Movement, Management and the Political System in Poland' in Koralewicz, Bialecki and Watson (eds), *Crisis and Transition: Polish Society in the 1980s*, pp.111–29.

— (1990), 'Transformations in the Polish Social Environment in the 1980s', *The Journal of Communist Studies*, vol.6, no.4 (December), pp.165–78.

'Państwo prawne i lustracja' (Interview with Adam Strzembosz) (1992), *Gazeta Wyborcza* 191, 14–16 August.

Papuga, J. (1992), 'Od orła do kosa', *Polityka* 37, 12 September.

Parysek, J.J. *et al.* (1991), 'Regional Differences in the Results of the 1990 Presidential Election in Poland as the First Approximation to a Political Map of the Country', *Environment and Planning*, vol.23, pp.1315–29.

Pawlowski, Witold (1992), 'Bizony na Sztorc', *Polityka* 27, 4 July.

Pęczak, M. (1993), 'Swoboda i dyktat', *Polityka* 7, 13 February,

Persky, S. and H. Flam (1982), *The Solidarity Sourcebook*, Vancouver: New Star Books.

Pilczyński, J. (1992a), 'Nie tylko ustawy', *Rzeczpospolita* 47, 25 February.

— (1992b), 'Powrót do trójpodziału', *Rzeczpospolita* 177, 29 July.

— (1992c), 'Reguły parlamentarnej gry', *Rzeczpospolita* 205, 1 September.

— (1993), 'Cena kompromisu', *Rzeczpospolita* 39, 16 February.

Podemski, S. (1992a), 'Rachunek za historię', *Polityka* 38, 19 September.

— (1992b), 'Ludzie, Historia, Przyszłość', *Polityka* 44, 31 October.

Polonsky, Antony and Boleslaw Drukier (1980), *The Beginnings of Communist Rule in Poland*, London: Routledge & Kegan Paul.

Poprzeczko, J. (1993), 'Sto milionów dla każdego', *Polityka. Prywatyzacja* (January).

Pravda, Alex (1982), 'Poland 1980: From "Premature Consumerism" to Labour Solidarity', *Soviet Studies*, vol.XXXIV, no.4, pp.162–99.

Prins, Gwyn (1990), *Spring in Winter: The 1989 Revolutions*, Manchester: Manchester University Press.

Przeworski, Adam (1991), *Democracy and the Market*, Cambridge: Cambridge University Press.

'Pucz czerwcowy?' (1992), *Nie* 25, 18 June.

Raina, Peter (1978), *Political Opposition in Poland, 1954–1977*, London: Poets and Painters Press.

— (1985), *Poland 1981: Towards Social Renewal*, London: Allen & Unwin.

Rakowski, Mieczysław (1991), *Jak to się stało*, Warsaw: BGW.

— (c. 1992), *Zanim stanę przed Trybunałem*, Warsaw: BGW (no date).

Ramet, Pedro (ed.) (1989), *Religion and Nationalism in Soviet and East European Politics*, Durham, NC, and London: Duke University Press.

Ramet, Sabrina P. (1991), *Social Currents in Eastern Europe*, Durham, NC, and London: Duke University Press.

Regulamin Sejmu Rzeczpospolitej Polskiej (1992), Warsaw: Wydawnictwo Sejmowe.

Remington, Robin (1990), 'Changes in Soviet Security Policy toward Eastern Europe and the Warsaw Pact' in Hudson (ed.), *Soviet National Security Policy under Perestroika*, pp.221–47.

Remmer, Alexander (1989), 'A Note on Post–Publication Censorship in Poland', *Soviet Studies*, vol.XLI, no.3 (July), pp.415–25.

Reykowski, Janusz (1992), 'Psychologiczne problemy okresu przemian' in Łukasiewicz and Zaborowski (eds), *Szanse i zagrożenia polskich przemian*, pp.50–56.

Richter, Emanuel (1991), 'Upheavals in the East and Turmoil in Political Theory: Comments on Offe's "Capitalism by Democratic Design?"', *Social Research*, vol.58 no.4 (Winter), pp.893–902.

Rigby, T.H. and Ferenc Fehér (eds) (1982), *Political Legitimation in Communist States*, London: Macmillan.

Rosati, Dariusz (1991), 'Poland: Systemic Reforms and Economic Policy in the 1990s' in Blazyca and Rapacki (eds), *Poland into the 1990s: Economy and Society in Transition*, pp.20–31.

Rose, Richard (1992), 'Escaping from Absolute Dissatisfaction: A Trial-and-Error Model of Change in Eastern Europe', *Journal of Theoretical Politics*, vol.4, no.4, pp.371–93.

Rostowski, Jacek (1989), 'The Decay of Socialism and the Growth of Private Enterprise in Poland', *Soviet Studies*, vol.XLI, no.2 (April), pp.194–214.

Rothschild, Joseph (1989), *Return to Diversity*, Oxford: Oxford University Press.

Ruane, Kevin (1982), *The Polish Challenge*, London: BBC.

Rupnik, Jacques (1986), 'Soviet Adaptation to Change in Eastern Europe', *The Journal of Communist Studies*, vol.2, no.3, pp.251–62.

— (1988), 'Totalitarianism Revisited' in Keane (ed.), *Civil Society and the State*, pp.264–71.

Rustin, M. (1992), 'No Exit from Capitalism', *New Left Review* 193 (May–June), pp.96–107.

Rychard, Andrzej (1991), 'Stare i nowe instytucje życia publicznego', in Adamski, Białecki, Jasiewicz *et al.*, *Polacy '90*, pp.47–60.

Sabbat-Swidlicka, Anna (1992a), 'Poland: Weak Government, Fractious Sejm, Isolated President', *RFE/RL Research Report*, vol.1, no.15 (10 April), pp.1–7.

— (1992b), 'Poland: Toward the Rule of Law', *RFE/RL Research Report*, vol.1, no.27 (3 July), pp.25–33.

Sachs, Jeffrey and David Lipton (1990), 'Poland's Economic Reform', *Foreign Affairs*, vol.69, no.3 (Summer), pp.47–66.

Sanford, George (1986a), *Military Rule in Poland: The Rebuilding of Communist Power 1981–1983*, London: Croom Helm.

— (1986b), 'Poland' in Martin McCauley and Stephen Carter (eds), *Leadership and Succession in the Soviet Union, Eastern Europe and China*, London: Macmilan, pp.40–63.

— (ed.) (1992), *Democratization in Poland, 1988–90*, London: St. Martin's Press.

Shils, Edward (1991), 'The Virtue of Civil Society', *Government and Opposition*, vol.26, no.1, pp.3–20.

Siemon, L. (ed.) (1989), *Propozycje przekształceń polskiej gospodarki*, Warsaw: Państwowe Wydawnictwo Ekonomiczne.

Sikorski, RAdek (1992), 'Poles Apart', *The Spectator*, 27 June., pp.9–12.

Simoneti, Marko (1993), 'A Comparative Review of Privatisation Strategies in Four Former Socialist Countries', *Europe–Asia Studies*, vol.45, no.1, pp.79–102.

Skilling, H.Gordon (1966a), *The Governments of Communist East Europe*, New York: Crowell.

— (1966b), 'Interest Groups and Communist Politics', *World Politics*, vol.18, no.3, pp.118–37.

Skubiszewski, K. (1991), 'New Problems of Security in Central and Eastern Europe', *East European Reporter*, vol.4, no.4, pp.61–4.

— (1992), 'Polityka zagraniczna RP w 1992', speech delivered in the *Sejm* on 8 May *Przegląd Rządowy*, no. 6 (June), p.27.

Slay, Ben (1992a), 'Poland: An Overview', *RFE/RL Research Report*, vol.1, no.17 (24 April), pp.15–21.

— (1992b), 'The Banking Crisis and Economic Reform in Poland', *RFE/RL Research Report*, vol.1, no.23 (5 June), pp.33–40.

— (1993), 'The Dilemmas of Economic Liberalism in Poland', *Europe–Asia Studies*, vol.45, no.2, pp.237–57.

Smith, M. (1992), 'Modernization, Globalization and the Nation-State', in McGrew, Lewis et al., Global Politics: Globalization and the Nation-State, pp.253–69.

Smolar, Aleksander (1983), 'The Rich and the Powerful' in Brumberg (ed.), Poland: Genesis of a Revolution, pp.42–53.

Snopkiewicz, Jacek et al. (1992), Teczki, czyli widma bezpieki, Warsaw: BGW.

Sokolewicz, Wojciech (1992a), 'The Polish Constitution in a Time of Change', International Journal of the Sociology of Law, vol.20, no.1, pp.29–42.

— (1992b), 'The Legal–Constitutional Bases of Democratisation in Poland: Systemic and Constitutional Change' in Sanford (ed.), Democratization in Poland, 1988–90, pp.69–97.

Solomon, Susan Gross (ed.) (1983), Pluralism in the Soviet Union, London: Macmillan.

Solska, Joanna (1991a), 'Sami Sobie', Polityka 35, 31 August.

— (1991b), 'Z lewej kieszeni', Polityka 48, 30 November.

'Sprawozdanie Rzecznika Praw Obywatelskich za okres 1 XII 1990 r. – 19 XI 1991 r.' (1992), Państwo i Prawo, vol.XLVII, no.2 (February), pp.3–16.

Staniszkis, Jadwiga (1978), 'On Remodelling of the Polish Economic System', Soviet Studies, vol.XXX, no.4 (October), pp.547–56.

— (1979), 'On Some Contradictions of Socialist Society: The Case of Poland', Soviet Studies, vol.XXXI, no.2 (April), pp.167–87.

— (1984), Poland's Self-Limiting Revolution, Princeton, NJ: Princeton University Press.

— (1989), 'The Obsolescence of Solidarity', Telos 80 (Summer), pp.37–50.

— (1990), 'Patterns of Change in Eastern Europe', East European Politics and Societies, vol.4, no.1 (Winter), pp.77–97.

— (1991), '"Political Capitalism" in Poland' East European Politics and Societies, vol.5, no.1 (Winter), pp.127–41.

— (1992), The Dynamics of Breakthrough in Eastern Europe, Oxford: Oxford University Press.

Stark, David (1992), 'Path Dependence and Privatization Strategies in East Central Europe', East European Politics and Societies, vol.6, no.1, pp.17–54.

Starski, Stanislaw (1982), Class Struggle in Classless Poland, Boston, MA: South End Press.

Stepan, A. (1986), 'Paths toward Redemocratization: Theoretical and Comparative Considerations' in O'Donnell, Schmitter, and Whitehead (eds), Transitions from Authoritarian Rule, pp.64–84.

Stokes, Gale (ed.) (1991), From Stalinism to Pluralism: A Documentary History of Eastern Europe since 1945, Oxford: Oxford University Press.

Syzdek, Bronisław and Eleonora Syzdek (1985), Polityczne Dylematy Władysława Gomułki, Warsaw: Czytelnik.

Szacki, Jerzy (1991), 'Polish Democracy: Dreams and Reality', Social Research, vol.58, no.4 (Winter), pp.711–22.

Szajkowski, Bogdan (1983), Next to God ... Poland, London: Pinter.

Szomburg, J. (1991), 'Prywatyzacja powszechna', Rzeczpospolita 167, 22 July.

Taras, Raymond (1984), Ideology in a Socialist State: Poland 1956–1983, Cambridge: Cambridge University Press.

— (1986), Poland: Socialist State, Rebellious Nation, Boulder, CO, and London: Westview.

Tarkowska, Elzbieta and Jacek Tarkowski (1991), 'Social Disintegration in Poland: Civil Society or Autonomous Familism', Telos 89 (Fall), pp.103–9.

Tarnowski, P. (1990), 'W oparach spiritusu', Polityka 32, 11 August.

Tarrow, Sidney (1991), 'Aiming at a Moving Target: Social Science and the Recent Rebellions in Eastern Europe', *PS: Political Science and Politics*, vol.24, no.1, pp.12–20.

Touraine, Alain *et al.* (1983), *Solidarity: The Analysis of a Social Movement*, Cambridge: Cambridge University Press.

Urban, Jerzy (c. 1992), *Jajakobyły*, Warsaw: BGW.

Vale, Michael (ed.) (1981), *Poland: The State of the Republic*, London: Pluto Press. (ch.1, n.23)

Vinton, Louisa (1990), 'The Politics of Property: Divesting the Polish Communist Party of its Assets', *RFE/RL Report on Eastern Europe*, vol.1, no.17 (27 April), pp.14–17.

— (1992a), 'Polish Government Proposes Pact on State Firms', *RFE/RL Research Report*, vol.1, no.42 (23 October), pp.10–18.

— (1992b), 'Poland's "Little Constitution" Clarifies Wałęsa's Powers', *RFE/RL Research Report*, vol.1, no.35 (4 September), pp.19–26.

— (1992c), 'Sejm Approves New Law on Radio and Television', *RFE/RL Research Report*, vol.1, no.43 (30 October), pp.32–4.

Walicki, Andrzej (1991), 'From Stalinism to Post-Communist Pluralism: The Case of Poland', *New Left Review* 185 (January–February), pp.93–121.

Walker, Rachel (1989) 'Marxism–Leninism as Discourse: The Politics of the Empty Signifier and the Double Bind', *British Journal of Political Science*, vol.19, no.2 (April), pp.161–89.

Waller, Michael (1981), *Democratic Centralism*, Manchester: Manchester University Press.

— and Bogdan Szajkowski (1986), 'The Communist Movement: from Monolith to Polymorph' in Stephen White and Daniel N. Nelson (eds), *Communist Politics: A Reader*, London, Macmillan, pp.9–26.

Wanless, P.T. (1980) 'Economic Reform in Poland 1973–79', *Soviet Studies*, vol.XXXII, no.1 (January), pp.28–57.

Warszawski, Dawid (1992), 'Regulamin', *Gazeta Wyborcza* 182, 4 August.

Wedel, Janine (1990), 'The Ties that Bind in Polish Society' in Gomułka and Polonsky (eds), *Polish Paradoxes*, pp.237–60.

Weitz, Richard (1992), 'The CSCE's New Look', *RFE/RL Research Report*, vol.1, no.6 (7 February), pp.27–31.

de Weydenthal, Jan B. (1992a), 'German Plans for Border Region Stirs Interest in Poland', *RFE/RL Research Report*, vol.1, no.7 (21 February), pp.39–42.

__ (1992b), 'Poland and Russia Open a New Chapter in Their Relations', *RFE/RL Research Report*, vol.1, no.25 (19 June), pp.46–8.

— (1992c), 'Polish–Russian Relations Disturbed by Troop Dispute', *RFE/RL Research Report*, vol.1, no.11 (13 March), pp.32–4.

— (1992d), 'Poland Free of Combat Troops', *RFE/RL Research Report*, vol.1, no.45 (13 November), pp.32–5.

— (1992e), 'Political Problems Affect Security Work in Poland', *RFE/RL Research Report*, vol.1, no.16 (17 April), pp.39–42.

— (1992f), 'Cross-Border Diplomacy in East Central Europe', *RFE/RL Research Report*, vol.1, no.42 (23 October), pp.19–23.

White, Stephen (1983), 'What Is a Communist System?', *Studies in Comparative Communism*, vol.16, no.4 (Winter), pp.247–63.

—, John Gardner and George Schöpflin (1982), *Communist Political Systems: An Introduction*, London: Macmillan (2nd edition 1987).

—, John Gardner, George Schöpflin and Tony Saich (1990), *Communist and Post-Communist Political Systems*, London: Macmillan.

Wiatr, Jerzy (1992), *Four Essays on East European Democratic Transformation*, Warsaw: Scholar Agency.

Widacki, Jan (1992), *Czego nie powiedział Generał Kiszczak*, Warsaw: BGW.

Wierzbicki, Piotr (1989), 'Familia, Świt, Dwor', *Tygodnik Solidarność* 23 (November), pp.1 and 5.

Winczorek, Piotr (1992a), 'The Internal Evolution and Changing Policies of the Democratic Party' in Sanford (ed.), *Democratization in Poland 1988–90*, pp.162–76.

— (1992b), 'Zagadki konstytucyjne', *Rzeczpospolita* 294, 15 December.

Włodek, Zbigniew (ed.) (1992), *Tajne dokumenty Biura Politycznego. PZPR a 'Solidarność' 1980–1981*, London: Aneks.

Wnuk-Lipiński, Edmund (1987), 'Social Dimorphism and its Implications' in Koralewicz, Białecki and Watson (eds), *Crisis and Transition: Polish Society in the 1980s*, pp.159–76.

Wolnicki, Miron (1991–92), 'The New Political Economy of Eastern Europe', *Telos* 90 (Winter), pp.113–28.

Wood, Ellen Meiksins (1990), 'The Uses and Abuses of "Civil Society"', *Socialist Register 1990*, London: Merlin Press, pp.60–84.

Woodall, Jean (ed.) (1982), *Policy and Politics in Contemporary Poland*, London: Pinter.

Wörner, Manfred (1992), 'A Vigorous Alliance – A Motor for Peaceful Change in Europe', *NATO Review*, vol.40, no.6, pp.3–9.

Zakrzewska, Janina (1991), 'Czas konstytucji', *Krytyka* 36, pp.69–78.

— (1992), 'Trybunał Konstytucyjny – Konstytucja – państwo prawa', *Państwo i Prawo*, vol.XLVII, no.1 (January), pp.3–12.

Za kulisami bezpieki i partii (1990), Warsaw: Biura Informacji Studenckiej Zrzeszenia Studentów Polskich.

Zinner, Paul (ed.) (1956), *National Communism and Popular Revolt in Eastern Europe: A Selection of Documents on Events in Poland and Hungary, February–November 1956*, New York: Columbia University Press.

Ziolkowski, Janusz (1990), 'The roots, branches and blossoms of Solidarność', in Prins (ed.), *Spring in Winter: The 1989 Revolutions*, pp.39–62.

Ziółkowski, Marek (1990), 'Social Structure, Interests and Consciousness: The Crisis and Transformation of the System of "Real Socialism" in Poland', *Acta Sociologica*, vol.33, no.4, pp.289–303.

Zubek, Voytek (1991), 'Walesa's Leadership and Poland's Transition', *Problems of Communism*, vol.XL, nos.1–2 (January–April), pp.69–83.

Żukowski, Tomasz (1991), 'Trzecia siła', *Krytyka* 37, pp.34–46.

Zuzowski, Robert (1991), 'The Origins of Open Organized Dissent in Today's Poland', *East European Quarterly*, vol.25, no.1, pp.59–90.

Index